ANALYSIS OF FOODS AND BEVERAGES

Headspace Techniques

ANALYSIS OF FOODS AND BEVERAGES

Headspace Techniques

EDITED BY

GEORGE CHARALAMBOUS

Anheuser–Busch, Inc.
Technical Center
St. Louis, Missouri

ACADEMIC PRESS   New York   San Francisco   London   1978
A Subsidiary of Harcourt Brace Jovanovich, Publishers

ACADEMIC PRESS, INC.
111 Fifth Avenue, New York, New York 10003

United Kingdom Edition published by
ACADEMIC PRESS, INC. (LONDON) LTD.
24/28 Oval Road, London NW1 7DX

Library of Congress Cataloging in Publication Data

Main entry under title:

Analysis of foods and beverages.

Proceedings of a symposium organized by the Flavor
Subdivision of the Agricultural and Food Chemistry
Division of American Chemical Society at the 174th
national meeting, Chicago, Aug. 29-Sept. 2, 1977.
 1. Food—Analysis—Congresses. 2. Beverages—
Analysis—Congresses. 3. Flavor—Congresses. 4. Gas
chromatography—Congresses. I. Charalambous, George,
Date II. American Chemical Society. Division of
Agricultural and Food Chemistry. Flavor Subdivision.
III. Title: Headspace techniques.
TX545.A5   664'.07   77-28841
ISBN 0-12-169050-4

PRINTED IN THE UNITED STATES OF AMERICA

CONTENTS

vi   **CONTENTS**

CONTRIBUTORS

Numbers in parentheses indicate the pages on which the authors' contributions begin.

Akiyama, H. (229), National Research Institute of Brewing (JOZO SHI-KENJO) 2-6-30, Takinogawa, Kita-ku, Tokyo 114, Japan

Alves, S. (1), College of Agriculture and Environmental Sciences, Department of Food Science and Technology, University of California, Davis, Davis, California 95616

Boyko, A. L. (57), Department of Food Science and Technology, Oregon State University, Corvallis, Oregon 97331

Chicoye, E. (187), Miller Brewing Company, Milwaukee, Wisconsin 53208

de Valois, P. J. (249), Naarden International N.V., P.O. Box 2, Naarden-Bussum, The Netherlands

Dinsmore, H. L. (135), Department of Chemistry, Florida Southern College, Lakeland, Florida 33801

Filsoof, M. (1), Department of Pharmacy, University of Tehran, Tehran, Iran

Helbert, J. R. (187), Miller Brewing Company, Milwaukee, Wisconsin 53208

Herwig, W. C. (187), Miller Brewing Company, Milwaukee, Wisconsin 53208

Hoff, J. T. (187), Miller Brewing Company, Milwaukee, Wisconsin 53208

Hruza, A. (81), International Flavors and Fragrances, IFF—R&D, Union Beach, New Jersey 07735

Hussein, M. M. (283), Life Savers, Inc., Port Chester, New York 10573

Jaegers, P. P. (249), Naarden International N.V., P.O. Box 2, Naarden-Bussum, The Netherlands

Jennings, W. G. (1), College of Agricultural and Environmental Sciences, Department of Food Science and Technology, University of California, Davis, Davis, California 95616

Klimes, I. (95), Givaudan Forschungsgesellschaft AG, CH - 8600 Düben-dorf/Zurich, Uberlandstrasse 138, Switzerland

Lamparsky, D. (95), Givaudan Forschungsgesellschaft AG CH - 8600 Dübendorf/Zurich, Uberlandstrasse 138, Switzerland

Libbey, L. M. (57), Department of Food Science and Technology, Oregon State University, Corvallis, Oregon 97331

Lund, E. D. (135), United States Department of Agriculture, Agricultural Research Service, Southern Region, Citrus and Subtropical Products Laboratory, Winter Haven, Florida 33880

Maarse, H. (17), Centraal Institut Voor Voedingsonderzoek TNO, Utrechtsweg 48, Zeist, The Netherlands

Mackay, D. A. M. (283), Life Savers, Inc., New York, New York 10019

Mookherjee, B. D. (81), International Flavors and Fragrances, IFF—R&D, Union Beach, New Jersey 07735

Morgan, M. E. (57), Department of Food Science and Technology, Oregon State University, Corvallis, Oregon 97331

Noble, A. C. (203), College of Agricultural and Environmental Sciences, Agricultural Experiment Station, Department of Viticulture and Enology, University of California, Davis, Davis, California 95616

Ouchi, K. (229), National Research Institute of Brewing (JOZO SHIKENJO) 2-6-30, Takinogawa, Kita-ku, Tokyo 114, Japan

Pattee, H. E. (359), United States Department of Agriculture, Agricultural Research Service, Southern Region, North Carolina State University, Raleigh, North Carolina 27607

Saleeb, F. Z. (37), General Foods Corporation, Technical Center, White Plains, New York 10625

Schaefer, J. (17), Centraal Institut Voor Voedingsonderzoek TNO, Utrechtsweg 48, Zeist, The Netherlands

Schenz, T. W. (37), General Foods Corporation, Technical Center, White Plains, New York 10625

Singleton, J. A. (359), United States Department of Agriculture, Agricultural Research Service, Southern Regions, North Carolina State University, Raleigh, North Carolina 27607

ter Heide, R. (249), Naarden International N.V., P.O. Box 2, Naarden-Bussum, The Netherlands

Timmer, R. (249), Naarden International N.V., P.O. Box 2, Naarden-Bussum, The Netherlands

Visser, J. (249), Naarden International N.V., P.O. Box 2, Naarden-Bussum, The Netherlands

Vitzthum, O. G. (115), Hag AG, Hagstrasse, D-2800 Bremen, Germany

Werkhoff, P. (115), Hag AG, Hagstrasse, D-2800 Bremen, Germany

Withycombe, D. A. (81), International Flavors and Fragrances, IFF—R&D, Union Beach, New Jersey 07735

Wyllie, S. G. (1), Department of Chemistry, Hawkesbury Agricultural College, Richmond, New South Wales 2753, Australia

Yoshizawa, K. (229), National Research Institute of Brewing (JOZO SHI-KENJO) 2-6-30, Takinogawa, Kita-ku, Tokyo 114, Japan

FOREWORD

Headspace sampling for gas chromatographic analysis, which in its truest sense implies the direct injection of the mixture of vapors in equilibrium with a sample held within a confined space, possesses a desirable and appealing simplicity. It also offers a distinct advantage in that sample work-up procedures have been avoided. These latter usually involve distillation, extraction, and/or adsorption processes, and almost invariably engender quantitative and, frequently lead to, qualitative changes in the composition of the sample, which are certainly good reasons to favor simple headspace injections.

Unfortunately, these simple headspace injections also suffer a disadvantage: To obtain optimum chromatographic results, it is necessary that the injected sample occupy a minimum length of column as the chromatographic process begins. If this concept is violated, one pays the price in broad, poorly resolved peaks; hence the size of gas sample that can be injected is seriously limited.

This in turn poses another problem: This limitation in the size of sample that can be injected also limits the components that can be detected. Only those components that, by virtue of their concentration and relative volatility, are present in quantities sufficient to activate the detector will be detected. Relatively low molecular weight and highly volatile compounds (e.g., C_2–C_8 esters, aldehydes, ketones) can be readily detected by the direct injection of these restricted quantities of headspace gas; larger or less volatile constituents cannot. The amounts present in the small volume of gas injected are simply too low for detection in most cases. While precolumn concentrations or splitless injection (in which the solvent effect is utilized to achieve a narrowband concentration of trace components on the head of the column) can sometimes be used to overcome these limitations, these techniques, however, are not universally adaptable.

The swing toward high-resolution gas chromatography, encouraged by the availability of columns possessing 2500–3500 effective theoretical plates per meter, draws renewed attention to this old problem, because the sample capacity of these high resolution systems is still smaller, reducing still further the size of sample that can be injected.

But headspace sampling is an area that most of us are loath to abandon.

In many cases, headspace compositions are much more meaningful than the total volatile analysis resulting from distillation or extraction procedures.

Fortunately, the situation is not hopeless; many investigators have been working on these problems, and many interesting results are beginning to emerge. This symposium is an attempt to bring some of those investigators together, and to explore methods of headspace concentration and headspace sampling that are producing results on a variety of products and model systems. The content of the following papers will, I believe, convince most readers that the prognosis for a bright future in headspace sampling is highly favorable.

WALTER JENNINGS
Davis, California

PREFACE

The merits and demerits of direct vapor analysis, or as it is more popularly known, the headspace method, have long been debated. Proponents of this technique cite the ease with which vapor analyses may be performed: The determination of volatile flavor components by direct chromatographic analysis is preferred by many to the classic methods involving distillation, adsorption, extraction, etc. On the other hand, the gain resulting from direct vapor analysis in eliminating the variability associated with multistep methods may be offset by nonreproducibility arising from inefficient sample preparation, even in a single-step procedure.

A symposium on the analysis of foods and beverages by headspace techniques was organized by the Flavor Subdivision of the Agricultural and Food Chemistry Division of American Chemical Society at its 174th National Meeting, August 29–September 2, 1977, in Chicago, Illinois, with the purpose of reviewing the latest developments in this field. This volume presents the proceedings of that symposium.

The current state-of-the-art points to a productive combination of techniques leading to the enrichment of headspace vapor components with gas chromatographic resolution followed by mass spectrometric identification. Such concentration techniques obviate the need for an increased sample size with its attendant drawback of a decrease in the minimum detectable amounts of flavor compounds of low vapor pressure. It may be concluded that headspace analysis is alive and well.

Flavor chemists in industry and academia from Europe, the United States, and Japan have contributed recent findings that cover the analysis by headspace techniques of mouth odors, vegetable flavors, lipoxygenase catalyzed reactions, the vanilla bean, coffee, tea, cocoa, beer, wine, and sake. Other contributors have dealt with general considerations such as the use and abuse of headspace sampling, statistical treatments of GLC headspace data, as well as quantitative aspects, new instrumentation, and techniques.

On behalf of the Flavor Subdivision, the editor wishes to thank the speakers, all experts in their fields, whose outstanding presentations made this symposium a considerable success; the papers presented in this volume will be of great value to the advancement of flavor research. The editor is also grateful to the contributors for their valiant and courteous responses to the numerous demands made on them for the preparation of this volume. He is particularly grateful to Professor Walter Jennings for contributing the foreword and to the publishers for their guidance and assistance.

HEADSPACE SAMPLING: USE AND ABUSE

S. G. Wyllie, S. Alves, M. Filsoof and W. G. Jennings[1]
*Department of Food Science & Technology, University
of California, Davis, CA 95616*

ABSTRACT

*As applied to gas chromatographic sampling methodology,
many of us frequently misuse the term "headspace". Most
precisely, it should denote that mixture of vapors existing
in equilibrium with a sample held in a closed system. Because
only the more abundant and more volatile compounds will exist
at detectable levels in the small samples that can be used for
direct injection, a variety of methods for achieving headspace
concentration have been proposed. When the vapor is removed
at a rate faster than the equilibrium can be maintained,
changes in the relative concentrations of individual components
can be expected to occur. Compositional changes can also be
engendered by discriminatory trapping; some trapping substrates
exhibit lower affinities for specific compounds, and similarly,
discrimination can be experienced in the recovery step.*

---

[1]To whom all inquiries should be directed.

1

I. INTRODUCTION

The analysis of the headspace vapors above foodstuffs by
gas chromatography or gas chromatography-mass spectrometry
(GC-MS) has been widely applied in flavor chemistry. A variety
of methods have been used to sample and/or isolate the trace
volatiles present in such headspace. However, the term "headspace" as applied to these sampling techniques has been used
to convey a number of different meanings. In the context of
this work we have defined headspace as the gaseous mixture
surrounding a sample within a closed system at equilibrium.

Some workers have suggested the use of displacement procedures to obtain larger volumes of a "true" headspace sample.
These have ranged from the displacement of a gaseous sample
within a confined space via a moveable piston or a liquid to
the inflation of a balloon within that space. When such procedures are used, attention should be directed to the possibility of preferential solubility or absorption of sample components in the rubber, lubricant or other parts of the system.
Preferential adsorption on the walls of the container or sampling system can also yield variable results. Chromatograms of
simple syringe injections from a standard headspace source frequently exhibit considerable scatter unless the syringe has
been filled and emptied several times to satisfy its adsorptive
demands.

Many "headspace" determinations involve the passage of a
non-condensible gas over the sample to sweep the volatiles into
a trapping device. Under these non-equilibrium conditions the
composition of the sample as subsequently determined--i.e. the
ratios of the individual volatiles--may bear little relation
to the true headspace composition. Additionally, the manipulations required to transfer the sample from the trap to the
chromatograph may also cause compositional changes.

Since in many cases the levels of volatiles in a headspace
sample are very low and since these volatiles are almost always
dominated by water, some method of preconcentration and cleanup
before analysis is usually required. The use of porous polymers
to affect these steps is now widespread (1, 2, 3, 4) and considerable work has been carried out on the relevant properties
of the available materials (5, 6).

Less attention has been paid, however, to the influence of
these adsorbants and of the sample manipulations required for
their use, on the composition of the sample. Of particular
concern is whether the adsorption and desorption processes are
quantitative under the conditions employed and the influence of
the subsequent sample collection procedure.

The usual procedures for sample recovery are heat desorption followed by collection in a cooled trap, or (less commonly)
solvent extraction. It is likely that either of these manipulations will have an influence on the sample composition.

A number of investigators have described methods for the
direct desorption of the collection traps in the inlet of a
gas chromatograph (4, 8). While this method obviously minimizes sample handling losses, it does have some disadvantages,
e.g., only one analytical run can be obtained from each collection. In our case we have been unable to obtain sufficiently
rapid desorption to meet the injection requirements for good
chromatography on small-bore capillary columns.

II. METHODS AND MATERIALS

A. Gas Chromatography

Analyses were performed on a Packard Model 427 gas chromatograph adapted to an improved version of a linear glass
inlet splitter (9) and a wall-coated open-tubular (WCOT) glass
capillary column, 0.24 mm i.d. X 40 m., coated with methyl

silicone SE-30 admixed with 7% Igepal CO 990. Inlet and
detector temperatures were maintained at 200°C. Unless otherwise specified the column was programmed from 70 to 160°C at
6°C/min after an initial delay of 4 min. Because the peaks
were narrow, sharp and symmetrical, and baseline separation was
achieved, the sample compositions were calculated from the
measurement of the peak heights.

B.   Model Systems

Two model systems, whose components were selected to
represent a range of functional groups and boiling point, were
used. Their components, in order of elution on these columns,
are shown in Table 1 and Table 2.

TABLE 1	TABLE 2
Components of Model System 1	Components of Model System 2
Ethanol	Ethyl butyrate
2-Pentanone	2-Pentanone
Heptane	Hexanol
Pentanol	Hexyl acetate
Hexanol	Limonene
Hexyl formate	
2-Octanone	
Limonene	
Heptyl acetate	
γ-Heptalactone	

C.   Porous Polymer Trapping Procedures

The traps were prepared by filling *ca.* 3 cm of a 15 cm
length of 6 mm o.d. Pyrex tubing with either 80-100 mesh
Porapak Q (Waters Associates) or 60-80 mesh Tenax GC (Enka,
The Netherlands) between glass-wool plugs. Traps were conditioned at 180° at a flow rate of 60 ml/min of purified N_2, for
8 hr. A similar tube packed only with glass wool was utilized

for the sample collection efficiency experiments.

The desorption-collection system used is shown in Figure 1.

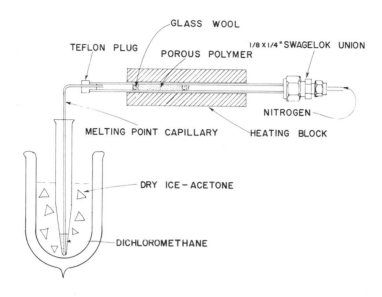

Fig. 1.   Apparatus used for desorption-collection from the porous polymer traps.   See text for details.

The heating block was maintained at 130°, the trap flow rate at 10 ml/min and the trapping time was 30 min unless otherwise specified.

For the through-flush experiments *ca.* 3 μl of the model system mixture was applied to one end of the trap with a microsyringe and the apparatus immediately assembled so that the gas flow swept the sample through the polymer trap, and the desorption-collection procedure commenced.

In the backflush experiments, the sample was applied as above but the sample was flushed into the polymer for 5 min then the trap reversed, placed in the desorption-collection apparatus and the sample collected as above.   For some experiments the bent capillary methylene chloride trap was replaced with a straight length of capillary tube (uncut melting point tubes, 20 cm), cooled by a glass-wool pad soaked in acetone and covered with dry ice.

D.   Headspace Sampling

Erlenmeyer flasks (250 ml) fitted with Teflon stoppers having a small central rubber septum were used for headspace analysis. The sample (3 ml) was added to the flask which was then equilibrated at room temperature for 1 hr. To satisfy adsorptive demand of the syringe, the plunger was reciprocated several times, filling and emptying the syringe while it remained attached to the sample vessel, before the removal of a 3.0 ml headspace sample for immediate injection.

For sweeping experiments, a stream of nitrogen was passed into the flask via a long hypodermic needle which terminated close to the surface of the liquid. The effluent gas was carried via a shorter needle to the polymer trap. Flow rates and trapping times are specified on the figures. The headspace vapors of canned Bartlett pears were trapped by passing a stream of purified N_2 over a pureéd sample of canned Bartlett pears contained in a three-neck 3 L flask. For the direct headspace determination of canned Bartlett volatiles a 3.0 ml sample was withdrawn from the headspace over the pureéd pears (500 g) contained in a 3 L flask and equilibrated at room temperature for 24 hr.

E.   Extraction

Distillation-extraction utilized a Nickerson-Likens apparatus (10) as modified by Maarse and Kepner (11). The material was mixed with water (100 ml) and continuously extracted with pentane (5 ml) for 2 hr.

III. RESULTS AND DISCUSSION

Figure 2 shows the influence of various sampling techniques on the composition of a model system (Table 1). This system was chosen to provide a range of volatilities and functionalities similar to those which may be encountered in a real system and has been the subject of a previous investigation (5). The composition determined by multiple injections of neat solution provides a reference. The effect of the final sample collection procedure was evaluated by injecting $ca.$ µl of sample into a trap packed with glass wool, and then subjecting it to the heat desorption-collection conditions as described in the experimental section. The changes in composition produced by this procedure were relatively minor and were due largely to losses of the more volatile compounds, particularly ethanol. These results indicate that the final collection procedure is of high efficiency.

The desorption characteristics of the polymer trapping material were tested with the trap in two different configurations. In one configuration the sample was applied at one end of the trap and flushed through the plug of porous polymer into the collection assembly. This was used in an attempt to duplicate the path of a sample component whose retention had almost been exceeded during the trapping procedure. The composition of the samples determined by this technique shows some loss of the less volatile constituents, particularly in the case of Porapak Q, where the considerable loss of limonene (peak 8) is notable. The superior desorption characteristics of Tenax GC for higher-boiling-point compounds has already been pointed out by Butler and Burke (4).

In the second configuration, the sample was applied to one end of the trap, swept onto the polymer, the trap reversed and the sample collected by backflushing.

The complete lack of ethanol in the backflushed Tenax

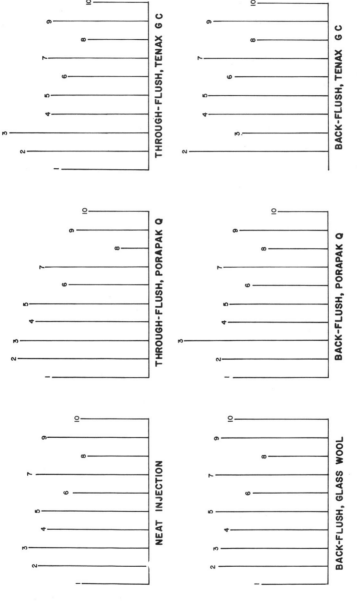

Fig. 2. Influence of through-flush or back-flush recovery from Porapak Q or Tenax GC, as compared with a neat injection and with recovery of sample placed directly on glass wool. Sample components appear in the order as listed in Table 1.

sample was found to be due to the breakthrough of this component while the sample was being swept onto the trap, and
reflects the very low adsorption of Tenax for the lower alcohols
(7). It is noteworthy that the loss of limonene observed in the
through-flush method is not apparent using the backflush procedures.

The recoveries of the higher boiling more polar compounds
(peaks 6, 7, 9, 10) from both Porapak Q and Tenax GC are not
quantitative, but the discrepancies are not large.

Since in some cases the presence of a solvent is undesirable,
the efficiency of sample desorption into a chilled glass
capillary was briefly evaluated. The composition of the
recovered sample was found to vary widely depending on the
desorption temperature and the flushing gas flow rate (Figure
3). At high temperature and/or flow rates the recovery of the
more volatile components was very low but at a lower flow rate
(10 ml/min) and desorption temperatures, compositions in reasonable agreement with that of the heat injection sample were
obtained. Considerable care is therefore required in the
control of these factors if a valid sample composition is to be
determined.

While direct injection of the equilibrated headspace vapors
over a sample in a gas chromatograph is a simple method of
determining the composition of those vapors, the method has
many disadvantages.

Particularly with capillary columns, the size of the
injected sample must be restricted or chromatographic resolution
is sacrificed. This practical limitation means that many
components, especially those of higher boiling points (i.e.
lower vapor pressures), may not be observed. Additionally, a
direct headspace usually contains large amounts of water vapor,
and the repeated injection of water-containing samples usually
leads to rapid deterioration of the column.

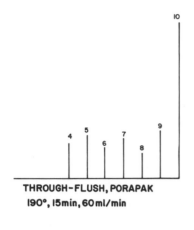

THROUGH-FLUSH, PORAPAK
190°, 15min, 60ml/min

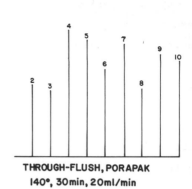

THROUGH-FLUSH, PORAPAK
140°, 30min, 20ml/min

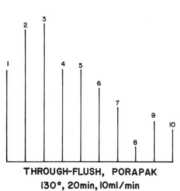

THROUGH-FLUSH, PORAPAK
130°, 20min, 10ml/min

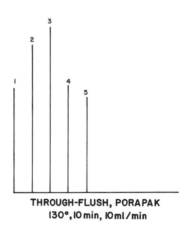

THROUGH-FLUSH, PORAPAK
130°, 10min, 10ml/min

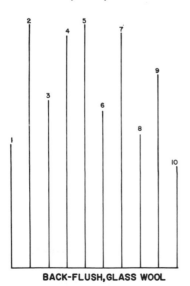

BACK-FLUSH, GLASS WOOL

Fig. 3. Effect of flushing gas flow rate and trap desorption temperature on component recovery. Eluted sample trapped in chilled glass capillary.

By sweeping an inert gas over the sample and trapping the resultant vapors on porous polymer traps, a considerable concentration can be achieved. When combined with a development step (Jennings, 2), this procedure enables both sample concentration and the removal of much of the water vapor. However, such a system is not at equilibrium and therefore the composition of the headspace vapors determined by this method may differ markedly from that determined on headspace vapors at equilibrium.

The composition of the collected headspace vapors would be expected to vary with the flow rate of the sweeping gas and the time of collection. The influence of these parameters on the composition of a model system has been determined and is shown in Figure 4. As expected, the composition of the equilibrated

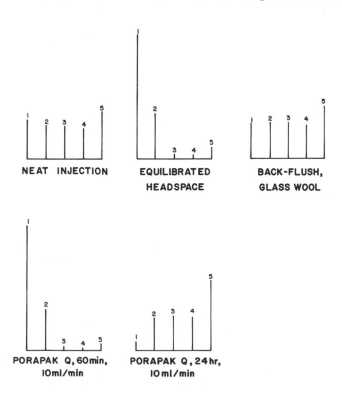

NEAT INJECTION   EQUILIBRATED   BACK-FLUSH,
                  HEADSPACE   GLASS WOOL

PORAPAK Q, 60min,   PORAPAK Q, 24hr,
    10ml/min   10ml/min

Fig. 4. Composition of headspace samples collected at low flow rates for extended periods, as compared to a neat injection, direct injection of the equilibrated headspace, and recovery of sample placed directly on glass wool. Sample components appear in the order listed in Table 2.

headspace sample reflects the vapor pressures of the sample
components. The composition of the headspace, as determined
by the gas sweeping method, closely resembled that of the
equilibrium headspace when the sample was collected for 1 hr at
a flow rate of 10 ml/min. However, when the sampling was continued for 24 hr, a completely different picture of the headspace composition is obtained. Clearly breakthrough has
occurred with some of the components and the resultant composition is completely distorted. Sampling time, sweeping gas flow
rate and trap capacity must, therefore, be carefully considered
if a composition reflecting that of the equilibrium sample is to
be obtained.

Examples of the results of various sampling procedures on
the composition of a complex system are shown in Figures 5 and 6,
which show the results of the analysis of the volatiles obtained
from canned Bartlett pears by several methods. The characteristic aroma of Bartlett pears is known to be due to the presence
of esters of <u>trans</u>:2-<u>cis</u>:4-decadienoic acid, and these could
readily be detected in the headspace by the nose. However, even
with the largest injection of the headspace vapors compatible
with chromatographic requirements, little of these compounds
could be detected; on the other hand they are present in sample
obtained by solvent extraction (Nickerson/Likens) in considerable
amounts (Figure 5).

Also it can be seen that some of the early peaks of the
direct headspace are lost or have been obscured by the solvent
in the solvent extraction sample. The essences obtained by gas
sweeping Bartlett pear headspace onto Porapak Q at a rate of
40 ml/min for 3 hr and 24 hr, respectively, are shown in Figure
6. The yield of the less volatile components is increased with
sweeping time.

We conclude that, in order to obtain a complete picture
of the volatiles present in a particular system, more than one

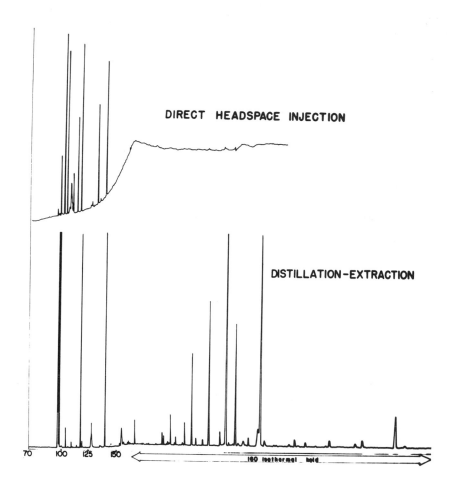

Fig. 5.   Chromatograms from (top) direct injection of head-space vapors, and (bottom) distillation-extraction of Bartlett pear.   0.25 X 40 m WCOT glass capillary column coated with methyl silicone SE 30; 70 to 160°C at 6°/min, after an initial hold of 4 min at 70°.

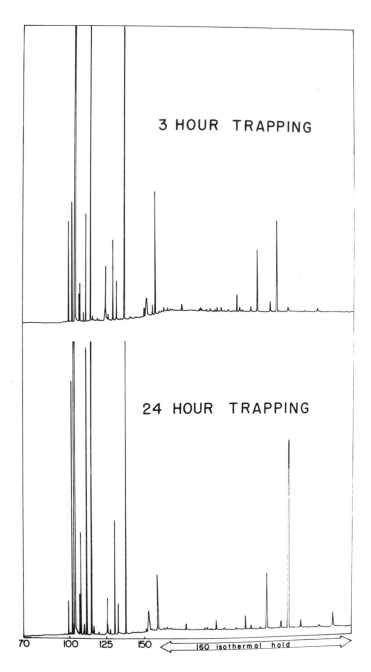

Fig. 6. *Chromatograms from Porapak Q essences of Bartlett pear volatiles, with trapping periods of 3 and 24 hrs. See text for details.*

sampling technique must be employed and the parameters of the
sampling procedures controlled carefully, if meaningful quantitative data are to be obtained.

ACKNOWLEDGEMENTS

S. G. Wyllie is on sabbatical leave from Hawkesbury
Agricultural College, NSW, Australia. S. Alves was supported
by an EMBRAPA Fellowship administered by the Brazilian Ministry
of Agriculture. M. Filsoof is on special leave from the College
of Pharmacy, University of Tehran.

REFERENCES

1. Dravnieks, A., Krotoszynski, B. K., Whitfield, J.,
    O'Donnell, A. and Burgwald, T. Environ. Sci. Technol.
    5, 1220 (1971).

2. Jennings, W. G., Wohleb, R. H. and Lewis, M. J. J. Food
    Sci. 37, 69 (1972).

3. Zlatkis, A., Bertsch, W., Lichenstein, H. A., Tishbee, A.,
    Shunbo, F., Liebich, H. M., Coscia, A. M. and Fleischer, N.
    Anal. Chem. 45, 763 (1973).

4. Schultz, T. H., Flath, R. A., Mon, T. R. J. Agr. Food Chem.
    19, 1060 (1971).

5. Butler, L. D. and Burke, M. F. J. Chromatogr. Sci., 14,
    117 (1976).

6. Jennings, W. G. and Filsoof, M. J. Agr. Food Chem. 25, 440
    (1977).

7. Kuo, P. P. K., Chian, E. S. K., De Walle, F. B., Kim, J. H.
    Anal. Chem., 49, 1023 (1977).

8. Murray, K. E., J. Chromatogr., 135, 49 (1977).

9. Jennings, W. G., Food Chem. , 2, 185 (1977).

10. Nickerson, G. B., Likens, S. T., J. Chromatogr. 21, 1 (1966).

11. Maarse, H., Kepner, R. E., J. Agric. Food Chem., 18, 1095
    (1970).

QUANTITATIVE HEAD SPACE ANALYSIS: TOTAL AND SPECIFIC GROUP ANALYSIS

H. MAARSE and J. SCHAEFER
Central Institute for Nutrition and Food Research TNO

Head space chromatograms of food and other products show large numbers of peaks of varying heights. Quantitative evaluation of these chromatograms is difficult as many small peaks are hidden under large ones. For those groups which possess a functional group in the molecule, this problem can be overcome by specific group analysis. Application is possible in those studies where only specific groups of compounds are of interest. Methods have been developed for quantitative measurement of a number of those chemical groups in the head space; they are applied both in the laboratory and in the field. In some model experiments quantitative determinations of a number of compounds were carried out in a total vapour sample as well as in isolated fractions. The method was used for measuring carbonyl compounds, pyrazines, acids and phenols in the process gases of a laboratory cocoa roast apparatus and in the emission gases of a cocoa factory. Another application was the determination of phenols and acids in the ventilation air of swine buildings.

INTRODUCTION

The era of identification of large numbers of compounds has been a very fascinating one and still the elucidation of the structure of an unknown compound is a satisfying result. However, with the use of the combination of gas chromatography, mass spectrometry and computer and the availability of large

numbers of reference spectra, identification is becoming more
and more a routine job. In our compilation of volatile compounds
in foods (1) almost 2900 compounds are listed, which have been
reported in the literature as constituents of food products
until October 1976. Contrary to these large numbers of data on
the qualitative composition, only of a limited number of foods
quantitative data have been published.

In exploring new fields in modern aroma research there is an
increasing need for these data e.g. in the study of the correlation of the results of sensoric and instrumental analysis.
The same need for quantitative data applies to odour pollution
studies which are carried out to find correlations between the
composition and the 'odour concentration'[x] of emission gases.
The vapour over a product, or the emission gases of a source of
malodour , generally consists of a large number of components in
varying concentrations. The quantitative analysis of the relevant
compounds, which often are the minor ones, is interfered with by
the major constituents or by compounds with the same chromatographic properties.

   We have been looking for methods which overcome these
problems, and we were successful in the analysis of some specific
groups of compounds, phenols, acids, saturated carbonyl compounds
and pyrazines, that were collected as groups and analyzed by gas
chromatography. No group separation is needed for the sulphur
compounds as these can be detected specifically by the flame
photometric or the microcoulometric detector (2).

   In this paper procedures for collection and analysis of the
above mentioned groups of compounds are discussed and applications
in odour pollution studies and in analysis of gases emitted
during the roasting of cocoa nibs are given.

---

x) the number of times the odorous air must be diluted to be
   undistinguishable from odour-free air by half of the panel
   members

EXPERIMENTAL

Sampling unit

The sampling unit (Figure 1) was portable and powered with a
12 V battery, so that it could be used also in the field. It
existed of a membrane pump with a capacity of 5 l/min, a flow
meter and a gas meter. The air was passed through a glass-fiber
filter to remove dust particles, through a trap and then through
the meters and the pump, thus preventing contamination of the trap.

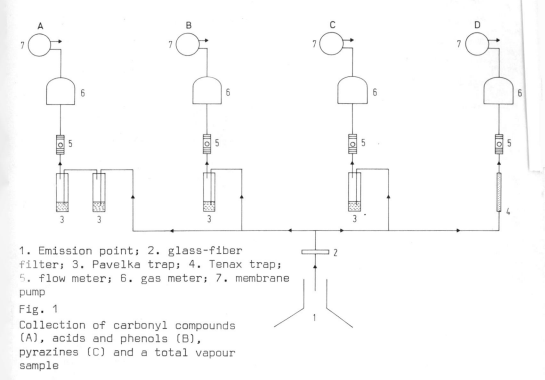

1. Emission point; 2. glass-fiber
filter; 3. Pavelka trap; 4. Tenax trap;
5. flow meter; 6. gas meter; 7. membrane
pump

Fig. 1
Collection of carbonyl compounds
(A), acids and phenols (B),
pyrazines (C) and a total vapour
sample

Samples were taken in the laboratory from a cocoa roast apparatus
and in the field the ventilation air of a swine building and the
emission gases of a cocoa factory were collected. In a schematic
drawing (Figure 1) it is indicated how at the cocoa factory,
carbonyl compounds (A), acids and phenols (B), pyrazines (C) and
a total vapour sample (D) were collected.

LABORATORY COCOA ROAST APPARATUS

For roasting cocoa nibs (batches of 400 g) obtained from
Ghana beans, a laboratory roast apparatus as shown schematically
in Figure 2 was used. Purified air entered the oven through the
heated (120°C) inlet. The temperature in the oven was
measured with the aid of a thermocouple and recorded. The ro-
tating oven was coupled with a special deviced coupling to the
heated (120°C) tubing which was connected with the trap. Carbonyl
compounds, pyrazines, phenols and acids were collected by passing
the process gases through the appropriate trap during the whole
process which lasted 1 h, including 0.5 h to reach the end
temperature.

Fig. 2   Laboratory cocoa roast apparatus

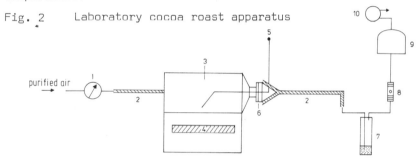

1. Flow meter; 2. heated tubes (120°C);3. oven;
4. heating element; 5. thermocouple; 6. coupling device;
7. trap; 8. flow meter; 9. gas meter; 10. membrane pump

TRAPPING PROCEDURES AND ANALYSIS

Carbonyl compounds were collected from a gas stream in two
liquid absorption traps according to Pavelka (3) ("Pavelka traps")
in series, filled each with 10 ml of an aqueous solution of
semicarbazide (10% w/w) and sodium acetate (10% w/w). After
passing 100-200 l through the traps with a flow of 2 l/min.,
the combined aqueous solutions were transferred to the flask of
a rotary film evaporator and the volume reduced to approximately

5 ml. This residue was transferred to a volumetric flask of
20 ml and diluted to volume with distilled water. Of this
solution 10 ml was pipetted into an infusion flask of 30 ml and
after addition of 1 ml of an internal standard solution,
5 g NaCl, 5 ml water and 2 ml concentrated H_2SO_4 the flask was
closed immediately, and then fully immersed in a thermostated
waterbath of $37^\circ C$. The concentration of the more volatile carbonyl compounds was determined by analyzing the vapour according
to the procedure described by Kepner et al. (4). To analyze
compounds with a low vapour pressure these compounds were extracted after regeneration with pentane/ether (2+1) (3x20 ml);
here n-decanal was used as internal standard. After drying
the extract on Na_2SO_4 the volume was reduced to 0.5 ml and
1 µl was analyzed. Gas chromatographic conditions are given in
Table 1.

Table 1. Conditions for the gas chromatographic analysis

	carbonyl compounds	pyrazines	phenols acids	Tenax concentrate
apparatus	Intersmat I.G.C. 16	Intersmat I.G.C. 16	Hewlett-Packard 7620	Hewlett-Packard 7620
column length (m)	90	150	50	50
int.diam. (mm)	0.5	0.75	0.75	0.75
material	glass	s.s.	s.s.	s.s.
stationary phase	Carb. 20M	Carb. 20M	F.F.A.P.	Carb. 20M
detector	F.I.D.	F.I.D.	F.I.D.	F.I.D.
flow (ml/min) carrier gas	4	10	10	10
H_2	25	25	30	30
air	400	400	500	500
temperature ($^\circ C$) column	70 or 110	120	150	70 (6 min) $\longrightarrow$ $\xrightarrow{2^\circ/min}$ 150
detector	150	150	200	200
injector	150	150	200	200
injected amount liquid (µl)	1	1	1	1
vapour (ml)	1	-	-	-

Standard solutions in ethanol of the compounds of interest were prepared, and 1 ml of these solutions was added to 10 ml of an aqueous solution containing semicarbazide (10% w/w) and sodium acetate (10% w/w). After a reaction time of 5 min this solution was treated as described above. The internal standard solutions were prepared as follows: 5 ml of a 1000 ppm solution of the internal standard in ethanol was added to 10 ml of an aqueous solution containing semicarbazide (10% w/w) and sodium acetate (10% w/w). After a reaction time of 5 min. the solution was transferred to the flask of a rotary film evaporator and the volume was reduced to approximately 5 ml. This residue was transferred to a volumetric flask of 50 ml and diluted to volume with distilled water.

Pyrazines were sampled from a gas stream in a Pavelka trap, filled with 10 ml 1N H_2SO_4. After passing 100-200 l through the trap, with a flow of 2 l/min, the acid solution was transferred to a separator funnel, brought up to pH=9 with 1N NaOH, and extracted three times with 20 ml of pentane/ether (2+1). The extract was dried on Na_2SO_4 and the volume reduced to 0.5 ml by evaporation through a Vigreux column. After addition of 5 µl of a 500 mg/l solution of n-pentadecane in pentane/ether (2+1), as an internal standard, 1 µl was analyzed by gas chromatography (conditions see Table 1). 5 µl of a standard solution of 2,5-dimethylpyrazine, trimethylpyrazine and tetramethylpyrazine were added to 0.5 ml of pentane/ether (2+1). After addition of 5 µl of the internal standard solution 1 µl of the solution was analyzed by gas chromatography.

Carboxylic acids and phenols were collected in a Pavelka trap, filled with 10 ml of a 2N NaOH solution. After passing 100-200 l through the trap with a flow of 2 l/min the solution was transferred to a separator funnel and extracted with pentane/ether (2+1) to remove all other trapped compounds.

1 ml of an internal standard solution of hexanoic acid in
2N NaOH (5 mg/l) was added and then the solution was acidified
to pH=2 by addition of 2N HCl and extracted three times with
10 ml of pentane/ether (1+1). The extract was dried over Na_2SO_4
and the volume was reduced to 0.5 ml by evaporation through a
Vigreux column and further to 0.1 ml by purging with a slight
stream of N_2. 1 µl was analyzed by gas chromatography (conditions
see Table 1).

Also a standard solution of acids and phenols, including hexanoic
acid, in pentane/ether (1+1), was analyzed by gas chromatography.

Total vapour samples were collected on a Tenax adsorption
trap, which consisted of a glass tube (10 cm x 6 mm i.d.) filled
with 200 mg Tenax. The gas stream was passed through this trap
with a flow of 2 l/min. In the laboratory the adsorbed compounds
were removed from the trap by elution with 5 ml ether. This
volume was reduced to 0.2 ml by evaporation through a Vigreux
column and finally to 0.1 ml by purging with a slight stream of
N_2. 1 µl of this concentrate was analyzed by gas chromatography
(conditions see Tabel 1). The calculation of the amount of the
components in the collected sample was made on basis of comparative peak heights or peak areas between standard and
unknowns.

TRAPPING EFFICIENCY

Trapping efficiencies were determined with the diffusion
apparatus described by Altshuller and Cohen (5) and schematically
shown in Figure 3. A diffusion tube was filled with a mixture
of the compounds of interest. Nitrogen was led over the tube,
with a flow of 100 ml/min, into an air dilution device and the
dilute gas stream passed through two or three traps in series.
The diffusion part of the apparatus was held at constant
temperature. Samples of the non diluted sample could be taken
with a syringe through a rubber cap and analyzed by gas

chromatography. From air and N_2 flow the dilution factor could
be calculated. The efficiency of the first trap was calculated
by comparing the amounts found in the other trap(s) to that
found in the first trap.

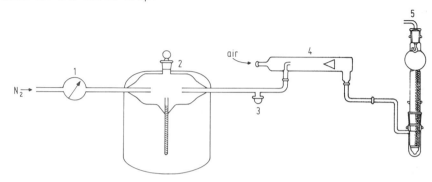

Fig. 3   Assembly for measurement of trapping efficiency
            1. Flow meter; 2. thermostated diffusion cell;
            3. sampling point for CG analysis; 4. air dilution
            device; 5. Pavelka trap

RECOVERY DETERMINATIONS

Carbonyl compounds

        Trapping of carbonyl compounds as a group from gas streams
has been tried by various authors using different absorbents:
        - a solution of $NaHSO_3$
        - a solution of 2,4-dinitrophenylhydrazine (DNPH)
        - a solution of an ammoniumacethylhydrazide (Girard T or P)
        - a solution of hydroxylamine
        - a solution of semicarbazide.
In air pollution studies bisulphite solutions have been used by
many investigators to trap carbonyl compounds from air streams
(6,7). The carbonyls were analyzed either directly as
derivative and regenerated with Na_2CO_3 in the injection port
(6,7) or after regeneration by the addition of sodium hydroxide

to the solution. Disadvantages of the method are that ketones are not efficiently collected and that only short collection periods can be applied; passing gas streams for longer periods (> 1h) through a bisulphite solution results in severe losses especially of the higher (> C_4) aldehydes (Dhont, personal communication). DNPH solutions cannot be used because of the low reaction rate at low concentration levels (table 2). Another disadvantage is the fact that a large number of artifacts is formed, which interfere with the determination (Dhont, personal communication, (9)).

Table 2. Reaction rates of several carbonyl compounds with 2,4-dinitrophenylhydrazine at $55^{\circ}C$ (8)

carbonyl compound	mol.% conversion to 2,4-DNPH after 24 h at a concentration of				
	$5 \times 10^{-2}M$	$5 \times 10^{-3}M$	$5 \times 10^{-4}M$	$5 \times 10^{-6}M$	$5 \times 10^{-8}M$
acetaldehyde	78	38	25	2	0
acetone	90	45	34	2	0
heptanal	70	30	15	2	0
2-octanone	80	36	24	2	0
cyclohexanone	100	100	95	10	0
benzaldehyde	100	100	90	5	0
piperonal	100	100	95	10	0
benzophenone	95	90	80	5	0

Table 3. Efficiency of trapping carbonyl compounds in semicarbazide solutions

compound	percentage found in		
	trap 1	trap 2	trap 3
acetaldehyde	95	5	-
propanal	86	12	-
2-methylpropanal	86	12	-
3-methylbutanal	88	11	-
benzaldehyde	96	4	-
2-butanone	83	15	2
2-pentanone	55	25	10
2-hexanone	79	16	4
acetophenone	84	14	2

Water soluble hydrazones are formed from carbonyl compounds and
Girard T or Girard P. Non carbonyl compounds can be removed by
extraction and then the carbonyls regenerated by addition of
acid. For trapping trace amounts of the low molecular carbonyl
compounds from gas streams these reagents are not suitable,
because of the large number of interfering compounds originating
from the reagents. Also the trapping efficiency is not high.
 Collection of carbonyl compounds, including unsaturated ones,
in hydroxylamine solutions and analysis of the oxime derivatives
by gas chromatography was described by Vogh (10,11). Using this
method he studied the carbonyl compounds in exhaust gases of
diesel engines. He found that the oximes were stable during
gas chromatographic analysis only if all-glass systems were used.
Contact with hot metal surfaces in the injector, the column or
the detector and with traces of metals or metal oxides in the
column support material caused decomposition of the oximes.
Most of the aliphatic aldoximes gave a peak of the syn and
anti isomer. This hampers quantitative analysis of complex
mixtures of aldehydes and ketones. Phenols in the exhaust gases
were collected also and could not be separated from the oximes
and therefore are potentially interfering compounds. The present
authors obtained best results with semicarbazide solutions.
In Table 3 the percentages found in three Pavelka traps in
series are given.

     The semicarbazone method is very well suited to determine the
concentration of saturated aldehydes and ketones. A great
disadvantage is, however, the fact that unsaturated carbonyl
compounds which play an important role in the aroma of food
products and in some odour pollution problems cannot be
determined in this way. We found that 2-propenal, 2-butenal,
trans-2-hexenal and cinnamaldehyde were apparently bound by the
semi-carbazide solution; this agrees with the results reported

by Cronin (12), who found that a number of unsaturated carbonyl
compounds were subtracted by a procolumn packed with semicarbazide on Celite 545. But after regeneration these compounds could not be detected in the vapour over the solution;
probably they are decomposed during regeneration.

ACIDS, PHENOLS AND PYRAZINES

    Collection of acids and phenols together, using aqueous
sodium hydroxide solution is a very simple and straightforward
method. With the acids the only problem arises during the
removal of the excess of solvent used to extract the free
acids and phenols from the aqueous solution after acidification.
Especially the lower aliphatic acids are rather volatile and
partially lost if the volume is reduced to 100 µl. The acids
are trapped with an efficiency of 90-100% and the low recoveries
are caused by the losses during evaporation (see Table 4).

Table 4. Trapping efficiencies and recovery of acids

compound	percentage found in			recovery in %
	trap 1	trap 2	trap 3	
acetic acid	91	8	1	50
propanoic acid	98	2	-	40
butanoic acid	99	1	-	83
2-methylpropanoic acid	99	1	-	77
pentanoic acid	95	-	-	90
3-methylbutanoic acid	95	-	-	83

Table 5. Efficiency of the trapping of pyrazines in
1N H_2SO_4 solutions

compound	percentage found in		
	trap 1	trap 2	trap 3
2,5-dimethylpyrazine	100	-	-
trimethylpyrazine	100	-	-
tetramethylpyrazine	100	-	-

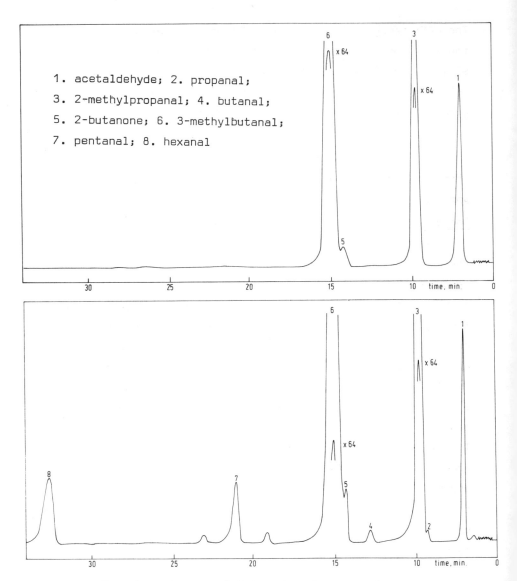

1. acetaldehyde; 2. propanal;
3. 2-methylpropanal; 4. butanal;
5. 2-butanone; 6. 3-methylbutanal;
7. pentanal; 8. hexanal

Fig. 4   Gas chromatogram of the carbonyl compounds
collected from process gases emitted during
the roasting of cocoa nibs. a) industrial roast
apparatus; b) laboratory roast apparatus.
Gas chromatographic conditions, see Table 1

The efficiency of the collection of phenols was compared with
the known efficiencies of collection on Tenax and found to be
95-100%. Recoveries of these compounds after evaporation of the
solvent were 95% for phenol and 83% for p-cresol. For three
pyrazines,which were the main ones in the process gases emitted
in the roasting of cocoa nibs, the trapping efficiency of the
acid absorption trap was determined. The results are given in
Table 5.

APPLICATIONS

Cocoa roast gases

In a study[x] which was aimed at finding a method for abating
the odour pollution caused by some cocoa factories, the concentrations of pyrazines, acids, phenols and carbonyl compounds
in the emission gases of a number of odour sources of a cocoa
factory were measured (Figure 1). Typical chromatograms of the
carbonyl compounds and the pyrazines are showns in Figures 4a
and 5, while in Figure 6 a chromatogram of a Tenax concentrate
is given. Also the process gases of a laboratory cocoa roast
apparatus were trapped and analyzed (Figure 4b). The concentrations of a number of compounds are given in Table 6.
To demonstrate the advantage of analyzing the pyrazines as a
group over their determination in a Tenax concentrate the
chromatogram in Figure 6 is given. Peaks nos. 1, 2 and 3 are the
three pyrazines which were quantitatively measured. In the total
vapour chromatogram too many compounds interfere with a
determination of the quantities of these pyrazines.

Of course, a preceding study of the composition of the
vapour must be carried out to make sure that no other compounds
with the same chromatographic properties will be trapped

---

[x] this study is carried out in cooperation with the Central
Technical Institute TNO and the Central Laboratory TNO

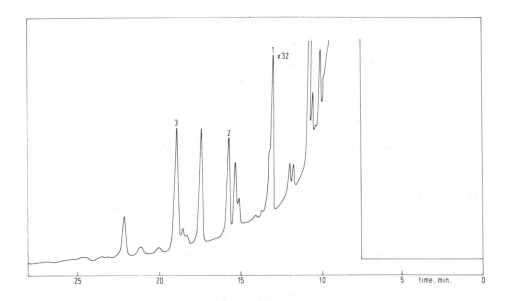

Fig. 5   Gas chromatogram of the pyrazines collected from process gases emitted during the roasting of cocoa nibs in an industrial roast apparatus

Gas chromatographic conditions, see Table 1

1. 2,5-dimethylpyrazine; 2. trimethylpyrazine;
3. tetramethylpyrazine

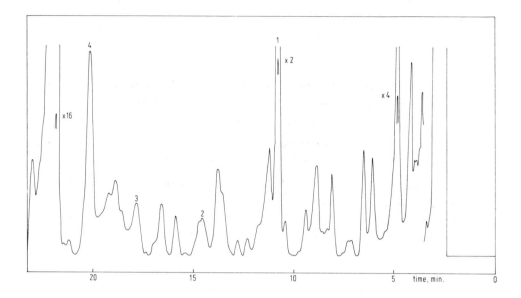

Fig. 6   Gas chromatogram of the compounds collected on a
Tenax trap from the process gases emitted during
the roasting of cocoa nibs in an industrial roast
apparatus. Gas chromatographic conditions, see
Table 1.
1. 2,5-dimethylpyrazine; 2. trimethylpyrazine;
3. tetramethylpyrazine

together with the pyrazines.

Table 6. Results of the quantitative analysis of process gases emitted
during the roasting of cocoa nibs in a laboratory cocoa
roast apparatus

compound	concentration $\mu g/m^3$		compound	concentration mg/m^3
acetaldehyde	3.7	10^{-3}	acetic acid	4.79
2-methylpropanal	6.3	10^{-3}	propanoic acid	
2-butanone	0.2	10^{-3}	butanoic acid	0.08
2-methylbutanal	9.0	10^{-3}	2-methylpropanoic acid	0.87
n-pentanal	0.3	10^{-3}	pentanoic acid	0.12
n-hexanal	0.4	10^{-3}	3-methylbutanoic acid	1.81
2,5-dimethylpyrazine	330		hexanoic acid	0.71
trimethylpyrazine	270		phenol	0.04
tetramethylpyrazine	270			

Table 7. Compounds contributing to the mal-odour of swine
buildings and their concentrations in the
ventilation air of a swine building

compound	concentration $\mu g/m^3$
indole	< 0.009
skatole	0.093
phenol	28.0
p-cresol	27.2
acetic acid	234.0
propanoic acid	< 0.02
2-methylpropanoic acid	20.8
butanoic acid	73.2
3-methylbutanoic acid	22.5
pentanoic acid	15.1

VENTILATION AIR OF SWINE BUILDINGS

In the Netherlands the malodours emitted by confinement
swine buildings have been studied[x] with the purpose to develop an
instrumental method for their measurement and for the
measurement of the efficiency of the method of abatement.
A number of compounds in the ventilation air of a confinement
swine building were identified; those which contributed
markedly to the malodour are given in Table 7 together with
the results of a typical quantitative measurement. To find
a possible correlation between sensoric measurements of the
odour of the ventilation air and the instrumental measurement
of these compounds, both were carried out in parallel at 20
swine buildings. The highest correlation value, 0.71, was found
for p-cresol. This compound is being measured now to check the
efficiency of a biological air scrubber which is applied to
abate the malodour of swine buildings. A rough estimation of the
mal odour concentration can moreover be obtained by determining
the average p-cresol concentration in the ventilation air.

CONCLUSIONS

Methods for collection and quantitative analysis of phenols,
acids, pyrazines and saturated carbonyl compounds in vapours
above food products and in gases emitted during the processing
of food were developed. Special attention was paid to the
collection of large samples during prolonged periods, in order
to enable:

- the quantitative analysis of compounds, occurring in
  low concentrations

---

x) this study was a cooperative project of the Central
   Institute for Nutrition and Food Research TNO, the Central
   Technical Institute TNO and the Institute of Agricultural
   Engineering

- obtaining quantitative data on compounds in a gas
  stream simultaneously with the determination of the
  odour concentration by a panel, so that possible
  correlations can be derived
- the collection and analysis of compounds, formed
  during processing or storage of food products and
  during the ripening of fruit.

No methods are available for e.g. the collection and separation
of unsaturated carbonyl compounds and amines, which are also
important compounds in the aroma of food as well as in
malodours produced by some industries.

A lof of work still has to be done to improve the quantitative analysis of compounds in large vapour samples.

ACKNOWLEDGEMENT

Grateful acknowledgement is made to Mr. J.H. Dhont and
Ir. J.A. Wijsman for useful discussions on trapping of
carbonyl compounds and roasting of cocoa nibs respectively.
We thank Mrs. H.E. Jansen, Mr. J. Rus and Mr. R. Wagenaar for
their technical assistance.

REFERENCES

1. Volatile compounds in food, Straten, S. van (ed.) pp. 320,
   Central Institute for Nutrition and Food Research TNO, Zeist,
   The Netherlands (1977)
2. Vitenberg, A.G., Kuznetsova, L.M., Butaeva, I.L., and
   Inshakov, M.D., Anal. Chem. 49, 128 (1977)
3. Pavelka, F., Mikrochim. Acta 6, 1121 (1969)
4. Kepner, R.E., Maarse, H., and Strating, J., Anal. Chem. 36,
   77 (1964)
5. Altshuller, A.P., and Cohen, I.R., Anal. Chem. 32, 802 (1960)
6. Levaggi, D.A., and Feldstein, M., J. Air Pollut. Control
   Assoc. 20, 312 (1970)

7. Levaggi, D.A., and Feldstein, M., J. Air Pollut. Control Assoc. 19, 43 (1969)

8. Cheronis, N.D., Proc. Int. Symp. Microchem. Techn. p. 117 (1962)

9. Hartung, L.D., Hammond, E.G., and Miner, J.R., Livest. Waste Manage. Pollut. Abatement, Proc. Int. Symp., (1971) p.105

10. Vogh, J.W., J. Air Pollut. Control Assoc. 19, 773 (1969)

11. Vogh, J.W., Anal. Chem. 43, 1618 (1970)

12. Cronin, D.A., J. Chromatogr. 64, 25 (1972)

A TECHNIQUE FOR THE DETERMINATION OF VOLATILE ORGANIC COMPOUNDS UNDER EQUILIBRIUM AND NON-EQUILIBRIUM CONDITIONS

Fouad Z. Saleeb and Timothy W. Schenz

General Foods Corporation

The DuPont 916 Thermal Evolution Analyzer (TEA) was modified for studying the concentration of volatile organic compounds (aromas) under dynamic as well as equilibrium conditions. The modified instrument is capable of measuring aromas in the gaseous phase, in aqueous and non-aqueous fluids, and in solid substrates continuously as a function of time and/or temperature. In this new technique, the nitrogen flow system of the TEA is diverted prior to entry into the flame ionization detector and allowed to pass through the appropriate sample cell. This allows the following measurements to be carried out:

(a)   the partition coefficients of various single aroma components between air/water and air/oil. The calculated coefficients are in good agreement with published data obtained by gas chromatography.

(b)   the diffusion coefficients (D) of volatile organic compounds present in solid substrates swept at known flow rates. This data approximates that of a desorption process making it possible to calculate D using appropriate diffusion equations. The energy of diffusion can be estimated from desorption experiments at more than one temperature.

*(c)   the prediction of the shelf life of systems con-
taining volatile compounds by examination of the
shape of the curves produced by sweeping nitrogen under specified conditions. This technique
was tested using model compounds on polymeric
and inorganic adsorbents as well as on starches.*

I.   INTRODUCTION

Most analyses and techniques of headspace aroma
have been concerned with measuring the absolute
amount of aroma as well as the composition of the
aroma. For many systems, valuable information can
be obtained using conventional gas chromatography
and the appropriate column for separation of components. However, it is often found that the information gained from the separation of the aroma into
its components does not give any indication of the
location of the aroma or the rate of release, both
of which are very critical, for example, for the
organoleptic acceptance of foods.

This paper presents a simple technique in which
the analysis of an aroma is carried out without
fractionation into its component parts. A modification of the DuPont Model 916 Thermal Evolution
Analyzer allows one to measure diffusion coefficients, energies of activation of diffusion processes, shelf life of aromas, and partition coefficients. This technique uses a flame ionization detector for sensitive response to volatile organic
compounds, and a precise, reproducible flow system
for quantitative measurements of concentrations in
dynamic systems. In addition, model systems may be
studied by using single components of an aroma.

Individual volatile organic compounds were used
to evaluate the partition coefficient between various phases. This was done in a static system.
Diffusion coefficients and energies of activation
for diffusion of the aroma from peppercorns were
measured using a dynamic flow system. A rapid,
accurate method for predicting the shelf life of
aroma was developed, also using a dynamic flow
system.

II. EXPERIMENTAL

A. Methods

The equipment employed was a DuPont Model 916
Thermal Evolution Analyzer (1). It is designed to
measure the release of organic carbon caused by
temperature-induced increases in volatility and by
thermal decomposition of samples (2). The amount
of total organic carbon is generally expressed as g
carbon/g sample. A schematic of the system is
shown in Figure 1. From the flow control, a flow
of nitrogen of 30 ml per minute is normally passed
to the sample oven (dotted line), where organic carbon from the sample is picked up by the carrier gas.
In the present system, the nitrogen flow was diverted using Teflon tubing prior to entry into the
sample oven and passed to various sampling devices.
A four-way miniature inert valve (Hamilton Co., Cat.
No. 86412) was placed in the system in order to provide continuous carrier flow and to permit isolation
of the sample from the system. The signal from the
flame ionization detector (FID) and electrometer
was sent to a digital electronic integrator and
strip chart recorder. The integrator, a Columbia
Scientific Model CS1-208, was equipped with a digi-

tize option, which enabled the area of a signal to be
printed at designated time intervals. In this way the
flux of the organic carbon (g carbon/sec) could be
measured. The system was calibrated by injecting with
a gas syringe a known volume of butane gas into the
gas injection port of the TEA.

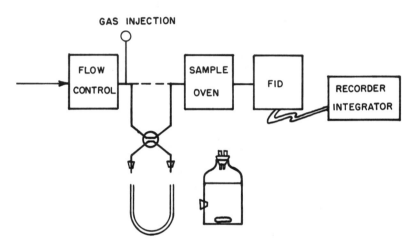

*Fig. 1. Schematic diagram of modified Thermal
Evolution Analyzer.*

Different sampling devices were used to determine
the following:

1. Partition Coefficients - The organic carbon
content of both the aqueous and air phases were
measured. A bottle equipped with a septum placed
below the water level and with one at the neck above
the water level was used (see Figure 1). Headspace
samples were taken directly from the bottle and
injected into the TEA. The analysis of the aqueous
phase required that a Hamilton Co. flash vaporization
inlet (Cat. No. 86800) be inserted into the sample
oven opening and the nitrogen flow directed through

it.   In this way, a few microliters of the aqueous
phase were withdrawn from the bottle and volatilized
upon injection into the flash vaporizer.   The
temperature of the bottle was controlled by placing
it in a thermostatted jacketed beaker.

2.   Diffusion Coefficients - For the calculation of
diffusion coefficients it was necessary to measure the
rate of organic carbon release from the material under
study.   This was accomplished by placing the material
in a simple glass U-tube (4mm ID) and flowing the
carrier gas through the tube.   Again, the
temperature of the tube was controlled by immersion
in a thermostatted bath.

3.   Shelf Life of Aroma - The shelf life of aroma was
predicted by observing the amount of organic carbon
that was swept from its substrate as a function of
sweeping time.   Again, the sample was placed in a
simple, glass U-tube and the quantity of aroma being
swept by the nitrogen from the substrate was
measured.

B.   Materials

Volatile organic compounds were used as
received.   Peppercorn samples were purchased from
retail outlets.   The substrates and their sources
were as follows:

Capsul, a modified food starch, and tapioca from
National Starch & Chemical Crop., Plainfield, N.J.;
potato starch, Accurate Chemical & Scientific Corp.,
Hicksville, N.Y.; polyvinyl pyrrolidone (PVP-360),
Sigma Chemical Co., St. Louis, MO.

III.   RESULTS AND DISCUSSION

A.   Partioning of Volatile Organic Compounds

Equilibrium partition coefficients of volatile organic compounds between the head space (air) and various liquids (e.g. water) were determined in a closed system by sampling the gaseous and liquid phases.

Table I shows typical data for the water-air partitioning coefficients (K_{wa}) of a number of volatile organic compounds at 22° and 90°C. K_{wa} is given by:

$$K_{wa} = \frac{solute\ concentration\ in\ water\ phase}{solute\ concentration\ in\ oil\ phase} \quad (1)$$

The experimental partition coefficients decreased, as expected, with an increase in the temperature of the system. For comparison, Buttery et al. (3) reported for 2-isobutyl-3-methoxy pyrazine a K_{wa} of 500 at 25°C.

TABLE I

PARTITION COEFFICIENTS (K_{wa}) OF VOLATILE ORGANIC COMPOUNDS BETWEEN WATER AND AIR

Compound	$K_{wa} = \dfrac{solute/cc\ water}{solute/cc\ air}$	
	22°C	90°C
3-hydroxy-2-butanone	7600	430
2-methoxy-5-ethylphenol	6640	426
2-isobutyl-3-methoxy pyrazine	725	28
methyl furfuryl sulphide	250	25

In many food systems, oil (fat) is present in addition to water. In such systems volatile organic

compounds are partitioned among three phases
(air/oil/water). When enough oil is present in these
systems, it is possible to analyze for the volatile
organic compound in the headspace as well as in the
oil and water phases and calculate directly the
various diffusion coefficients. On the other hand,
if the oil is present in a dispersed form (emulsion)
or in minute quantities, the analysis becomes more
difficult. However, oil/water distribution
coefficients of volatile organic compounds in these
three phase systems can be readily calculated from
a knowledge of the distribution coefficients of the
two-phase systems, namely, K_{wa} and K_{oa}, using the
simplified relationship given by Buttery et al. (4).
The partition coefficient, K_{am}, of volatile organic
substances between air and the liquid mixture is
given by:

$$K_{am} = \frac{1}{F_w/K_{wa} + F_o/K_{oa}} \qquad (2)$$

where F_w and F_o are the fractions of water and oil in
the mixture, respectively, and:

$$K_{oa} = \frac{solute\ concentration\ in\ oil\ phase}{solute\ concentration\ in\ air\ phase} \qquad (3)$$

The solute concentration in the oil phase can be
easily determined by sweeping with nitrogen a known
weight of oil containing solute placed in a glass
U-tube.

B. Diffusion of Volatile Organic Compounds Through
    Solid Substrates

Very useful information can be obtained from

studying the rate of desorption of volatile
component(s) from solid substrates at different
temperatures and particle sizes. The TEA provides a
continuous recording of the concentration of volatile
compounds released on sweeping a given weight of solid
at a fixed nitrogen flow rate (normally 30 cc/min).
The integrator provides a printout of these data at
specified time intervals (2 to 200 sec). This
technique has been applied to natural and synthetic,
inorganic and organic substrates. Results obtained
from peppercorns are given here as an example.

1. *Diffusion Coefficients of Aroma in Peppers*

Pepper was used in this study because of its
aromatic character and its availability in two
different forms, black and white. Black pepper is
the mature fruit of the plant Piper Nigrum. The fruit
is removed from the plant, soaked in boiling water
for 10 minutes and dried for 3 to 4 days. The
process yields peppercorns that are dark brown to
black in color with deep-set wrinkles formed on the
surface. White pepper is obtained from the same
plant except that the fruit is soaked in water for 2
to 3 days until most of the dark outer coating, or
pericarp, can be removed mechanically from the berry.
Subsequent washing and drying complete the process.
The difference, then, between black and white
peppercorns is that black peppers have their entire
pericarp intact, whereas in white peppers about half
of the pericarp has been removed. In both black
and white peppers, the seed coat and perisperm, or
flesh, are left undisturbed (5).

Figure 2 gives results showing the cumulative

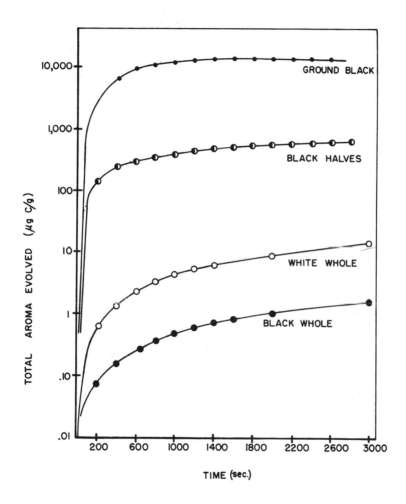

Fig. 2.   Rate of aroma release for various
forms of pepper.

(total) aroma evolved from four pepper samples at
30°C. The four curves in Figure 2 are for whole
black pepper, whole white pepper, black pepper halves
and very finely ground black pepper. The last sample
was prepared by grinding whole black pepper at liquid
nitrogen temperature in a Spex Mill. These fine
particles had an average particle size of 19 microns
as determined by Coulter Counter analysis.

The semi-logarithmic plot of Figure 2 shows the
significant differences between the rate of release
(desorption) of aromas from the different forms of
pepper. On one hand, the aromas released by whole
white pepper are about one order of magnitude higher
as compared to those given by whole black pepper. On
the other hand, the aromas desorbed from whole corns
are at least two orders of magnitude lower than those
released by pepper halves. The data clearly indicate
the very important role that the pericarp of the
pepper plays in preserving and retarding the rate of
loss of aromas from these spices, as will be
discussed later.

Figure 3 shows a scanning electron microscope
(SEM) photomicrograph of a black peppercorn cut in
half. The pericarp, or outer covering, can be seen
in the photomicrograph, which provides the dimensions
needed for the calculation of diffusion coefficients.

The aroma desorption curves given in Figure 2
were used to calculate the diffusion coefficient of
pepper aroma for diffusion through the different
regions of the pepper, namely diffusion through
pericarp and through the internal cellular matrix
(flesh).

a. *Diffusion through Whole Peppers.* From the

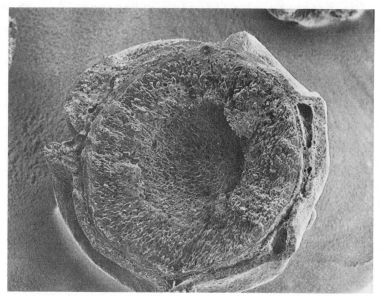

Fig. 3.   Scanning electron photomicrograph of black pepper half, magnification 20X.

inspection of (a) the difference in the magnitude of the desorption data between whole and broken peppers as outlined above and (b) the linear relationship between aroma losses and time for the whole white and whole black pepper, it was concluded that aroma losses in the case of whole peppers approximated that of a steady state diffusion in a sphere. This was arrived at because of the 3 orders of magnitude increase in aroma loss upon exposure of the inner surface of the black pepper halves. This increase cannot be accounted for by considering only the essentially 2-fold increase in surface area upon halving the pepper. Obviously, the pericarp, or outer covering, of the pepper controlled the diffusion of aroma, leading to the application of the diffusion equations for a hollow sphere (6).

The quantity of diffusing substance, Q_t, which passes through a spherical wall in time t, is given by:

$$Q_t = 4\pi Dt \frac{ab}{b-a} (C_1 - C_2) \qquad (4)$$

where D is the diffusion coefficient (cm^2/sec), b and a are the outer and inner radii of the sphere (b-a is the wall thickness) and C_1 and C_2 are the aroma concentrations of the inner and outer surfaces of the hollow sphere.

Since, in the present case, $C_1 >> C_2$, Equation 4 reduces to

$$Q_t = 4\pi Dt \frac{ab}{b-a} C_1 \qquad (5)$$

Equation 5 was used to calculate the diffusion coefficient of pepper aroma through white and black pepper. The inner radius (a) and pericarp thickness (b-a) were estimated from SEM photomicrographs and are as follows:

inner radius	a = 0.1675 cm.
white pericarp	b-a = 0.00374 cm.
black pericarp	b-a = 0.00935 cm.
	C_1 = 0.016 gm aroma (as carbon)/gm pepper)

The value of C_1 was obtained by exhaustive sweeping of finely divided pepper and by calculating the aroma evolved as grams of carbon per gram of pepper.

It should be mentioned that the size of peppercorns varies from one corn to the next. However, corns of a very narrow range of particle sizes were selected for this work and the values of a and pericarp thicknesses (b-a) should be considered to have an error of less than 10%.

b. *Diffusion through broken (ground and half peppers*. The average diffusion coefficients of aromas in black halves and finely ground pepper were calculated from the initial slopes of plots of the quantity of aroma desorbed versus the square root of time. Thus, in the early stages of desorption, for a constant diffusion D and a sheet of thickness ℓ, we have:

$$M_t/M_\infty = \frac{4}{\pi^{\frac{1}{2}}} \left(\frac{Dt}{\ell^2}\right)^{\frac{1}{2}} \tag{6}$$

where M_t/M_∞ was the fraction of the total aroma desorbed in time t. The ℓ values were 19×10^{-4} cm and 1.05×10^{-1} cm for finely divided and black halves, respectively.

c. *Values of Diffusion Coefficients*. Table II shows the calculated diffusion coefficients of aroma for the different forms of pepper.

Table II

DIFFUSION COEFFICIENTS (D) OF AROMAS IN PEPPER AT $30^\circ C$

Pepper Form	Region of Interest	D in cm^2/sec.
Black Whole	entire pericarp	1.73×10^{-11}
White Whole	pericarp fraction	6.6×10^{-11}
Black Halves	perisperm	1.4×10^{-9}
Black Fine Grind	perisperm	0.9×10^{-9}

The D values of Table II clearly show two major points. First, the pepper pieces have almost the same diffusion coefficient (approximately 1×10^{-9}

cm^2/sec) whether one considers finely divided
pepper or black halves, the latter being about 50
times as large in thickness as the former. This
fair agreement confirms the use of Equation 6 for
the diffusion of aroma within the pepper matrix.
Secondly, the diffusion of aroma through the pericarp (black or white) was very slow. The pericarp,
then, was the major factor in retarding the aroma
losses from whole pepper corns.

It should be mentioned, however, that although
the D value for the ground pepper is almost two
orders of magnitude higher than that for the
whole pepper, this does not mean that ground pepper
will lose all of its aroma very quickly even in an
open container. This is evident from the following
relationship between the diffusion path (d) and the
average diffusion coefficient D where:

$$d = \sqrt{Dt} \tag{7}$$

Taking $D = 1 \times 10^{-9}$ cm^2/sec at $30^{\circ}C$ and $t = 1$ day
($\sim 10^5$ sec), the aroma diffuses only a distance d of
0.01 cm in one day. For a period of 100 days, the
diffusion path is only 0.1 cm.

2. *Activation Energies of Diffusion*

The TEA was also found to be very useful in
measuring volatile organic compound losses at
different temperatures. This provides information
for determining activation energies of different
mass transfer processes involved in foods. Figure
4 shows an Arrhenius-type plot of the log of aroma
flux (F) from whole black pepper at 4 different
temperatures. As mentioned earlier, the aroma
that diffuses through the pericarp per unit time is
fairly constant (up to 2000 sec) at a given

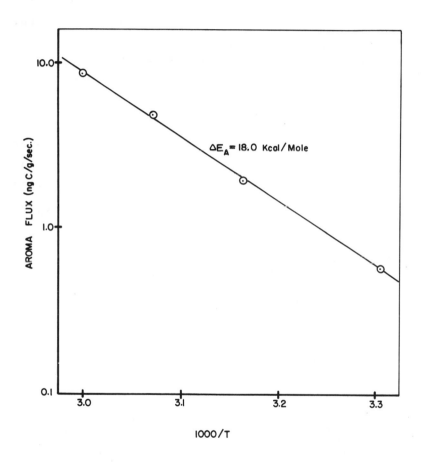

Fig. 4.   Arrhenius-type plot for aroma from peppers.

temperature.   The fluxes given in Figure 4 were
determined on the same peppercorn sample.   The
units of flux are nanograms aroma (as carbon) per
gram of pepper per second.   The fluxes were plotted
rather than the diffusion coefficients (D) in order to give an idea of the order of magnitude of
aroma losses from pepper (Equation 4 shows a direct
relation between flux (Q_t) and D).

The data in Figure 4 satisfied the relationship

$$\frac{d\ln F}{d(1/T)} = -\frac{\Delta E_a}{R} \qquad (8)$$

where R is the gas constant and ΔE_a is the activation energy of diffusion.   The slope of the curve in
Figure 4 gives (using a least squares method) an
activation energy of 18.0 kcal/mole for the diffusion of pepper aroma through the pericarp.

The organic carbon that was measured presumably included components which do not contribute
to the characteristic pepper aroma.   For work in
which the quality of an aroma is a factor, independent verification of aroma composition should be
made.

C.   Prediction of Aroma Shelf Stability from
     Sweeping Curves

Volatile organic materials are generally held
by solid substrates.   The extent of volatile loss
as a function of time at a given set of conditions
is mainly determined by the energies of interaction
of these volatile materials with the substrate.
The TEA provides, therefore, a very quick test for
predicting shelf stability.   This was achieved by
sweeping a known weight of the substrate containing

the volatile organic compound with a stream of
nitrogen (30 cc/min) at a given temperature. The
volatile organic compounds removed under such conditions were continuously recorded by the TEA
system.

Figure 5 shows typical results for
isobutyraldehyde fixed in four different substrates.
The data are presented as % isobutyraldehyde remaining in the solid as a function of sweeping
time. The TEA analysis indicates that isobutyraldehyde is retained to a greater extent by PVP
(polyvinyl pyrrolidone) than by potato starch. The
retention capacity of tapioca for isobutyraldehyde
is much less than that of potato starch but is
slightly greater than that of Capsul.

After a 10 minute sweep at 30°C the PVP re-
tains about 75% of its original isobutyraldehyde
compared with less than 25% retained by tapioca
under the same experimental conditions. The
total isobutyradehyde content of these four substrates were as follows: 4560, 12.9, 38.9, and
99.7 µgm C/gm solid for PVP, potato starch, tapioca,
and Capsul respectively.

Organoleptic evaluation over extended periods
(months) of some of the systems shown in Figure 5
as well as of other food systems confirmed the
predictions obtained from the TEA sweep curves.
The advantages of using the TEA are that the
results can be obtained in a period of about 10-30
minutes with a minimum of material and attention
with or without a knowledge of the total aroma
present and/or composition. Even though the data
presented in Figure 5 required a knowledge of the
total isobutyraldehyde level in the substrate,

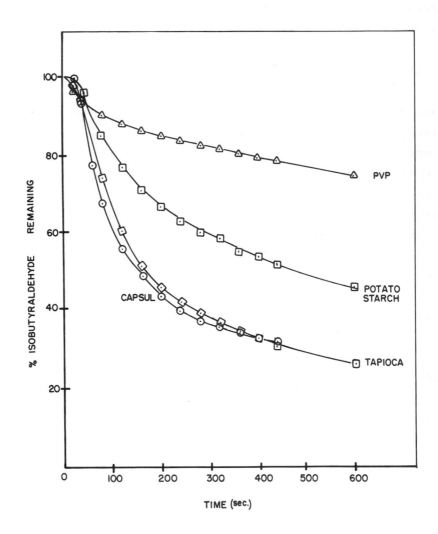

Fig. 5.   Rate of isobutyraldehyde release from various substrates.

equally important information on storage stability
can be obtained by observing the rate at which an
unknown quantity of aroma is released from a given
substrate. A system with a very steeply declining
loss of aroma curve indicates a poorly held aroma.
Good retention is characterized by sweeping curves
with slowly decreasing slope.

In summary, with slight modification, the Thermal Evolution Analyzer has had many uses in the
analysis of the interaction of volatile organic
compounds with their substrates, either natural
or synthetic. Partition coefficients of volatile
organic compounds between air/water, air/oil, and
air/oil/water can be found relatively easily. Diffusion coefficients of aromas can be determined as
well as energies of activation of the diffusion process. Owing to the accurate flow system, shelf-
like stability and other storage parameters can be
quickly and accurately measured and extrapolations
can be made.

IV. ACKNOWLEDGEMENTS

We wish to thank Elie Hayon for his encouragement and helpful discussions. We also are grateful
to General Foods Corporation for permission to publish this work.

V. REFERENCES
1. E. I. DuPont de Nemours & Co. (Inc.), Instrument Products Division, Wilmington, DE, 19898;
   Brochure A-78114.
2. Stapp, A. C., and Carle, D. W., "A New Thermal
   Analysis Instrument" presented at the Pittsburgh
   Conference of Analytical Chemistry and Applied

Spectroscopy, Cleveland, OH, March 1969.

3. Buttery, R. G., Bomben, J. L., Guadagni, D. G., and Ling, L. C., J. Agr. Food Chem., 19, 1045 (1971).

4. Buttery, R. G., Guadagni, D. G., and Ling, L. C., J. Agr. Food Chem., 21, 198 (1973).

5. Parry, J. W., "Spices: Their Morphology, Histology, and Chemistry", Chemical Publishing Co., Inc., New York (1962).

6. Crank, J., "The Mathematics of Diffusion", Oxford University Press, 1956, Page 84.

POROUS POLYMER TRAPPING FOR GC/MS ANALYSIS OF
VEGETABLE FLAVORS

Alayne L. Boyko, Max E. Morgan, and Leonard M. Libbey
Department of Food Science and Technology
Oregon State University

Flavor profiles of canned and frozen whole kernel sweet corn were obtained by entraining the volatile compounds on Porapak Q traps and by subsequent analysis on temperature-programed, 500' x 0.03" ID capillary columns (SF-96 or Carbowax 20M). Identification was based on GC/MS data, retention indices (I_E's), and retention times. The new compounds identified in canned corn included pyridine, methional, dimethyl sulfoxide, and dimethyl sulfone. Various sulfur, nitrogen, and nitrogen-sulfur heterocyclic compounds were also present as previously mentioned by Libbey et al. (1). Qualitative and quantitative varietal differences were observed in both frozen and canned samples. Many of these compounds were typical of roasted foods, such as nuts or roasted meats, and were not found to any extent in samples of frozen or fresh corn. New compounds found in frozen corn included acetoin, 3-methyl-2-cyclohexenone, and dimethyl sulfone. Various model systems were heated to simulate the canning process of sweet corn. Mixtures of water, corn starch, and sulfur-containing

(1) Libbey, L.M., M.E. Morgan, L.A. Hansen, and R.A. Scanlan. *Higher-Boiling Volatiles in Canned Whole Kernel Sweet Corn. A.C.S. Atlantic City, N.J. 1975.*

*amino acids produced the most corn-like aromas. Systems contain-
ing glutamic acid, asparagine, proline, aspartic acid, and other
amino acids produced earthy, parsnip, or vegetable notes. Pyrazines, furans, and thiophenes were among the compounds identified.
Other experiments were conducted to elucidate mechanisms of flavor
formation and to simulate sweet corn flavor.*

I. INTRODUCTION

The analysis of vegetable flavor has been the subject of many
studies during the last 20 years. Isolation and identification of
volatile compounds present in trace quantities in vegetables has
been greatly facilitated by the advent of GC, GC/MS, and headspace techniques. Salunkhe and Do (1) reviewed the biogenesis
of aroma constituents of fruits and vegetables and stated that
these products have genetically controlled, characteristic
flavors. The cultivar, maturity, and horticultural practices
also influence aroma. They concluded that much more research is
needed to elucidate the processes of aroma formation and degradation in vegetables in order to develop means to control the
production of flavor, to maintain the flavor produced, and to
improve the flavor of these nutritious products.

The relative quantities of low-boiling compounds present in
cooked sweet corn were measured by Self et al. (2) by GC. High
levels of dimethyl sulfide, hydrogen sulfide and acetaldehyde,
and low levels of methanethiol, ethanethiol, acetone and methanol
were found. Bills and Keenan (3), Williams and Nelson (4), and
others have emphasized the significance of dimethyl sulfide in
the top note of sweet corn flavor. More recent work by Ishii (5)
identified ethanol, butanol, pentanol, cis-3-hexene-1-ol, hexanal,
limonene, 2-3, 2,5- and 2,6-dimethylpyrazine, and α and β-ionone
as the main flavor constituents of corn powder. Loss of low-
boiling compounds and increase of hexanal; trans, trans-3,5-
octadiene-2-one; trans, trans-2,4-heptadienal; trans, cis-2,4-

and trans, trans-2,4-decadienal were reported to cause off-flavor
of sweet corn powder. These researchers used temperature-
programed capillary columns with SF-96 and headspace techniques.

   In our laboratory we have used headspace sampling and porous
polymer trapping techniques. Earlier work by Libbey et al. (6)
indicated the presence of dimethyl sulfide, acetaldehyde, methyl
acetate, methanol, acetone, ethyl acetate and ethanol by on-column
trapping. Extremely volatile compounds such as hydrogen sulfide
or methyl mercaptan were lost during trapping. Temperature-
programed, 500 ft x 0.03 in ID capillary columns wall-coated with
Carbowax 20M were used to investigate canned corn aroma. A series
of alkyl pyrazines was detected and because of their low threshold
values, were thought to contribute significantly to the background
flavor of canned corn. Diacetyl was reported for the first time.
Diacetyl and other α-dicarbonyls were believed to be important
both as flavoring agents and as participants in Strecker degradation reactions. Numerous other compounds were characterized in
16 GC/MS runs, including alcohols, methyl ketones, furans, etc.
These were thought to be minor contributors to canned corn flavor.

II. EXPERIMENTAL

   In our sampling procedure, 50 ml of vegetable liquor was
decanted into a screw-cap, 100 ml bottle equipped with a magnetic
stirrer (Figure 1). Corn liquor was taken directly from the canned samples and saturated with Na_2SO_4. Frozen samples were
thawed with 100 ml of hot distilled water and allowed to sit
at refrigerator temperature before the liquor was removed. The
entrainment assembly was held at 60°C with a water bath. Volatile
organic compounds were entrained using prepurified N_2 at 30 ml/
min for 30 min or longer. The nitrogen entrainment gas was
purified by passage through a 20 ft x 0.25 in OD firebrick trap
immersed in a Dry-Ice-2-methoxyethanol slurry. The N_2 swept the
volatile compounds onto a porous polymer precolumn trap. The

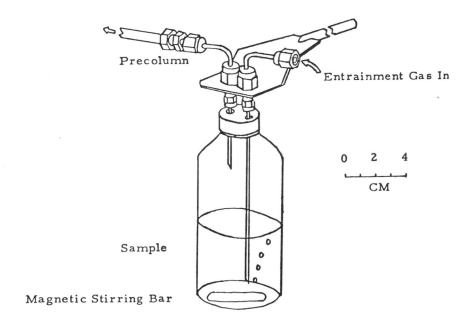

Fig. 1. Entrainment assembly

trap was 4 in x 0.24 in ID packed with 100/120 mesh Porapak Q,
100/120 mesh Chromosorb 102, or 60/80 mesh Tenax GC. Selection
of a particular porous polymer depended on the application and
will be discussed later. The precolumns were previously conditioned by purging with prepurified N_2 at a flow rate of 30 ml/
min--first for 4 hr at 200°C, and finally for 12 hr at 100°C.
During the 30-min entrainment process, the precolumn was maintained at 55°C. This prevented water condensation in the trap
and subsequent water interference in the analysis. After entrainment the polymer trap was removed from the entrainment assembly and
a solution of various ethyl esters in ethanol was applied to the
upstream end of the precolumn. Ethyl esters were used in calculating I_E values as discussed by Van Den Dool and Kratz (7).
When working with polar compounds, ethyl esters were a more useful
retention index system than the Kovats index which utilized non-

polar hydrocarbons as reference compounds. Next the trap was
purged with prepurified N_2, in the same direction as before, at
30 ml/min for an additional 20 min to remove any residual water.
Excessive purging resulted in loss of low-boiling compounds.

The compounds on the precolumn were transfered to a capillary U-tube trap by reversing the precolumn, raising its temperature to 135°C and reducing the N_2 flow to 12 ml/min for 45 min.
The 10 in X 0.03 in ID stainless steel, Dexsil-coated U-tube trap
was immersed in a slurry of Dry Ice and 2-methoxyethanol during
trapping. Such U-tube traps could be stored about a week in a
freezer without sample loss. The volatile compounds
were then flashed onto the GC and GC/MS using the inlet system
described by Scanlan et al. (8) and pictured in Figure 2.

Fig. 2. GC inlet system

Volatile materials collected from vegetables in this manner
were chromatographed on wall-coated, 500 ft X 0.03 in ID stainless steel, capillary columns. Columns were wall-coated with
6:1 Carbowax 20M and Versamid 900 or with SF-96 and 5% Igepal 880.

The columns were held at 80°C for 5 min and then programed at
1°C/min to 145°C with He flowing at 15 ml/min. The column
effluent entered the ion source of a Finnigan Quadrupole
electron impact MS via a glass jet separator. Electron voltage
was 70 ev. Spectra were scanned from m/e 15-250, and data was
collected by a System Industries Model 250 data system in the
IFSS mode. The IFSS or Integration-Time-as-a-Function-of-Signal-
Strength mode results in a nearly constant signal-to-noise
ratio and is useful in trace analyses. Analysis of data was
accomplished using this data system in conjunction with a Tek-
tronix model 4010-1 display terminal.

III.   RESULTS AND DISCUSSION

In a preliminary study, the behavior of some typical
flavor compounds on porous polymer precolumns was investigated.
The choice of porous polymer trap was made on the basis of these
retention characteristics. Table 1 shows retention times (T_R)
in minutes of various compounds on Porapak Q, Chromosorb 102
and Tenax GC precolumns under simulated sampling and water
removal conditions.

Retention performance on Porapak Q and Chromosorb 102 was
similar, while retention times exhibited on Tenax GC were considerably shorter. Thus during the 20-min water removal step,
greater losses of low-boiling compounds would occur with use of
Tenax GC traps. Porapak Q traps were used for vegetable sampling
since we were interested in compounds with a wide range of
boiling temperatures. Tenax GC traps would be useful in applications where high-boiling compounds were a major concern.

Recoveries of n-undecane from these porous polymers were measured. A known quantity was introduced onto a precolumn and after simulated sampling and water removal, the compound was desorbed
and trapped on-column as described by Morgan and Day (9). Digital
integrator response was measured and compared to a standard curve

TABLE 1

Retention Times on Precolumns Under Simulated Loading and Water Removal Conditions[a]

Compound	BP °C[b]	Retention time (Min)								
		Porapak Q			Chromosorb 102			Tenax GC		
		First Det[c]	TR	Last Det	First Det	TR	Last Det	First Det	TR	Last Det
Water	100	0.63	1.44	6.0	0.63	1.38	6.0	0.25	1.0	5.5
Methanol	64.6	2.13	3.36		1.25	2.13		0.44	0.75	
Ethanol	78.5	8.5	11.63[d]		5.25	7.0[d]		1.12	1.5[d]	
Formic acid	100.7	14.63	20.0[e]		12.0	15.75[e]		2.0	3.25[d]	
Acetic acid	118.1		>34					8.25	10.0[e]	
Acetaldehyde	21	3.63	5.0[d]		2.13	3.0[d]		0.5	0.75	
Propanal	48.8	18.0	22.75[e]		12.0	15.0[e]		2.0	2.63[d]	
N-butanal	75.7							5.5	6.5[e]	
Isobutanal	61.5							4.5	6.0[e]	
Methyl mercaptan	7.6	3.0	3.75[d]		5.13	6.75[d]		1.25	1.88	
Ethyl mercaptan	34.7	23.5	29.13[e]		10.75	13.75[d]		1.75	2.5[d]	
Isobutyl mercaptan	98							8.5	12.5[e]	
Dimethyl sulfide	37.5	23.63	28.5[e]		17.0	21.0[e]		1.69	2.13[d]	
Diethyl sulfide	92							14.38	17.38[e]	
Methyl formate	31.5	6.5	8.63[d]		3.5	4.5[d]		0.81	1.25	
Ethyl formate	54	33.0	37.0[e]		16.5	19.25[e]		2.0	3.38[d]	
Methyl acetate	57.5				17.0	20.5[e]		2.5	3.38[d]	
Ethyl acetate	77.2							7.38	9.0[e]	

[a] Precolumn conditions:

Column temperature   55° C   He flow rate   12 ml/min
Injection port temperature 120° C
Detector temperature   160° C

[b] From Handbook of Chemistry and Physics. Cleveland: Chemical Rubber Publishing Co. 1960.

[c] Det = Detected

[d] Moderate tailing

[e] Extreme tailing

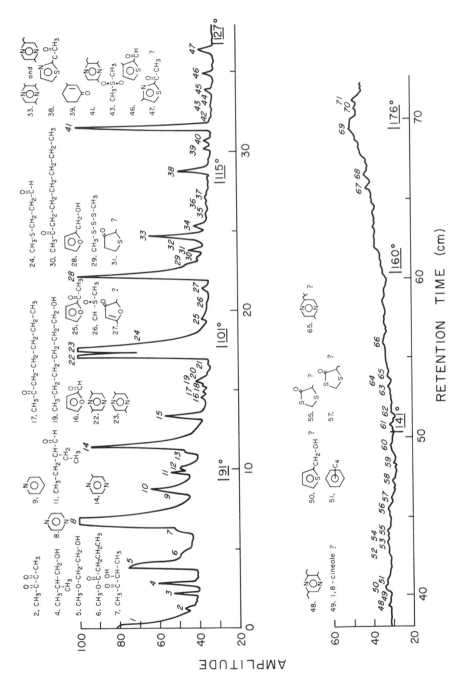

Fig. 3. Total ionization chromatogram of canned Jubilee sweet corn

prepared by direct injection. Recoveries of n-undecane were nearly 100% from these three porous polymers;however, recoveries of other compounds may not be as complete. Particular care must be exercised when using porous polymer trapping in quantitative studies.

We investigated four varieties of canned corn: Jubilee, Fanfare, Stylepak and No. 70-2367. Figure 3 shows a typical total ionization chromatogram of the volatile compounds entrained from Jubilee. Table 2 lists the compounds we identified, their I_E values and odor descriptions. Odor assessments were made by sniffing GC effluent from an effluent splitter. Pyrazine and a series of alkyl pyrazines were found. These compounds have been

TABLE 2

Compounds Detected in Canned Jubilee Sweet Corn

Compounds Detected	Retention Index[d]		Odor Description
	GC-MS	Literature[b]	
1. water	d		
2. diacetyl	d	1.69	butter
3. unidentified			
4. 2-methylpropanol	d		
5. 2-methoxyethanol			(artifact)
6. methyl butyrate	d		
7. acetoin	d	3.08	
8. pyrazine	d		corn-like with bitter note
9. pyridine	d		
10. C(4) ethyl ester	4.00	4.00	
11. 2-ethylbutanal	d		
12. unidentified			
13. unidentified			
14. methylpyrazine	4.32	4.38	grassy
15. unidentified			
16. furfural	4.70	4.62	
17. unidentified			
18. 2-heptanone	4.89	4.95	
19. 1-hexanol	4.90	4.87	
20. C(5) ethyl ester	5.00	5.00	
21. unidentifed			
22. 2,6-dimethylpyrazine	5.14	5.12	ether-like with corn note
23. 2,5-dimethylpyrazine	5.19	5.17	grassy, "corn nuts"
24. methional	5.21	5.21	
25. 2-acetylfuran	5.37	5.29	
26. dimethyl sulfoxide	5.49[d]	5.41	burned egg shell
27. 2,5-dimethyldihydro-2H-furan-3-one	5.60[d]		corn-like
28. 2-furfuryl alcohol	5.70	5.33	sweet mild odor
29. dimethyl trisulfide	5.76[d]	5.90	corn-like, musty
30. 2-octanone	5.90[d]		fruity
31. 2-methyltetrahydrothiophen-3-one	5.94[d]		
32. C(6) ethyl ester	6.00	6.00	
33. trimethyl- and 2-ethyl-5-methylpyrazine	6.06(6.06)	6.07(6.07)	grassy
34. unidentified			
35. unidentified			
36. unidentified			
37. unidentified			

(Continued)

TABLE 2 (Continued)

Compounds Detected in Canned Jubilee Sweet Corn

	Retention Index[a]		
Compounds Detected	GC-MS	Literature[b]	Odor Description
38. 2-acetylthiazole	6.51	6.30	taco, grassy
39. 3-methyl-2-cyclohexenone	6.69	6.64	pleasant, corn-like
40. unidentified			
41. 2-ethyl-3,6-dimethylpyrazine	6.84	6.83	roasted, pungent
42. unidentified			
43. dimethyl sulfone	6.98	7.06[c]	sulfury, taco
44. C(7) ethyl ester	7.00	7.00	
45. unidentified	7.07		old socks
46. 2-methylfurfural	7.19$_d$	7.48	corn note
47. 2-acetyl-4-methylthiazole	7.35^d		
48. 2,6-diethyl-3-methylpyrazine	7.66$_d$	7.64	grassy
49. 1,8-cineole	7.71^d		fruity
50. 2-thienyl alcohol	7.79$_d$		
51. butyl benzene	7.84^d		(artifact)
52. C(8) ethyl ester	8.00	8.00	
53. unidentified			
54. unidentified			
55. 5-methyl-4-one-1,3-dithialane	8.14^d		corn-like
56. unidentified			
57. 5-ethyl-4-one-1,3-dithialane	8.34^d		
58. unidentified			
59. unidentified			
60. unidentified			
61. unidentified			
62. unidentified			
63. unidentified			
64. C(9) ethyl ester	9.00$_d$	9.00	
65. C(6) substituted pyrazine	9.11^d		

[a] I_E values were for a 500 ft x 0.03 in ID SF-96 stainless steel open-tubular column.

[b] Literature I_E values were taken from Katz et al. (28), Kinlin et al. (29), Wal radt et al. (30) or Mussinan et al. (31).

[c] I_E was measured with authentic compound.

[d] Tentative identification, MS only, retention index not used or not available

characterized by Maga and Sizer (10) as significantly contributing to the unique flavor and aroma associated with roasting or toasting of numerous foods. Because of their low odor thresholds, characteristic odors and the relatively large amounts present, we believe these to be important contributors to the odor of canned corn. Using the odor unit concept of Guadagni et al. (11) the major flavor contributors were calculated to be 2,5- and 2,6-dimethyl-, 2-ethyl-5-methyl- and 2-ethyl-3,6-dimethylprazine. 2-Acetylthiazole and 2-acetyl-4-methylthiazole were also present. Pittet and Hruza (12) described the sensory properties of thiazoles as being green, roasted, or nutty, with some vegetable notes. Libbey et al. (6) suggested these compounds may add to the flavor of canned corn. Furan derivatives including 2-furfural, 2-furfuryl alcohol, 2-acetylfuran and 2,5-dimethyldihydro-

2H-furan-3-one, were also detected. According to Stahl (13),
flavor thresholds in water range from 30 ppm for 2-furfural to
410 ppm for 2-acetylfuran. Thus these compounds are thought to
play relatively minor roles in corn flavor. Maga (14) noted
that except in raw onion, thiophenes have been reported only in
heated products. Canned corn contained 2-methyltetrahydro-
thiophen-3-one, 5-methyl-2-thiophene-carboxaldehyde, 4- or 5-
methylthiophen-3-one and 2-thienyl alcohol. More work needs to
be done on the sensory properties and thresholds of thiophenes
before their importance to corn flavor can be assessed.

    The following compounds were identified for the first time in
canned sweet corn: pyridine, methional, dimethyl sulfone, dimethyl sulfoxide (DMSO), acetoin, and 3-methyl-2-cyclohexenone
(MCH). Pyridine has an odor threshold in water of 82 ppm and was
found to be an important constituent of canned snap bean aroma by
Stevens et al. (15). Pyridine and related compounds were also
found in roasted pecans by Wang (16) and in cocoa by Vitzthum (17).
Methional has been identified in tomato by Buttery et al. (18),
chocolate by van Pragg (19), beef by Watanabe (20), and in other
products. Guadagni (21) identified methional as the characteristic flavor in potatoes. Strecker degradation of methionine is
the generally accepted mechanism of formation. Because of its
low taste threshold-50 ppb in skim milk (Stahl, (13))-methional
may contribute to canned corn flavor. However, it is present only
in trace quantities. Dimethyl sulfoxide is formed from the oxidation of dimethyl sulfide. It was found by Ralls et al. (22) in
the volatile compounds from a commercial pea blancher and by
Liebich et al. (23) in roast beef. Dimethyl sulfone, an oxidation
product of DMSO, was also found in roast beef as well as in stale
non-fat dry milk by Ferretti and Flanagan (24). Dimethyl sulfone,
DMSO, acetoin and 3-methyl-2-cyclohexenone are not flavorful
compounds and probably contribute little to canned corn flavor.
A single peak with characteristic "canned-corn" odor has not been

identified. Instead, corn aroma appears to be a blend of many compounds peculiar to corn with dimethyl sulfide as the sweet top note.

In the four varieties we investigated, a total of 76 components was detected (Table 3). All however, were not present in each variety. Of the 38 identified compounds, only two were missing from certain varieties. 5-Ethyl-3-one-1,2-dithialane was not detected in Stylepak or 70-2367, and 2-furfuryl alcohol was

TABLE 3

Varietal Differences in Canned Sweet Corn

Peak Number	Fanfare	Jubilee	Stylepak	70-2367	I_E [a]	Compound
1	VL [b]	VL	L	L		diacetyl
2	VL	M	L	L		2-methyl-1-propanol
3	VL	VL	VL	VL		ethanol
4	VL	M	VL	T		
5	VL	VL	L	VL		
6	?	L	S,Sh	L,Sh		
7	?	L	L	L,Sh		
8	VL	VL	VL	L		
9	VL	VL	L	VL		
10	?	VL	L	L,Sh		
11	?	T	L	?		
12	VL	VL	VL	VL		2-methoxyethanol (artifact)
13	?	VL	?	L,Sh		
14	?	?	?	L,Sh		
15	M	S	L,Sh	L,Sh		
16	M	S	L,Sh	L,Sh		
17	L	M	L,Sh	N		
18	S	S	L,Sh	M		
19	VL	VL	VL	VL		pyrazine
20	L,Sh	?	L,Sh	M,Sh		pyridine (?)
21	VL	L	L,Sh	M		
22	VL	L	L,Sh	L		
23	L,Sh	L	M,Sh	M,Sh		
24	VL	VL	T,Sh	M		
25	T	T,Sh	T	T		
26	S	T	T	T		
27	VL	VL	L	L		methylpyrazine
28	S,Sh	S,Sh	T,Sh	M		
29	T	T	N	T		
30	S	S	T	S		
31	T	T	N	N		
32	L	L	T	M		2-heptanone
33	T	S	T	S		
34	S,Sh	T	S	T	5.10	2,6-dimethylpyrazine
35	VL	VL	VL	VL	5.18	2,5-dimethylpyrazine
36	S,Sh	S,Sh	S,Sh	S,Sh	5.26	methional
37	N	N	L,Sh	L	5.36	
38	M,Sh	M,Sh	S,Sh	M	5.43	dimethyl sulfoxide
39	S	T	T	M	5.57	2,5-dimethyldihydro-2H-furan-3-one
40	N	N	N	T	5.66	
41	T	T	M	N	5.70	2-furfuryl alcohol
42	M	VL	L	M	5.77	dimethyl trisulfide
43	L	S	S	S	5.88	2-octanone
44	T	S	T	T	5.92	2-methyltetrahydrothiopen-3-one
45	M	T	T	T	6.04	
46	L	L	VL	L	6.09	trimethyl-and 2-ethyl-5-methylpyrazine

(Continued)

TABLE 3 (Continued)

Varietal Differences in Canned Sweet Corn

Peak Number	Fanfare	Jubilee	Stylepak	70-2367	$I_E{}^a$	Compound
47	T	S	T	T	6.18	
48	T	T	T	T	6.24	
49	T	T	T	T	6.33	
50	N	T	N	T	6.40	
51	L	M	L	M	6.53	2-acetylthiazole
52	S	S	S	S	6.70	3-methyl-2-cyclohexenone (MCH)
53	VL	VL	VL	VL	6.82	2-ethyl-3,6-dimethylpyrazine
54	L	T	L	L	6.94	dimethyl sulfone
55	L	T	T	M	7.07	
56	T	N	N	N	7.15	
57	S	S	S	T	7.20	3-methyl-2-thiophene-carboxaldehyde (?)
58	T	T	N	T	7.27	
59	M	S	L	S	7.34	4-methyl-2-acetylthiazole
60	T	T	T	T	7.41	
61	T	T	N	N	7.53	
62	N	N	T	N	7.57	
63	S	T	L	S	7.63	2,6-diethyl-3-methylpyrazine
64	L	T	S	M	7.83	C(4)-benzene (artifact)
65	S	S	N	N	8.06	
66	S	T,Sh	M	S	8.09	
67	T	T	L	T	8.17	5-methyl-4-one-1,3-dithiolane (?)
68	T	T	N	N	8.44	5-ethyl-4-one-1,3-dithiolane (?)
69	T	N	N	N	8.67	
70	T	N	L	T	8.80	
71	T	N	T	N	8.85	
72	T	T	T	T	9.11	C(6)-pyrazine
73	T	T	T	T	9.18	
74	N	T	M	N	9.28	
75	N	T	N	N	9.73	
76	T	N	T	?		

[a] I_E's on SF-96 500 ft capillary column

[b] Relative Peak Heights
 N = Not detected
 T = Trace, less than 1 cm
 S = Small, greater than or equal to 1 cm and less than or equal to 2 cm
 M = Medium, greater than 2 cm and less than 5 cm
 L = Large, greater than or equal to 5 cm and less than 20 cm
 VL = Very Large, greater than or equal to 20 cm
 Sh = Shoulder peak

not detected in 70-2367.   Eleven unidentified peaks were missing from various varieties.   Using ethyl octanoate as an internal standard, relative peak heights were measured and assigned various letter designations.   "Trace" designated a peak height of less than one cm.   Criteria for small, medium, large and very large were also established (see Table 3).   For 13 of the components, the peaks were in the same size designation for all varieties.   For 24 components three out of four designations were the same.   One component had different peak sizes for each variety, and in the remaining 38 components, two of the four

varieties had similar peak size designations. These qualitative
and quantitative similarities for the four varieties were expected, since these varieties all had good canned corn flavor.
The variations present in compounds and quantities would account
for the subtle flavor differences.

Nine varieties of frozen blanched corn were investigated.
In frozen Jubilee a total of 38 compounds was detected, and 14 of
these were subsequently identified (Table 4). Figure 4 shows a
typical total ionization chromatogram of frozen Jubilee. Relatively large amounts of alcohols, diacetyl, acetoin, and dimethyl
sulfone were detected. Other compounds including pyridine,
pyrazines, a furan and a thiazole were present only in trace
quantities. New compounds found in frozen corn included acetoin,
pyridine, 3-methyl-2-cyclohexenone and dimethyl sulfone. The
flavor of frozen corn is much less developed than that of canned
corn and can be described as rather bland. Important flavor contributors to frozen corn were the low-boiling compounds such as
alcohols, diacetyl, and certainly dimethyl sulfide, etc. Forty
eight peaks were detected with I_E values of 5.00 or greater
(Table 5). The varieties had from 16 to 38 peaks present in
their respective chromatograms; 88.5% of these peaks were present
only in trace quantities. Two of the varieties, NCO4 and white
field corn, had poor texture, and flavor characterized as chalky,
grassy, straw-like. Little difference in higher-boiling
compounds was observed between those frozen samples with good
and poor flavor. 2-Ethyl-3,6-dimethylpyrazine, trimethylpyrazine
and and 3-methyl-2-cyclohexenone were not detected in those
samples with poor flavor. Presumably lower-boiling compounds
and bitter non-volatile compounds present in the raw corn were
mainly responsible for the off-flavors.

Major qualitative and quantitative differences occurred in
the compounds present in canned and frozen corn and were
responsible for the different flavors of these products. Frozen
Jubilee with 38 compounds had one furan, one thiazole and no

TABLE 4

Compounds Detected in Frozen Jubilee Sweet Corn

	Retention	Index[a]
Compounds Detected	GC-MS	Literature[b]
1. water	d	
2. diacetyl	d	1.69
3. 2-methylpropanol	d	
4. 2-methoxyethanol		
5. acetoin	d	3.08
6. 1-pentanol	d	3.88
7. unidentified		
8. unidentified		
9. pyridine	4.02	
10. furfural	d	4.62
11. unidentified		
12. unidentified		
13. unidentified		
14. unidentified		
15. 2,5-dimethylpyrazine	5.18	5.17
16. unidentified		
17. unidentified		
18. unidentified		
19. unidentified		
20. unidentified		
21. trimethylpyrazine	6.09	6.07
22. unidentified		
23. 2-acetylthiazole	6.51	6.30
24. 3-methyl-2-cyclohexenone	6.70	6.64
25. unidentified		
26. 2-ethyl-3,6-dimethylpyrazine	6.83	6.83
27. dimethyl sulfone	6.92	7.06[c]
28. unidentified		
29. unidentified		
30. unidentified		
31. unidentified		
32. unidentified		
33. unidentified		
34. unidentified		
35. unidentified		
36. unidentified		
37. unidentified		
38. unidentified		

[a] I_E values were for a 500 ft x 0.03 in SF-96 stainless steel open-tubular column.

[b] Literature I_E values were taken from Katz et al. (28), Kinlin et al. (29), Walradt et al. (30) or Mussinan et al. (31).

[c] I_E was measured with authentic compound.

[d] Tentative identification, MS data only

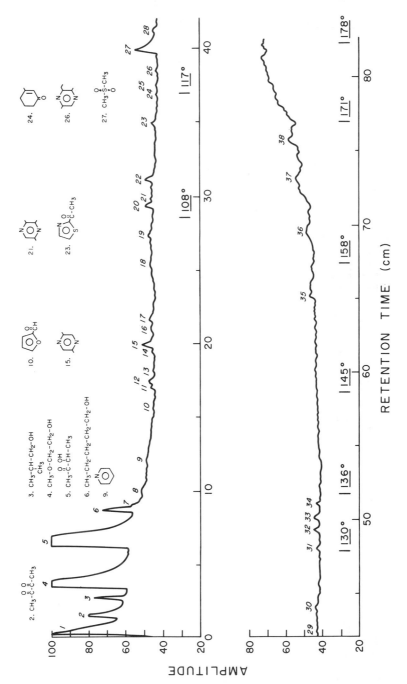

Fig. 4. Total ionization chromatogram of frozen Jubilee sweet corn

thiophenes while canned Jubilee with 65 compounds had four, two and five, respectively. Thiophenes, furans and thiazoles result from interactions during the thermal exposure of amino acids and carbohydrates and thus greater numbers and/or amounts of these compounds were expected in canned corn. The most outstanding difference between the two Jubilee corns was in the pyrazines. In canned corn nine pyrazines were present with relatively large peaks, in frozen only trace amounts of 2,5-dimethyl-, trimethyl- and 2-ethyl-3,6-dimethylpyrazine were present. These trace amounts may have been formed during blanching or sampling. As mentioned previously, pyrazines were thought to play a major role in canned corn flavor.

To investigate the source of the flavor compounds in canned

TABLE 5

Varietal Differences in Frozen Sweet Corn

I_E^d	Stylepak	Goldie	Commander	70-1631	Illan Chief	FM Cross	Jubilee	White Field Corn	NCO4	Compound
5.05	T[b]	M,Sh	T	T,Sh	M	T	T	S,Sh	S	
5.08	N	N	N	T	N	S	N	T	N	
5.12	T	T	M	T	S	S	T	T	T	
5.18	S	T	S	T	T	T	S	T	T	2,5-dimethyl-pyrazine
5.22	T	S	S	N	S	N	T	N	N	
5.28	N	N	T	N	N	N	T	N	N	
5.33	T	N	N	T	N	T	T	T	N	
5.36	N	L	N	N	T	N	N	N	N	
5.39	T	N	T	T	N	T	T	T	T	
5.44	N	N	N	N	N	T	N	N	T	
5.51	N	N	T	T	N	T	T	T	N	
5.58	T	T	T	N	T	T	N	N	T	
5.68	T	N	T	T	N	T	T	T	T	
5.75	N	N	T	T	T	T	N	T	N	
5.82	N	N	N	N	N	T	T	T	N	
5.89	T	T	T	N	T	N	T	N	T	
5.93	N	N	T	T	T,Sh	T	T	T	N	
6.05	T	M	N	T	M	T	S	S	S	
6.09	T	N	T	N	N	T	T	N	N	trimethyl-pyrazine
6.14	N	T	T	N	T	N	T	N	T	
6.19	N	T	T	T	N	T	T	T	N	
6.26	N	N	N	T	T	T	T	T	T	
6.30	T	N	T	N	N	T	T	N	N	
6.35	N	N	N	N	N	T	N	T	N	
6.40	T	N	T	N	T	N	T	T	T	
6.47	N	N	N	N	N	T	N	N	N	
6.51	T	T	T	N	T	T	T	T	T	2-acetyl-thiazole
6.61	N	T	T	T	T	T	T	T	T	
6.70	N	N	T	T	T	N	T	N	N	3-methyl-2-cyclo-hexenone
6.79	N	N	N	T	T	T	T	T	N	
6.84	T	N	T	T	T	T	T	N	N	2-ethyl-3,6 di-methyl-pyrazine

TABLE 5 (Continued)

Varietal Differences in Sweet Corn

$I_E{}^a$	Stylepak	Goldie	Commander	70-1631	Illan Chief	FM Cross	Jubilee	White Field Corn	NCO4	Compound
6.92	T	N	T	N	N	T	S	T	N	dimethyl sulfone
7.06	T	S	S	T	S	T	T	S	M	
7.21	N	N	N	N	N	T	N	N	N	
7.27	T	N	T	T	T	T	T	T	T	
7.34	T	T	N	N	N	N	T	N	N	
7.41	T	N	T	T	T	N	T	T	N	
7.58	N	N	T	T	N	T	T	N	N	
7.65	T	T	T	N	T	N	T	T	T	
7.73	N	N	N	N	N	N	T	T	N	
7.82	T	N	T	N	T	T	T	N	T	
7.95	N	N	T	N	N	N	T	N	T	
8.09	T	T	T	N	T	T	T	T	T	
8.17	T	N	N	N	T	N	T	T	N	
8.28	N	N	N	N	T	N	T	T	N	
8.80	N	N	N	N	T	N	T	N	N	
Flavor	Good	Good	Good	Good	Good	Good	Good	Straw-like		Grassy Chalky
Texture	Good	Good	Good	Good	Good	Good	Good	Tough		Tough

^{a} I_E's on SF-96 500 ft capillary column

^{b}Relative Peak Heights:
  N = Not detected
  T = Trace, less than 1 cm
  S = Small, greater than or equal to 1 cm and less than or equal to 2 cm
  M = Medium, greater than 2 cm and less than 5 cm
  L = Large, greater than or equal to 5 cm and less than 20 cm
  VL= Very Large, greater than or equal to 20 cm
  Sh= Shoulder peak

corn 17 model systems were prepared and examined. In the abstract we mentioned that the model systems with the most peaks were those made with corn starch and amino acids. Later we found that most of the peaks were coming from the corn starch alone. We then abandoned the use of corn starch and used sucrose, fructose and glucose as the carbohydrate sources. These were found to be the primary sugars in corn by thin layer chromatography. A typical model system consisted of 100 ml of distilled water buffered to pH 7.0, 0.1 mole of sugar and 0.1 mole of amino acids. The model systems were autoclaved in sealed bottles at 120°C at 20 psi for 0.5 to 2.5 hours. The amino acids chosen for the model systems were listed by Sodek and Wilson (25) as the free amino acids present in normal and opaque-2 corn.

    Model system 13 which had a slight corn-like aroma contained the following compounds in 100 mls of buffer solution (pH 7.0):

d-glucose (0.022 mole) , d-fructose (0.022 mole), sucrose (0.058
mole), L-proline (0.038 mole), L-cystine (0.012 mole),
L-alanine (0.014 mole) and L-glutamic acid (0.038 mole). The
resulting pH was 6.2; the pH of canned Jubilee liquor was 6.3.
After autoclaving for 1.5 hrs, the model system was subjected to
headspace analysis. Some of the major peaks identified by MS
and confirmed by comparing I_E values were: 2-furfural, 2,5-
dimethylpyrazine, furfuryl alcohol (slight amount), 2-ethyl-?-
methylpyrazine, 2-acetylthiazole, 2-ethyl-?,?-dimethylpyrazine and
2,5-dimethyl-3-thiophene carboxaldehyde. Acetoin and 2-acetyl-4-
methylthiazole were tentatively identified. A sulfur-containing
compound (I_E = 6.84) and a large peak (I_E = 6.37) which contained
oxygen and had a MW 98 were not identified. All of these identified compounds were detected in canned corn except for 2,5-
dimethyl-3-thiophene carboxaldehyde. Although the compounds in
the model system were not formed in the same proportions as those
in canned corn, a corn-like aroma was still present and the
importance of amino acid-carbohydrate interactions to corn flavor
was demonstrated.

Odors of some of the other model systems were described as
burned popcorn, toasted nut, cold cauliflower, butter-like, musty,
sulfury vegetable and meaty. Pyrazines, furans, thiazoles,
thiophenes and other compounds were tentatively identified. The
precursors and their relative proportions in the model systems
naturally determined the flavors formed upon heating.

Using the same porous polymer sampling techniques, the flavor
of fresh parsnip roots was investigated in our laboratory by
Grieco et al. (26). Previous work was done by Self (2), Johnson
et al. (27) and Cronin (28). Cronin stated that parsnip-like
aroma was only associated with the largest peak, terpinolene.
However, we noted that pure terpinolene does not have a parsnip-
like odor, and that Cronin had concluded that the terpinolene
peak was masking an unknown parsnip-like compound. Table 6
shows some compounds we identified in parsnips. There was a

TABLE 6

Compounds Identified in Parsnips

Compound	GC-MS Identification	Flavor Contribution
1-pentanol	a	no
methional	a	yes
3-methylthiopropanal	a,b	yes
dimethyltrisulfide	a	yes
dimethylsulfide	a	yes
dimethyl sulfoxide	a	no
limonene	a	yes
α-phellandrene	a	yes
terpinolene	a,b	yes
α-terpineol	a	yes
p-cymen-8-ol	a	yes
biphenyl	a	no
methyl eugenol	a	yes
butylated hydroxy toluene	a	no
myristicin	a,b	yes

a = Compound identified by data system flavor file.

b = Spectrum matches that of authentic compound.

pungent note to this aroma which resembled myristicin more than terpinolene. However, the background was terpenoid and was similar in some respects to the flavor of raw carrots. The spiciness of methyl eugenol also contributed to the unique pungency of parsnip, but myristicin was the most characteristic and strongest component of parsnip odor. Through olfactory analysis of the split GC effluent, we concluded that myristicin was the chracteristic parsnip aroma.

The previous inability to identify myristicin as the

parsnip compound may have been due to the method of isolation. Porous polymer trapping has several advantages over steam distillation, extraction, etc. An isolate is produced which more closely resembles the aroma that the nose perceived, and artifact formation is minimized. Other advantages include preliminary separation of water from organic compounds, ease of sample handling, relatively short analysis times, lack of water vapor interference, reproducibility and sensitivity. Of course, porous polymers are not without problems. Oxidizing atmospheres, high MW compounds, deposition of salts and excessive temperature are detrimental to porous polymers. Other problems include artifacts, irreversible adsorption, tailing, peak broadening and reactions with the polymer. However, we have found porous polymer trapping a very useful technique for investigating vegetable flavors.

IV. REFERENCES

(1) Salunkhe, D.K. and J.Y. Do, Critical Reviews in Food Science and Nutrition 8 (2), 161 (1977).

(2) Self, R., J.C. Casey and T. Swain, Chem. Ind. 35, 863 (1963).

(3) Bills, D.D. and T.W. Keenan, J. Agr. Food Chem. 16, 643 (1968).

(4) Williams, M.P. and P.E. Nelson, J. Food Sci. 38, 1136 (1973).

(5) Ishii, T., T. Yamanishi, T. Mochizuki and B. Toi, J. Agr. Chem. Soc. Japan 48, 637 (1974).

(6) Libbey, L.M., M.E. Morgan, L.A. Hansen and R.A. Scanlan, Proceedings A.C.S. Atlantic City, N.J. (1975).

(7) van Den Dool, H. and P.D. Kratz, J. Chromatog. 11, 463 (1963).

(8) Scanlan, R.A., R.G. Arnold and R.C. Lindsay, J. Gas Chromatog. 6, 372 (1968).

(9) Morgan, M.E. and E.A. Day, J. Dairy Sci. 48, 1382 (1965).

(10) Maga, J.A. and C.E. Sizer, CRC Critical Reviews in Food Tech. 4, 39 (1973).

(11) Guadagni, D.G., R.G. Buttery and J. Harris, J. Sci. Food Agr. 17, 142 (1966).

(12) Pittet, A.O. and D.E. Hruza, J. Agr. Food Chem. 22, 264 (1974).

(13) Stahl, W.H., Ed., "Compilation of Odor and Taste Threshold Values Data", American Society for Testing and Materials, Baltimore, Md., 1973.

(14) Maga, J.A., CRC Critical Reviews in Food Tech. 6, 153 (1975).

(15) Stevens, M.A., R.C. Lindsay, L.M. Libbey and W.A. Frazier, Proc. Am. Hort. Sci. 91, 833 (1967).

(16) Wang, P. and G.V. Odell, J. Agr. Food Chem. 20, 206 (1972).

(17) Vitzthum, O.G., P. Werkhoff and P. Hubert, J. of Food Sci. 40, 911 (1975).

(18) Buttery, R.G., R.M. Seifert, D.G. Guadagni and L.C. Ling, J. Agri. Food Chem. 19, 524 (1971).

(19) van Pragg, M., H.S. Stein and M.S. Tibetts, J. Agr. Food Chem. 16, 1005 (1968).

(20) Watanabe, K. and Y. Sato, J. Agr. Food Chem. 20, 174 (1972).

(21) Guadagni, D.G., R.G. Buttery and J.G. Turnbaugh, J. Sci. Food Agr. 23, 1435 (1972).

(22) Ralls, J.W., W.H. McFadden, R.M. Seifert, D.R. Black and P.W. Kilpatrick, J. Food Sci. 30, 228 (1965).

(23) Liebich, H.M., D.R. Douglas, A. Zlatkis, F. Muggler-Chavan and A. Donzel, J. Agr. Food Chem. 20, 96 (1972).

(24) Ferretti, A. and V.P. Flanagan, J. Agr. Food Chem. 20, 695 (1972).

(25) Sodek, L. and C.M. Wilson, J. Agr. Food Chem. 19, 1144 (1971).

(26) Grieco, M., L. Libbey and M. Morgan, Unpublished data, Oregon State University (1976).

(27) Johnson, A.E., H.E. Nursten and A.A. Williams, Chem. Ind. 43, 1212 (1971).

(28) Cronin, D.A., 4th Inter. Cong. Food Sci. and Tech. la, 41 (1974).

(29) Katz, I., R.A. Wilson, C.J. Mussinan and A. Sanderson,
J. Agr. Food Chem. 21, 873 (1973).

(30) Kinlin, T.E., R. Muralidhara, A.O. Pittet, A. Sanderson and
J.P. Walradt, J. Agr. Food Chem. 20, 1021 (1972).

(31) Walradt, J.P., A.O. Pittet, T.E. Kinlin, R. Muralidhara,
and A. Sanderson, J. Agr. Food Chem. 19, 972 (1971).

(32) Mussinan, C.J. and J.P. Walradt, J. Agr. Food Chem. 22,
827 (1974).

ISOLATION OF TRACE VOLATILE CONSTITUENTS OF HYDROLYZED VEGETABLE PROTEIN VIA POROUS POLYMER ENTRAINMENT

D. A. Withycombe, B. D. Mookherjee, A. Hruza
International Flavors and Fragrances, Inc.

Three porous polymer adsorbents were evaluated for use in obtaining volatile headspace isolates from hydrolyzed vegetable protein. Detailed GC-MS analyses were performed on Tenax-GC, Chromosorb 105, and Porapak Q isolates resulting in the identification of 77 volatile constituents, 64 of which have not previously been reported in HVP. Tenax-GC was found to produce the most organoleptically characteristic isolate even though a greater number of constituents were identified from the Porapak Q isolate than from either the Chromosorb 105 or Tenax-GC isolates.

I. INTRODUCTION

The analysis and recreation of complex food and beverage flavors cannot be satisfied by a single isolation or analytical approach. The analyst must draw upon an arsenal of methodologies which, when the results are collated in an artistic manner, result in a product which is not only true to nature but, ideally, organoleptically indistinguishable. The analysis of flavors may be delineated into at least four different, though not distinct areas (1).

1) The qualitative and quantitative composition of the volatile constituents of the food itself.

2) The qualitative and quantitative composition of the vapors over, and in equilibrium with, the food as perceived by our sense of smell.

3) The non-volatile constituents which contribute to, among other things, mouth feel and possibly tri-

geminal nerve response.

4) The physical environment in which these constituents are present in the food.

This paper deals with methodologies described in Item 2 -- a discipline we refer to simply as "Headspace Analysis".

Headspace technology evolved early in the development of sensitive gas chromatographic instrumentation. Early techniques were primarily limited to static headspace sampling via gas-tight syringes and subsequently to on-column entrainment techniques which permitted approximately a 25-50 fold concentration. The need for sufficient quantities of volatile isolate for gas chromatography-mass spectrometry (GC-MS) and further nuclear magnetic resonance (NMR) and infrared (IR) characterization of trace constituents demanded the concentration and trapping of much larger volumes of headspace volatiles.

Porous polymer chromatographic adsorbents were introduced in the late 1960's with the ability to efficiently and selectively retain organic molecules yet exhibit a low affinity for water and low molecular weight alcohols frequently encountered in food and beverage analysis (2). The physical characteristics of the adsorbents may be summarized as follows:

1) Efficient concentration of volatile constituents from large volume headspace samples with minimum interference from water vapor or volatile constituents (i.e., alcohols).

2) High adsorptive capacity.

3) Non-specific adsorption of organic constituents at ambient temperature.

4) Quantitative release of trapped volatiles at moderate temperatures without an appreciable chromatographic process.

5) No (low) chemical or catalytic activity at operating temperatures.

6) Amenable to quantitative and non-destructive

transfer to chromatographic apparatus.

In addition, the ultimate test for any isolation process requires that the recovered volatile isolate must be organoleptically characteristic of the food from which it was obtained. It is important to note that this requirement is not for complete flavor capture. The isolate must, however, exhibit the dominant and characteristic organoleptic attributes of the sample. Failure to achieve this objective will not be corrected during subsequent analytical techniques.

The physical techniques of porous polymer headspace collection and transfer to a suitable chromatographic system are as diverse and numerous as the number of scientists collecting headspace volatiles. The four essential components of a system are 1) a constant flow high purity purge gas, 2) a sample vessel, 3) an adsorbent trap, and 4) a constant temperature desorption oven. These elements are typified by the system described by Jennings et al. (3) for beverage analysis. An extension of this system is the adaptation of the GLC heated injection port to accept the adsorbent trap, thereby serving as the desorption oven (4, 5). These systems are contrasted by the completely automated and sometimes elegant systems reported for quantitative environmental and biological analyses (6, 7). These systems incorporate the precision flow control, absolute temperature regulation and sequence timing essential for reproducible quantitative applications.

We have not found the design of the sample vessel to be critical except that it should provide a suitably controlled temperature environment, and a high surface area:sample volume ratio. When aqueous samples are studied, a controlled temperature double coil condenser should be provided to eliminate a portion of the water vapor before the adsorbent trap.

Our laboratory has used two transfer techniques which we have found to be suitable for the qualitative isolations required by our analytical approach. Small isolates are readily handled in

1/8" o.d. glass adsorbent traps which are directly inserted into
the heated injection port of GLCs equipped with carrier gas by-
pass lines. These 1/8" traps also serve as suitable secondary
traps when transferring volatiles from high volume traps for subsequent injection or when collecting chromatographically resolved
components for reinjection on a second analytical column. Direct
injection is the procedure of choice when larger volume isolates
have been obtained. The trap introducer designed by Murray (8)
has been adapted for use on our Varian Model 3700 gas chromatographs. This procedure is useful for transfer of volatiles to
0.032" i.d. glass capillary columns used routinely in our laboratories.

II. EXPERIMENTAL

     In order to evaluate the effectiveness of the porous polymer
resins in obtaining organoleptically acceptable isolates and providing adequate sample for characterization of trace constituents,
our laboratory utilized a hydrolyzed vegetable protein (HVP) product as a model system. The prior literature is limited to the
study by Manley (9) who identified 60 volatile constituents from
a laboratory produced soybean isolate and the subsequent work of
Markh and Vinnikova (10) who reported the identification of 35
constituents of a commercial Russian soybean hydrolyzate. The
diverse origins of these protein isolates makes correlation with
a "standard" product less meaningful. Nestle 4-BE "Maggi" paste
was therefore used for this investigation due to its extensive
use by the food industry.

     The collection apparatus (Fig. 1) utilizes a 22 liter, 3-
necked reaction flask fitted with a mechanical stirrer operated
at ca. 120 rpm, a 50 cm double coil condenser maintained at 15°C,
and a 1/16" teflon helium purge line. The high purity helium
flow was maintained at 60 ml/min by a constant-flow flow control-
ler   while the heating mantle surrounding the sample flask was

controlled to maintain a sampling temperature of 75°C. The condenser was fitted with a teflon thermometer adapter bored through to accept the 1 cm adsorbent traps. The oven assembly and collection apparatus was conveniently adapted from a Kontes Model K-500500 sweep co-distillation apparatus. This provided a four place flow control module and oven for trap conditioning and desorption. Adsorbent traps were prepared by packing a 15 cm section of the trap (Part No. K-898600) with the porous polymer contained between two plugs of silinized glass wool.

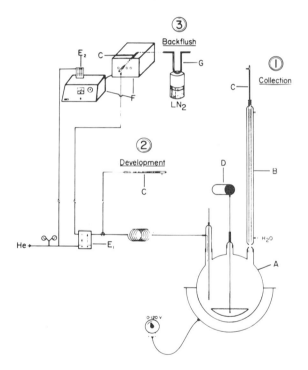

Fig. 1. Headspace collection and entrainment apparatus. A-22 liter sample flask, B-50 cm double coil condenser, C-adsorbent trap, D-mechanical stirrer, E₁-constant-flow flow meter, E₂-constant pressure flow meter, F-Kontes Model K-500500 sweep co-distillation apparatus, G-1/8" o.d. glass U-trap.

Tenax-GC, Chromosorb 105, and Porapak Q were selected from the available resins for comparison. Table 1 indicates the details of the resins and the temperatures used for each.

TABLE 1 *Porous Polymer Resins Used for Comparison*

RESIN	MESH	RESIN WEIGHT (gm)	CONDITIONING TEMPERATURE	BACKFLUSH TEMPERATURE
Tenax-GC	60-80	0.7	230°C	220°C
Chromosorb 105	80-100	1.6	230	200
Porapak Q	120-150	1.3	200	150

Samples were prepared by bringing 300 grams of Nestle 4-BE paste into solution in 6000 gm of distilled water. The flask was charged with the sample, equilibrated to 75°C with continuous stirring, and the thermometer adapter fitted with an adsorbent trap. Volatiles were collected for a period of 24 hours, the total volume equivalent to ca. 85 liters. Traps were subsequently purged of residual water vapor by disconnecting them from the collection apparatus and continuing the 60 ml/min flow for an additional 20 min. Volatiles were immediately recovered by backflushing them into 1/8" o.d. glass U-traps cooled in liquid nitrogen. Transfer time was 60 min at a helium flow rate of 15 ml/min. U-traps were flame sealed and the volatiles centrifuged into the conical tip where they could be readily recovered by a dry ice-cooled 10 microliter syringe. Analyses were immediately performed on a 500' x 0.03" i.d. stainless steel Carbowax-20M capillary column operated at 17 ml/min He and temperature programmed from 70-190°C at 2°/min. The Hewlett-Packard 5750 GLC was interfaced to a Hitachi RMU-6E mass spectrometer via a Watson-Biemann separator and spectra were obtained by a Varian SS-100 mass spectral data system. Alternately, 0.1% solutions of the recovered volatiles were made in spring water for organoleptic evaluation by a panel of experienced flavorists.

III. RESULTS AND DISCUSSION

The system described provides a convenient and easily manip-
ulated method for the collection of 3-5 milligrams of volatile
headspace isolate. Of the three resins investigated, Tenax-GC
provided an estimated 60% more isolate than either of the other
resins. The physical appearance of the Tenax-GC trap was unchanged following conditioning and use, whereas both the Chromosorb 105 and Porapak Q traps appeared discolored. The deterioration did not appear to affect subsequent isolations in that
sequential gas chromatograms were essentially superimposable.

Flavor evaluations of the three isolates are summarized
below:

Tenax-GC - Substantially characteristic of HVP in aroma and
taste at 5 ppm with distinct cocoa aroma and taste components and a bitter cocoa aftertaste. 2 ppm - a baked goods
aroma with characteristic chocolate aroma and taste. 1 ppm
- sweet, brown sugar, caramel notes. The most product-
characteristic of the isolates.

Chromosorb 105 - Similar in character to Tenax-GC isolate
but dominated by chocolate/cocoa aroma and taste at 0.5 ppm,
retaining the characteristic chocolate/cocoa aroma and taste
at 0.02 ppm. The Chromosorb 105 isolate seems more milk
chocolate in nature. Not as well balanced in HVP character.

Porapak Q - Lacks the dominant HVP character of the other
two isolates having similar cocoa/chocolate-like aroma and
taste at 5 ppm and 1 ppm but unbalanced toward butyraldehyde.
The least interesting of the isolates.

Based upon these evaluations it became apparent that Tenax-GC
was the preferred resin for this application.

The chromatograms from the GC-MS analyses are shown in Fig.
2. Although no internal standard was present in the sample it is
apparent that the qualitative profile and relative quantitative
profile are almost superimposable with the exception of the three

large peaks eluting from Porapak Q between 63 and 78 minutes.
These components are unidentified aromatic resin decomposition
products of Mole Wt. 210. In addition, a number of other trace
decomposition products appeared in the baseline of the Porapak Q
isolate between 40 and 60 minutes.

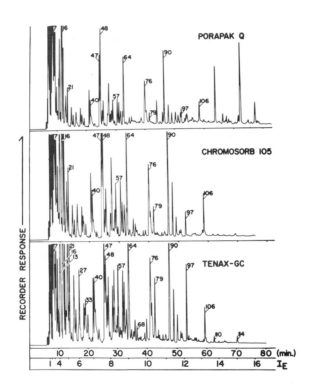

Fig. 2.   Chromatograms of HVP headspace entrainment isolates analyzed on a 500' x 0.03" i.d. s.s. Carbowax-20M capillary column operated at 70-190°C at 2°/min.

The compounds which were identified from these three isolates
are listed in Table 2. Quantitatively, 8 aldehydes compose approximately 32% of the total volatiles with isovaleraldehyde
being the single largest component of the sample. The second
most abundant class of chemicals are the 12 sulfur-containing

constituents representing 31% of the total volatiles. Previous experience did not lead us to anticipate either this number of sulfur components or the quantity in which they were isolated. Based upon the flavor balance perceived by our flavorists we feel that the ability to concentrate sulfides is not indicated as a unique feature of the resins, but is truly representative of the sample. As anticipated of this product, the pyrazines were the most numerous of the components yet comprise only 19% of the total isolate. Although no novel or unusual pyrazines were identified, they are felt to be primarily responsible for the characteristic nutty, chocolate note. The furan derivatives were again numerous but composed only 4.5% of the volatiles. The furans contribute to the sweet, baked, roasted notes which are class characteristic. The ketones are responsible for 5.5% of the volatiles and are dominated quantitatively by the alpha-beta diketones and qualitatively by the branched chain $C_{6,7,8}$ methyl ketones. In addition to these constituents, a number of miscellaneous compounds were identified, many of which are indicative of polymer decomposition and/or sampling environment contamination.

TABLE 2 *Compounds Identified from HVP Headspace Entrainment*

| Peak No.[1] | Compound | *Compound Identified from:* | | |
		TENAX-GC	*PORAPAK Q*	*CHROMOSORB 105*
	ALDEHYDES			
	Acetaldehyde		x	
4	Isobutyraldehyde	x	x	x
7	Isovaleraldehyde	x	x	x
	2-Methyl butanal		x	
17	2-Methyl-2-butenal	x	x	x
	2-Pentenal		x	
	Heptanal			x
64	Benzaldehyde	x	x	x

TABLE 2   *Compounds Identified from HVP Headspace Entrainment*

Peak No.[1]	Compound	TENAX-GC	PORAPAK Q	CHROMOSORB 105
	FURANS			
	Furan		x	
	2-Methyl-T.H.-furan		x	
5	2-Methyl furan	x	x	x
8	2,5-Dimethyl furan	x	x	x
13	2,3,5-Trimethyl furan	x	x	x
21	5-Methyl-2-vinyl furan	x	x	x
27	2-n-Pentyl furan	x	x	x
31	2-Methyl-T.H.-furan-3-one	x	x	x
	2-Vinyl-3,4(5)-dimethyl furan		x	x
61	2-Acetyl furan	x	x	x
62	Benzofuran	x		
	5-Methyl-2-furfural			x
	2-Methyl-5-propionyl furan			x
94	5-Methyl-2-furfuryl furan	x		x
97	3-Phenyl furan	x	x	x
	KETONES			
	Acetone		x	x
6	2-Butanone	x	x	x
9	2,3-Butanedione	x	x	
11	4-Methyl-2-pentanone	x	x	x
	2,3-Pentanedione		x	x
20	5-Methyl-2-hexanone	x	x	
23	2-Heptanone	x	x	
	3-Methyl-3-penten-2-one		x	x
28	6-Methyl-2-heptanone	x		

TABLE 2   *Compounds Identified from HVP Headspace Entrainment*

Peak No.[1]	Compound	Compound Identified from:		
		TENAX-GC	PORAPAK Q	CHROMOSORB 105
	PYRAZINES			
32	Methyl-	x	x	x
39	2,5-Dimethyl-	x	x	x
43	Ethyl-	x	x	x
41	2,6-Dimethyl-	x	x	x
	2,3-Dimethyl-		x	x
44	Isopropyl-	x	x	x
48	2-Ethyl-6-methyl-	x	x	x
49	2-Ethyl-5-methyl-	x	x	
50	2-Methyl-5(6)-isopropyl-	x	x	x
52	3,5(6)-Dimethyl-2-isopropyl-	x	x	x
56	2-Ethyl-3,6-dimethyl-	x	x	x
	2-Ethyl-3,5-dimethyl-		x	x
	2-Isobutyl-6-methyl-	x	x	x
57	2-Isobutyl-5-methyl-	x	x	x
	2-Propyl-5(6)-methyl-		x	
	Propyl dimethyl- (Isomer)			x
112	2-(2'-Furyl)-5(6)-methyl-	x		
	SULFUR			
	Hydrogen sulfide		x	
2	Methyl mercaptan	x	x	x
	Carbon disulfide		x	
3	Dimethyl sulfide	x	x	x
4	Ethyl methyl sulfide	x	x	x
	Diethyl sulfide		x	
16	Dimethyl disulfide	x	x	x
19	2-Methyl-T.H.-thiophene	x	x	x
48	Dimethyl trisulfide	x	x	x
	Furfuryl methyl sulfide		x	x

TABLE 2   *Compounds Identified from HVP Headspace Entrainment*

Peak No.[1]	Compound	Compound Identified from:		
		TENAX-GC	PORAPAK Q	CHROMOSORB 105
	Dimethyl sulfoxide		x	
110	Benzyl methyl disulfide	x		x
	MISCELLANEOUS			
1	Diethyl ether	x		
8	Benzene	x		
10	Trichloroethylene	x		x
	Chloroform		x	
14	Toluene	x	x	x
	o-Xylene			x
31	Styrene	x	x	x
	Naphthalene		x	
98	2-Methyl naphthalene	x		
101	1-Methyl naphthalene	x		
102	Ionol	x		
109	Biphenyl	x		
110	Ethyl naphthalene (Isomer)	x		
	Methyl fluorene (Isomer)		x	
	1,2-Diphenyl propane		x	
	Diethyl phthalate			x

[1]*Corresponds to peak designations of Tenax-GC isolate in Fig. 2*

Of the flavor components identified (excluding the miscellaneous components), 10 were identified exclusively in the Porapak Q isolate whereas 4 were identified only in the Chromosorb 105 and 3 in the Tenax-GC isolates. It would appear from these data that Porapak Q is the more efficient adsorbent. However, 80% of these compounds were present at levels of less than 0.1% and none represented more than 0.5% of any isolate. When dealing with trace concentrations in a semi-quantitative manner, injection technique, relative sample composition, and spectra procurement become increasingly important to the "odds" of obtaining an identifying mass spectrum. These observations should not, therefore, be superficially attributed to selective adsorption by the respective resin.

Of the 77 volatile components reported, 64 have not previously been identified in HVP. As has been the case with other complex food flavor systems, many of the compounds identified are considered to contribute to the overall flavor but none was isolated which would be considered to be typical of HVP.

We have demonstrated through the application of porous polymer headspace entrainment technology that it is possible to obtain sufficient quantities of volatile isolate for detailed mass spectral identifications. Our experience cautions the analyst to satisfactorily demonstrate that the resin selected for a specific application provides the most organoleptically characteristic isolate. It must be recognized that headspace isolation is only one approach to a much larger analytical problem if complete flavor recreation is the final objective.

IV. REFERENCES

1. Weurman, C., J. Agric. Food Chem. 17, 370 (1969).

2. Jennings, W. G., Filsoof, M., J. Agric. Food Chem. 25, 440 (1977).

3. Jennings, W. G., Wohleb, R., and Lewis, M. J., J. Food Sci. 37, 69 (1972).

4. Bertsch, W., Chang, R. C., and Zlatkis, A., J. Chromatogr. Sci. 12, 174 (1974).

5. Zlatkis, A., Lichtenstein, H. A., and Tishbee, A., Chromatographia 6, 67 (1973).

6. Dowty, B., Green, L., and Laseter, J. L., J. Chromatogr. Sci. 14, 187 (1976).

7.   Robinson, A. B., Partridge, D., Turner, M., Teranishi, R. and Pauling, L., <u>J. Chromatog</u>. 85, 19 (1973).

8.   Murray, K. E., <u>J. Chromatog</u>. 135, 49 (1977).

9.   Manley, C., "A Study of the Volatile Compounds and Chemical Reactions of Hydrolyzed Soybean Protein", Ph.D. Dissertation, University of Massachusetts, Amherst, Massachusetts, 1969.

10.   Markh, A. T. and Vinnikova, L. G., <u>Prikl. Biokhim. Mikrobiol</u>. 9, 913 (1973).

HEADSPACE TECHNIQUES UTILIZED FOR THE DETECTION OF

VOLATILE FLAVOR COMPOUNDS OF THE VANILLA BEAN

Ivan Klimes and Dietmar Lamparsky
Givaudan Research Co. Ltd., Dübendorf/Switzerland

Abstract

The commercial extracts of vanilla are often devoid of sensorially important trace components compared to the original vanilla bean. In order to define the differences we analyzed headspace samples of vanilla beans. Several difficulties were encountered, especially in connection with the handling of very small amounts of material without losses. Therefore, special but simple microtechniques were developed which allow a further working with the headspace samples previously collected in the usual way on charcoal filters and subsequently extracted with solvents.

A modification of the GLC injection port gives the possibility of utilizing the full amount of material available for injection even on hot glass capillary columns. In order to check GLC peaks for uniformity, a capillary glass tube serves as trapping vial which subsequently can be used as reinjection device. The conditions worked out to reach up to 100% substance recovery will be given. The microanalytical tool utilizing the capillary trap as reaction vial for the purpose of an identification aid will be discussed in view of the detection of functional groups of unknown constituents.

I. INTRODUCTION

Nowadays the trend in analytical chemistry to work with very small amounts of material, especially in the case of natural substrates, becomes more and more important. Our work on analytical problems in connection with the identification of trace components in vanilla beans, as well as in other flavor or fragrance bearing materials not well suited for common analytical procedures, has forced us to develop methods in the general field of headspace and microchemistry techniques in order to reach the goal given by the needs of the flavorist.

Vanilla is one of the most popular flavors throughout the world. Synthetic vanillin has been known for nearly 100 years, but this main component of the natural substrate by itself does not give the characteristic smell we like in real, natural vanilla flavors. So, it is clear that other trace components must be responsible for the better overall sensation when vanilla beans are utilized for flavoring of our baked goods or ice-creams.

We decided a few years ago to attack this problem by analysis of the headspace of vanilla beans, thus hoping that we also could find those volatile trace components always lost by producers during the concentration step in manufacturing so-called folded extracts.

II.   HEADSPACE OF VANILLA BEANS

The headspace analysis was chosen for the following two reasons:

The most volatile components can readily be isolated and enriched by this method.

The non-volatiles as well as excessive amounts of vanillin do not enter into the sample to be analyzed.

It is known that the analysis of vanilla extracts, for instance, with the aim of identification of trace components will be rendered troublesome because of the large amounts of vanillin, waxes and fats present as undesirable ingredients from the viewpoint of an analytical chemist.

A. Experimental

The headspace is taken by means of an all-glass apparatus (Fig. 1) developed in our laboratories by M. Hrivnac (1) and now utilized in all laboratories concerned with corresponding problems. The vanilla beans are placed on the grate. Nitrogen is passed through the system at the rate of 40 ml/min and a temperature of about 45± 5°C (by irradiation with an infrared lamp).

All volatile flavor substances are adsorbed on two charcoal filters (Fig. 2) connected to the vessel by Teflon shrinking tubes.

We have slightly modified the filter construction first proposed by K. Grob (2) for use in headspace sampling. Each of our filters contains 10 mg charcoal placed between two sieves as indicated in the figure. This amount of charcoal is sufficient for a total of about 100 μg of headspace substances without any loss of material as seen from experience. We can also completely saturate the filter with respect to each substance. Thus, we obtain more material for qualitative analytical purposes. For quantitative measurements such a "supersaturation" is not desirable. The filter is extracted ten times with separate 10 μl portions of carbon disulfide. This solvent has - apart from its good solvent properties - the advantage of giving only a small response in the

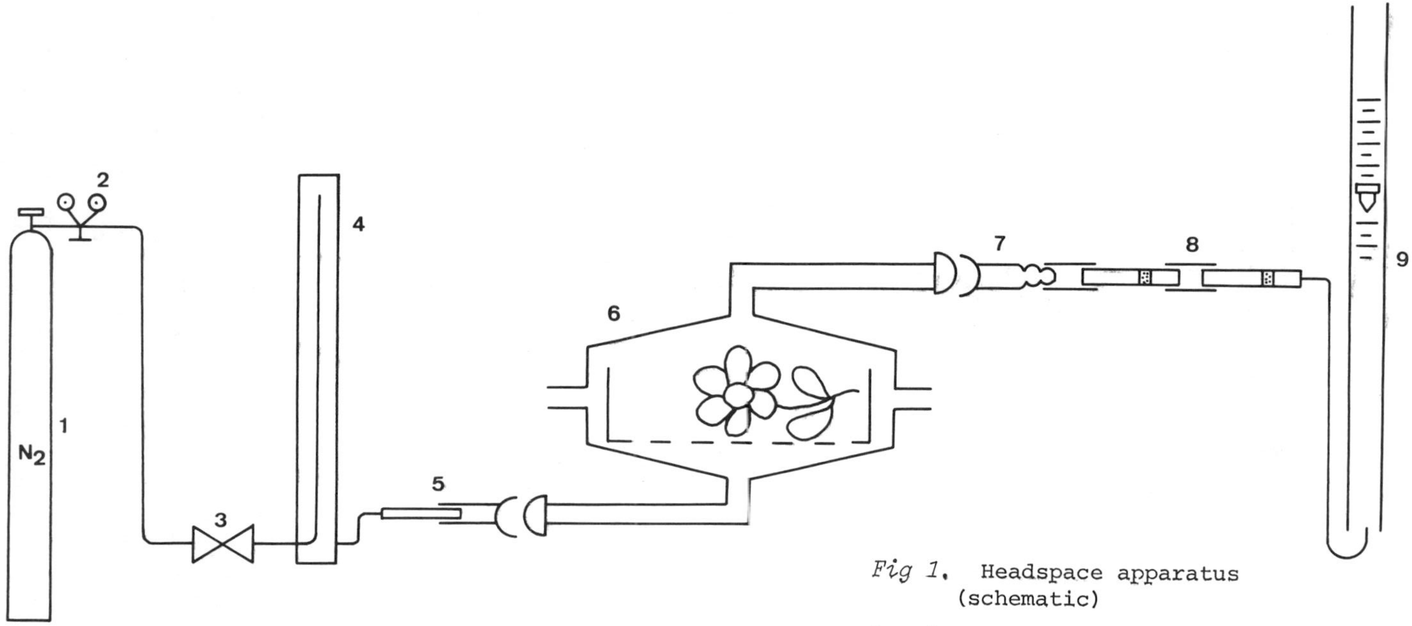

Fig 1. Headspace apparatus (schematic)

1 Nitrogen cylinder
2 Reducing valve
3 Needle valve
4 Tower with molecular sieves
5 Connection
6 Vessel with grate
7 Connection
8 Charcoal filters (two)
9 Rotameter

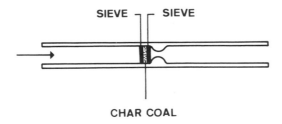

Fig 2. Charcoal filter

GLC utilizing a flame ionization detector. The solutions coming from the repeated extraction of the charcoal are collected in a microvial (Fig. 3). This tool enables us to work also in a quantitative manner with aliquot parts of a given total amount obtained from a not supersaturated headspace sample.

B. Results

   Just for illustration, we show a gas chromatogram (Fig. 4) obtained with a glass capillary column of 50 m length, internal diameter 0.31 mm, UCON HB 5100 as stationary phase, temperature range from 20 to 180°C   with a program rate of   3°C/min, with splitless injection of a 0.8 µl sample onto the cold column.
   The enrichment of trace components as well as the lack of high-boiling materials, including vanillin, are very well shown by this chromatogram.
   The analysis of the headspace of vanilla beans has revealed the presence of many constituents detected for the first time in vanilla. The chemical results have been published by us (3). We would therefore like to discuss here in more detail all additional microtechniques we needed to obtain these results which represent the most comprehensive compilation of vanilla components.

III.   MICROTECHNIQUES DEVELOPED TO FACILITATE IDENTIFICATION OF
       SUBMICROGRAM QUANTITIES

   The sophisticated instrumental possibilities of today permit us to obtain valuable results even in the nanogram (10^{-9} g) range. First of all, the combination of GLC with mass spectrometry allows highest sensitivity and will therefore be the appropriate technique to get the best information on the structures of the individual components of a well separated mixture. Infrared or NMR spectra need much more of each substance than is present in the injected amount of the mixture.
   If mass spectrometry is not able to give immediately the right answer and we have only a quantity of material far below

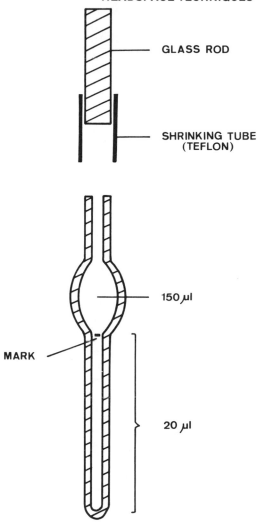

GLASS ROD

SHRINKING TUBE
(TEFLON)

150 µl

MARK

20 µl

Fig. 3 Microvial

the microgram range, then we have to consider in which way we can
solve the identification problems. We first analyzed the possible reasons for this situation and came to two points of primary importance:

A) The substances are not well separated on the chosen GLC
column. A single peak can be composed of two or more components,
thus preventing an immediate interpretation of the mass spectra
taken at several points on the peak.

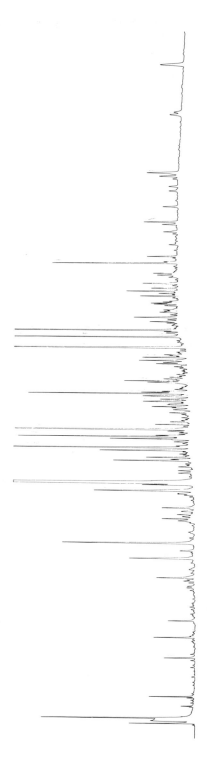

Fig. 4 Gas chromatogram of vanilla bean headspace.

B) The substance is pure but unknown with respect to the registered mass spectrum. The interpretation offers several structures belonging to different classes of organic functional groups.

A. <u>Separation Problems</u>

A complex natural mixture normally also gives complex GLC curves on almost all columns. It will not be sufficient to change only the stationary phase because the sensorially important trace components will then be overlapped by other main constituents of the mixture. We must have some preselection for which column chromatography or gas chromatography on a preparative scale are good examples in the field of the macro-range.

In the nanogram range, first of all we have the great advantage of the better resolving power of analytical packed or capillary GLC columns in comparison with "macro" preparative gas chromatography. But we have also to insure that any loss of material is avoided; otherwise we will not have sufficient quantities even for identification by mass spectrometry. Thus, the goals to be reached for efficient headspace analysis are clearly indicated:

Use of capillary GLC columns
Avoidance of material losses

1. Principle
The principle of our proposed technique is simple: the same glass capillary tube is used for collecting and reinjecting the substances first separated on appropriate analytical GLC columns. This micropreparative technique is already described by us in full detail (4).

2. Trapping
The substances are trapped at the FID outlet utilizing a special adapter instead of the flame ionization detector (Fig. 5). The trapping vial is filled with cotton wool in order to avoid formation of aerosols and subsequent losses.

We have achieved a nearly 100% recovery of injected materials with this filling of the trap, whereas we have to expect a 50% loss during collection without the cotton. We refer here to our publication (4) for more details.

The capillary trapping vial with the collected substance is now sealed by melting the tube in front of and behind the substance (Fig. 6).

3. Injection
We have not found any reference in the literature indicating how one could inject very small amounts of organic substances without diluting the test material. Working with nanogram quan-

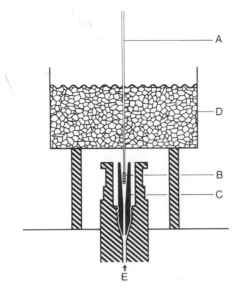

A Glass capillary tube (trap)

B Teflon shrinking tube

C Replacement device for FID outlet

D Cooling device

E Capillary GLC column

Fig. 5 Collecting of preseparated GLC effluents

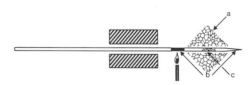

Fig. 6 Subsequent treatment of the trapping vial

a)   Cooling

b)   Melting zones

c)   Trapped substance

tities, the research chemist often encounters the fact that only a slight mist on the walls of a capillary tube represents the sample to be analyzed. Until now, a dilution of this mist with solvents was normally necessary in order to bring the material onto the GLC column. This dilution is not always desirable in view of losses on the surface of the syringe by capillary elevation or during a following concentration step. Another source of loss lies in the transfer of trapped material to the next operation step. It therefore seems ideal to utilize only one vial for trapping, possible reacting and subsequent reinjecting of nanogram quantities to be handled by the analytical chemist.

For the last mentioned purpose the melted end point of the capillary tube is broken before injecting. The tube is then inserted through the septum which will surely be more damaged than by a normal injection with the aid of a syringe. Therefore, one has to avoid excessive tightening of the septum cap in order to keep the septum in a soft state for convenient introduction of the capillary tube. The temperature of the injection port should be 50° higher than the boiling point of the injected substances so that they can evaporate immediately from the capillary tube onto the column.

This method of injecting also helps to overcome what we have seen at the beginning of the use of capillary GLC columns: the loss of material when only 1 to 10% of the injected (and diluted) sample goes to analysis whereas the greatest part is blown off by a splitter. The development of headspace analysis has forced the analytical chemist to treat his starting material in a more economical way. K. Grob and G. Grob (5) have shown that a splitless injection of a diluted sample on a cold column permits the utilization of the full amount of the analytical specimen. Modifications of the injection port were necessary to apply the splitless injection on hot columns (6,7).

We, on our side, have solved the problem by utilizing a double cone device as a modification of the injection port (Fig.7).

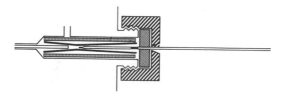

Fig. 7 Adaption of the injection port

The double cone device inserted between the septum and the end of the glass capillary GLC column diminishes the dead volume in the injection port in such a manner that a direct injection on a <u>hot</u> column gives the same separation efficiency as by injecting the sample in the usual way with use of a splitter. The capacity of our double cone device lies between 50 and 100 µl depending on the construction. A simple calculation shows that the injected amount of substances or solvents like pentane, diethyl ether or carbon disulfide give, under the experimental conditions (0.1 µl liquid injected, 1 atm pressure, 200°C in the injection port), about 20 to 30 µl of vapor. The volume of the adapter, therefore, is sufficient to hold the total of injected material and to bring it quantitatively onto the separation column.

The carrier gas flow of about 3 ml/min (= 50 µl/sec) will be rapid enough to transport the whole sample in less than 1 sec to the column which is sufficient for a good separation efficiency during analysis.

4. *Syringe with Lengthened Piston*

As we have seen in the preceding sections, the dilution of submicrogram quantities is not always the best way for the detection of trace components. It is, therefore, an advantage of our method that the isolated peak is available in its undiluted form for further studies. If we have, however, isolated the peak by means of a separation on a packed analytical GLC-column, then we often have more material than we need for a single reinjection on a column of other polarity. To use this material in undiluted form for several future experiments, we have developed a syringe with lengthened piston (Fig. 8).

A 1 µl-syringe (HAMILTON or the like) was shortened by about 10 mm by cutting or sawing the external needle. The side of the exposed length of the piston was ground with abrasive paper in such regular manner that a narrow space between needle and piston will be formed when the latter is drawn back. The slot offers enough space to hold the material and to protect it during the insertion passage through the septum.

We can also use our method for the injection of less volatile substances in dilution. We obtain GLC curves without solvent peak if we use the aforementioned tool and technique in a slightly modified manner. The lengthened piston is dipped in the solution and then held in the same position for about 5 seconds in the air to allow the solvent to evaporate. After this evaporation time the injection into the gas chromatograph is performed as indicated above.

Another advantage of the lengthened piston lies in the fact that it permits the separation of volatiles from the non-volatile substances often encountered in small samples obtained by extraction procedures from plant material. Thus, we do not overload the glass capillary GLC columns with extraneous material extracted together with olfactorily interesting compounds.

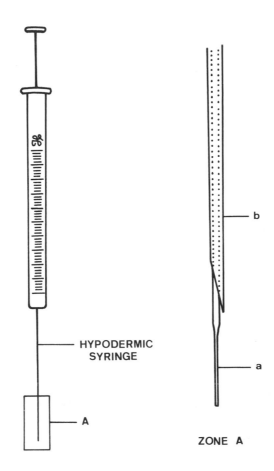

Fig. 8 Modified syringe

Headspace sampling is also possible with the modified syringe. In this case, we apply a stationary phase, e.g. UCON, SF 96 or the like, to the ground part of the piston. It was very interesting to see that the choice of stationary phases influences the sorption of different substances according to their polarity. Utilizing a polar phase, one observes increased peaks for all the more polar components of a mixture and vice-versa.

Exposure from 1 to 30 seconds, according to the concentrations expected to be present in the vapor phase, is enough to collect sufficient material for the injection method as indicated above. The results obtained with model substances, their mixtures, and also with essential oils were in most of the cases in good agreement with each other. The reproducibility looks, therefore, very promising in the time range up to 30 seconds.

5. *Practical Example*

In Fig. 9, the peak marked "1" could not be interpreted by mass spectrometry, probably owing to its being a mixture of substances. In order to verify this suspicion, the peak was collected according to our method and reinjected onto a more polar glass capillary column (Fig. 10).

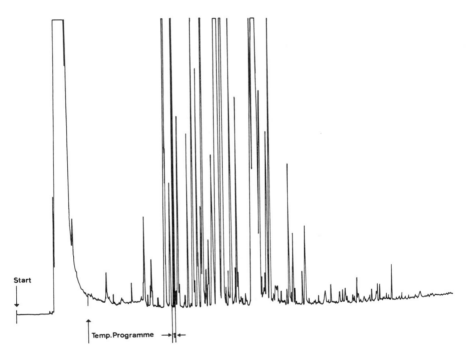

Fig. 9 GLC of a natural extract

Glass capillary column (50 m length i.d. 0.35 mm) with OV-01. Injection: 0.8 µl of a 0.5% solution in diethyl ether on cold column. Temperature: 50–220° with ΔT=5°/min. Carrier gas: Helium (1 atm)

The single peak on OV-01 is now separated into several distinct peaks which, after collection (area "1" of Fig. 10) and reinjection on the OV-01 column, give once again a single peak (Fig. 11). For further discussion of findings in our laboratory we refer to the review publication of P. Schudel (8).

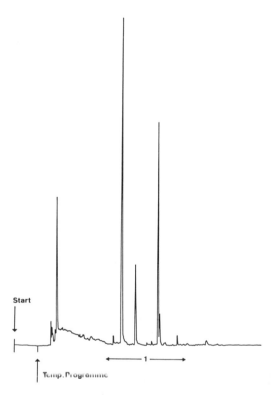

Fig. 10 GLC of peak "1" from **Fig.** 9

Glass capillary column (50 m length, i.d.
0.33 mm) with UCON HB 5100. Injection:
undiluted peak "1" on cold column with
the aid of the trapping vial utilized as
syringe.

B. Identification Aids

Up to now we have discussed some tools and methods utilized
routinely to achieve better separation of very complex mixtures
of natural origin. But what can we do to improve the identification of really pure compounds on a submicrogram level? In these
cases we find not easily interpretable mass spectra exhibiting
some unknown structural features. Thus, we need more information
about the functionality of the molecule. Because we have isolated the compound in our capillary trapping vial which we used for
reinjection, as previously described, we had in mind to use the
same vial for some chemical reactions before the reinjection.

Just for illustration, we have chosen the reaction of lithi-
um aluminum hydride with the various functional groups present in
organic molecules (Fig. 12).

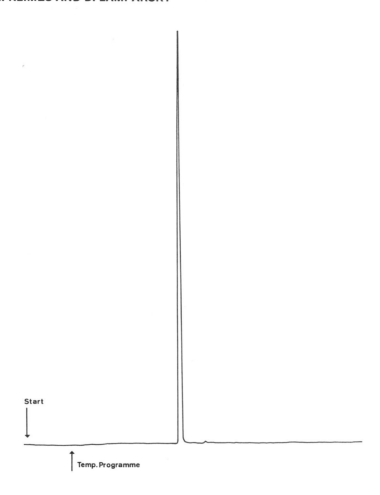

Start

Temp. Programme

Fig. 11 GLC of area "1" of Fig. 10

Glass capillary column and conditions
as in Fig. 9

Hydrocarbons and ethers do not react with the reagent. Alcohols form thermostable complex compounds degradable to the original substances by water. Aldehydes, ketones, esters, lactones
and carboxylic acids are reduced to the corresponding alcohols.

1. Experimental
One μl of a 0.3% solution of LiAlH$_4$ in diethyl ether is added to the trapped substance. The capillary trapping vial is sealed off at the end and just after the deposit of the material as
described above. The reaction proceeds at 140°C and after about
1 hr reaction time, the capillary vial is chilled with dry ice,

the point is broken and the reacted material introduced into the
gas chromatograph by syringe (first injection). With the aid of
a syringe we add 1 μl of a methanol-water 1:1 mixture to the reacted material after the first injection experiment.

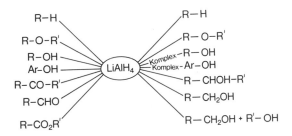

Fig. 12   Reaction of LiAlH$_4$ with various functional groups

1st INJECTION GIVES	2nd INJECTION GIVES PEAK WITH RETENTION TIME		SUBSTANCE CONTAINS FUNCT. GROUP
	AT ORIGINAL PLACE	AT OTHER PLACE	
+	−	−	HYDROCARBON
+	−	−	ETHER
−	+	−	ALCOHOL
−	+	−	PHENOL
−	−	+	ALDEHYDE
−	−	+	KETONE
−	−	+	CARBOXYLIC ACID
(+)	(+)	+	LACTONE
−	−	+ and +	ESTER

Fig. 13   Identification aids on the basis of a nanogram
level (GLC only)

The capillary tube is once again sealed off and the decomposition reaction is allowed to proceed for 1 hr at 140°C. After this time the reaction vial is cautiously opened (hydrogen pressure !) and a portion of the contents injected for the second time. The alcoholic complexes are now destroyed and furnish distinct GLC peaks according to their original chemical nature (Fig. 13).

Thus we achieve the result of a functional group analysis with a minimum of substance, one chemical reaction on the isolated substance and two GLC injections only. For more details we refer to a paper given by one of us at the International Symposium on Microchemical Techniques, Davos/Switzerland, May 1977, which will be published soon (9).

In comparison to the well known reaction gas chromatography, our method shows several advantages with respect to the performance (no change of columns necessary, no exposure of reagents to long temperature influence, etc.).

2. *Some Practical Examples*
In the following figures (Fig. 14-17) we show some practical examples of the behaviour of model compounds under our experimental conditions.

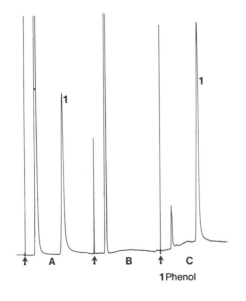

A Starting material

B First injection (after reaction with $LiAlH_4$)

C Second injection (after reaction with H_2O)

1 Phenol

Fig. 14 Behaviour of a phenol
Model: Phenol

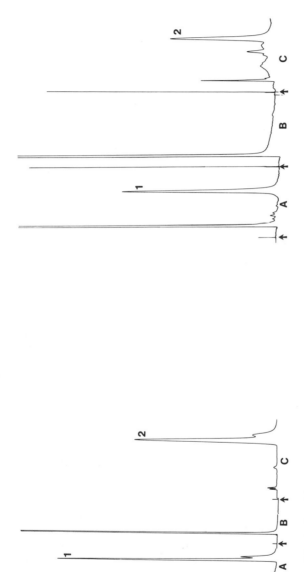

Fig. 15 Behavior of an aldehyde

Model: 3,5-Dimethylcyclohex-3-ene-1-carboxaldehyde (Cyclal)

1. Aldehyde
2. Alcohol

Fig. 16 Behaviour of a ketone

Model: Davanone

1. Ketone
2. Alcohol

A Starting material
B First injection (after reaction with LiAlH$_4$)
C Second injection (after reaction with H$_2$O)

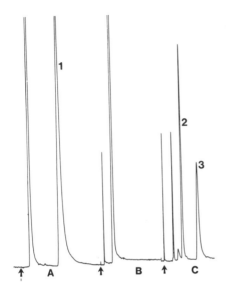

1. Ester

2. Isobutanol

3. n-Pentanol

A. Starting material

B. First injection (after reaction with LiAlH$_4$)

C. Second injection (after
   reaction with H$_2$O)

Fig. 17 Behaviour of an ester

Model: Isobutyl n-valerate

The peak(s) after the second injection will easily be interpreted with respect to their retention time as being primary or
secondary alcohols. The ratio

$$X = \frac{\text{Retention time of reacted derivative}}{\text{Retention time of starting material}}$$

is normally greater when an aldehyde is reduced to a primary alcohol than when a ketone is reduced to the corresponding secondary
alcohol.

At the end of our presentation we will focus our attention
once again on the vanilla flavor analysis. By utilizing the described new tools and useful microtechniques we gained results
clearly indicating that headspace analysis alone cannot give the
complete answer to a problem like the determination of vanilla
volatiles. Just to give an impression of how the composition can
change, even in a qualitative manner, from one substrate to the
other in spite of their common natural origin (vanilla bean), the
following table compiles several findings with respect to three
classes of functional groups (phenols, carbonyls, esters) and
without pretension of completeness.

TABLE 1   Some examples of new compounds identified
in different vanilla substrates

Headspace	Extract (MeOH)	Vapor Condensate
a) Phenols		
Phenol	p-Vinyl phenol	
	p-Vinyl guaiacol	
	p-Ethyl guaiacol	
b) Carbonyls		
Pentanal	Heliotropin	2-Pentenal
Salicyclic aldehyde		Safranal
β-Cyclocitral		
Hexan-2-one	6,10,14-Tri-methyl penta-decan-2-one	4-Methylpentan-2-one
Heptan-2-one		Methylheptadienone
Octan-2-one		Acetophenone
c) Esters		
Amyl acetate	Ethyl 2-Methyl-butyrate	Propyl senecioate
Hexyl acetate	Ethyl levulate	Methyl decanoate
Methyl valerate	Ethyl lactate	
Methyl lactate	Methyl vanillate	
Phenylethyl acetate	Methyl phenyl-acetate	

We have compared not only the headspace but also a methanol-
ic extract especially prepared for our analytical purposes and a
vapor condensate coming from the production of so-called folded
extracts. The latter contains some preferentially steam-distill-
ed constituents which are enriched only in this special form of a
vanilla flavor bearing substrate. In order to identify these
trace substances in the aqueous-alcoholic vapor condensate, we
have obtained, after careful concentration, about 1 mg of a complex mixture. Needless to say, the identification of 74 components, with some new compounds never before found in vanilla and
therefore not previously reported in the literature, was achieved
only by means of several of our aforementioned microtechniques.
    We close with the remark that we have been convinced by the
facts that even trace components in the concentration range of
about 0.1 ppb are of sensory importance and can be detected by
the human senses as well as by the analytical chemist of today.

IV   REFERENCES

1. Hrivnac, M., unpublished.
2. Grob, K., J. Chromatogr. 84,255 (1973).
3. Klimes, I., Stünzi, W., Lamparsky, D., Intern. Flav. and
    Food Add. 7, 272 (1976).
4. Klimes, I., Stünzi, W., Lamparsky, D., J. Chromatog. 136,
    12, 23 (1977).
5. Grob, K., Grob, G., J. Chromat. Sci. 7, 584 (1969).
6. Cronin, D.A., J. Chromatogr. 52, 375 (1970).
7. Verzele, M., Verstappe, M., Sandra, P., van Luchene, E.,
    Wuye, A., J. Chromat. Sci. 10, 668 (1972).
8. Schudel, P., Chimia 31, 155 (1977)
9a. Klimes, I., "Chemical Identification Reactions for Deter-
    mination of Organic Functional Groups at the Nanogram
    Level", Intern. Symp. on Microchemical Techniques, Davos,
    May, 1977.
9b. Klimes, I., Stünzi, W., Lamparsky, D., to be published
    in J. Chromatogr.

AROMA ANALYSIS OF COFFEE, TEA AND COCOA
BY HEADSPACE TECHNIQUES

Otto G. Vitzthum, Peter Werkhoff

HAG AG, Research Laboratories

The greatest part of the numerous volatile components from coffee, tea and cocoa has been analysed in the past after pre-concentration by known procedures as extraction or steam distillation. Thus compounds with wide boiling range are iso-lated, which normally were identified by GC/MS combination. Though the human nose, a specific multicomponent trace detector can perceive and recognize yet the characteristic food aroma from the surrounding atmosphere of a product only little attention up to now has been paid to the investigation of the headspace aroma of coffee, tea and cocoa. This is due to the fact that there were no detectors selective and sensitive enough to analyse completely the ultra traces in gas samples directly.

In the last few years there have been developed some sophisti-cated techniques which may help to overcome these difficulties and to give additionally highly efficient resolutions of complex mixtures i.e. 1) enrichment of headspace vapors on porous poly-mers with direct transfer to the GC column 2) separation of the components on high performance capillary columns including low temperature GC 3) complete resolution of overlapped peaks on GC columns by using the valveless switching technique according to Deans 4) localization and indication of ultra trace components

by specific detectors prior to MS identification. Examples ob-
tained by conventional headspace analysis and after application
of the techniques as described above are given for coffee
(staling of roast beans), tea and cocoa aroma.

Soon after introduction of gas chromatography in aroma research first attempts were made to analyse the aroma components
from headspace of stimulant beverages. Such procedures had already been described in 1958 for coffee (1), in 1962 for cocoa
(2), and in 1965 for tea (3).

These experiments demonstrated, however, that the elucidation
of the aroma impact compounds was more complicated than origi-
nally thought. Single substances which could be correlated
directly with the characteristic beverage aromas have not been
found. Gas chromatographic detectors were not sensitive or specific enough to indicate headspace components present only in
traces; gas chromatographic columns at that time on the other
hand did not offer adequate resolution efficiency to separate
them.

As a consequence the research efforts in this field were concentrated more in a total exploration of all the volatile components contained in stimulant products. Well known isolation procedures like solvent extraction, vacuum and steam distillation
were applied to coffee (4-7), tea (8-12) and cocoa (13-16) in
order to obtain aroma samples in high concentrations. The result
to now has been a total of 610 volatiles identified from roasted
coffee, 360 from tea, and 370 from cocoa.

The following disadvantages of these procedures have to be
considered in search for authentic natural aromas :

- higher risk of artifact formation
- insufficient quantities of high volatiles in the concentrates
- shift of concentration ratios from the original aroma
  compounds.

Some newly developed techniques that can help to overcome
these hindrances are :
- enrichment of headspace vapors on porous polymers (17) and
  transfer of the adsorbate to a cooled glass capillary column
  (18)
- "heart cutting" of overlapped peaks and subsequent resolution
  on a second column using the valveless switching technique
  according to Deans (19), or as described by Zlatkis (20);
  intermediate trapping of small traces, i.e. sulphur compounds,
  on the second column for further ms investigations (21)
- installation of specific detectors after the capillary column
  for selective registration of nitrogeneous or sulphurous
  compounds (22).

EXPERIMENTAL METHODS

A. Enrichment Procedures

1. *Isolation of the Aroma Volatiles*

For investigation of the aroma volatiles from coffee, tea and
cocoa, headspace samples were taken by passing purified helium
over the samples or their aqueous suspensions (Fig. 1).
Fifty gms. samples of fresh ground coffee, tea leaves or a cocoa
mass were placed into a gas washing bottle. The volatile compounds
were aspirated into a porous polymer adsorption column (Tenax) by
a pump at a rate of 0.5 l/min. The gas volumes that passed
through the adsorption tube were 0.5 l for coffee and 40 l for
tea and cocoa. Aroma headspace isolation from the beverages was
accomplished by making a fresh brew of 2 gms. of coffee or 10 gms.
of tea in 150 ml of hot water (90°C) and sweeping He over the

solution at a rate of 50 ml/min for 20 minutes.

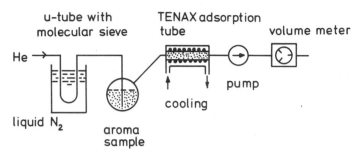

Fig. 1. Schematic of sampling unit for headspace volatiles from ground roast coffee, tea leaves, and cocoa mass respectively the beverages.

2. Adsorption on Tenax

The adsorbing tube (60 mm x 4 mm i.d.) was filled with 90 mgs. Tenax (60/80 mesh). Two small plugs of glass wool kept the adsorbent in place. Before the first use Tenax was conditioned for 24 hours at 300°C in a stream of He.

This porous polymer was used because it is hydrophobic and has a low adsorption strength, thus allowing thermal desorption of relatively high boiling compounds. It shows an excellent thermal stability and does not react with most organic aroma substances; furthermore Tenax doesn't contain volatile byproducts and is easily regenerated.

3. Desorption and Transfer to GC Capillary Column

After completion of the adsorption the Tenax tube was removed from the sampling unit and installed at the entry of a gas chromatograph (Fig. 2). One end of the tube was connected to a He source, the other end to a glass capillary which was inserted through the injection septum of the instrument.

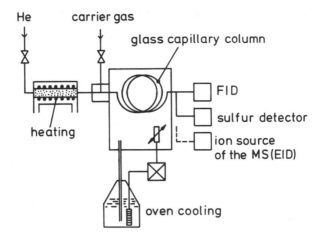

Fig. 2. Schematic of transfer of the adsorbate from the porous polymer into the cooled glass capillary column.

By using the splitless injection device from Carlo Erba, a direct transfer of the substances to the glass capillary column was accomplished. As the column was cooled to -60°C and the injector heated to $+170^\circ$C the volatiles were condensed in the column in a very narrow band thus avoiding spreading effects before starting the GC. During sample transfer the He carrier gas flow through the capillary column was turned off. The desorption temperature of the Tenax tube was 150°C. A He flow of 6 ml/min through the tube was maintained for a period of 20 min. At the end of the desorption the transfer capillary was pulled out of the injector and the carrier gas supply of the gas chromatograph was turned on.

B. Instrumentation

1. GC Detection

A Carlo Erba 2101 AC gas chromatograph especially designed for operation with glass capillary columns and FID was used. The FID that was mounted at the column outlet on top of the oven could be easily replaced by the sulphur specific flame photometric detector (FPD) from Tracor. The latter was adjusted by an adaptor

from Carlo Erba. For the multidimensional GC a modified Carlo
Erba 2350 all glass double column instrument with 2 FIDs was employed.

2. GC/MS Identification

A modified Varian MAT 111 gas chromatograph/mass spectrometer-
combination as described previously (11) was utilized for identification. The headspace samples were introduced into the gas
chromatograph the same way as mentioned above. For separations a
glass capillary column 100 m x 0.3 mm i.d. coated with Ucon HB
5100 was used. The He flow rate was 4.5 ml/min. The oven temperature was programmed from $-60^{\circ}C$ to $+180^{\circ}C$ at $2^{\circ}C/min$.

3. Multidimensional Gas Chromatography

Fig. 3 shows a schematic of a double column gas chromatograph
modified to employ the"heart cutting" technique. We used a valveless system according to Deans (19) as described in detail by
Schomburg et al. (21).

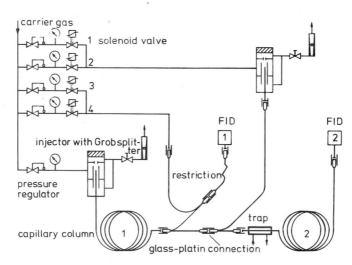

Fig. 3. Schematic of valveless switching
technique for multidimensional gas chromatography.

The enriched headspace samples were first chromatographed on
column 1 and registered in FID 1. Interesting sections with over-

lapping peaks were transferred in a second run from the first to
the second glass capillary column which possessed different polarity characteristics. Thus a rather complete separation of coeluting substances from column 1 could be achieved. The diversion
of the substances into the second column was performed by flow
inversion operations with help of solenoid valves, that were lo-
cated outside the oven. The programmable flow switching unit with
electronic timer was obtained from Siemens. The two FID's permitted control of separation on each column. Band spreading in
column 2 was minimized by keeping the dead volume of the coupling
capillary between the two columns small.

C. Applications

1. Coffee

Enrichment of headspace volatiles from coffee brew in cooling
traps (23) and on Porapak Q (24) before GC characterisation is
described in the literature.

We tried to transfer the headspace aroma from coffee in its
original composition into the analytical system. Fig. 4 shows
aroma chromatograms of fresh ground roast coffee isolated in two
different ways. By means of a steam distillation procedure there
were obtained numerous compounds with a wide range of boiling
points; only small amounts of light volatiles were present,
because the majority of them was lost during isolation. On the
other hand the headspace enrichment technique with Tenax resulted in a great number of very low boiling components which
approximated the impression of light fresh coffee aroma if
checked organoleptically. - As test coffee we used a commercial
blend of Arabicas (Columbia,Brazil) of medium roast, screened
after grinding through a No. 30 ASTM sieve.

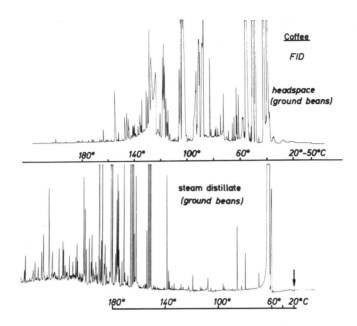

Fig. 4. Chromatogram of headspace volatiles from
ground coffee beans adsorbed on Tenax. GC-conditions:
100 m x 0.3 mm i.d. glass capillary column coated with
Ucon HB 5100, Helium flow rate 3.5 ml/min., injector
and detector temperature 170°C, temperature program
10°/min from -60°C to +20°C and 2°/min up to 180°C
(above). - Steam distillate chromatogram from ground
coffee, conditions see previous publication (11)(below).

Tassan and Russel (24) investigated headspace samples from
coffee brew after enrichment on Porapak Q by GC on packed columns.
The advantage of our work lies in the fact that we achieved better aroma protection by our all glass system and an improved resolution of the aroma mixture on the capillary column starting
with low temperature GC.

2. Tea

Trapping of headspace volatiles from the beverage by cooling
on the GC column (25) and in cooling traps (26,27) is mentioned
in literature.

For the tea beverage we found similar results as for coffee.
Fig. 5 shows comparative chromatograms of headspace and steam

distillation concentrates.

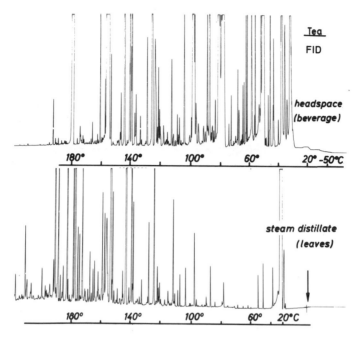

Fig. 5. Chromatogram of headspace volatiles from
tea beverage enriched on Tenax (above). GC-conditions
see Fig. 3. - Chromatogram of steam distillation from
tea leaves (below).

The high amount of low volatile compounds in the headspace run is
clearly visible. As the aroma complex in the atmosphere over the
tea beverage is in equilibrium with the tea solution, samples
drawn carefully from the headspace may well represent an important part of the specific tea flavour.

In contrast to the coffee aroma, tea aroma contains only a
few sulphur compounds as is shown in Fig. 6. On the other hand
these chromatograms point out the high selective specificity of
the flame photometric detector for sulphur compounds towards the
numerous other non sulphur containing coeluting substances. The
first large peak in the headspace chromatogram of the beverage
represents dimethylsulfide. During brewing of tea a considerable

amount of it must be liberated because dimethylsulfide is practi-
cally non-detectable in the headspace of tea leaves.

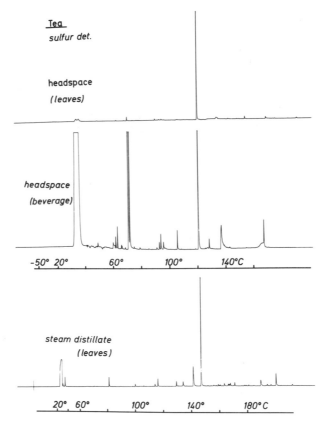

Fig. 6. Chromatograms of sulphur compounds obtained
by headspace enrichment and steam distillation from tea
leaves respectively beverage. Flame photometric detector
from Tracor. GC-conditions see Fig. 4

A test run of the headspace sample from tea leaves in our
gc/ms-combination confirmed several tea components already previously known (Table 1). Ten sesquiterpenes $C_{15}H_{24}$ out of 18
have not yet been reported (28). A structural elucidation was not
possible, however, as reference samples were not available.
No sesquiterpenes were found in the headspace sample of the tea
beverage. In the steam distillate they are present in small

amounts. - In all experiments the same black tea product was
used : Darjeeling, flowery orange pekoe, first flush 77, plan-
tation Bannuckburn.

TABLE 1

CHEMICAL COMPOUNDS IDENTIFIED IN BLACK TEA HEADSPACE
AROMA (TENAX TRAP)

Hydrocarbons	*Carbonyls*
Benzene	4-Pentenal
Toluene	2-Hexenal
o-Xylene	Phenylacetaldehyde
m-Xylene	2,2,6-Trimethylcyclohexanone
p-Xylene	2,6,6-Trimethylcyclohex-2-en-2-one
Ethylbenzene	Benzaldehyde
Styrene	Dimethylbenzaldehyde
Naphthalene	3,5-Octadien-2-one
2 x Methylnaphthalene	ß-Cyclocitral
8 x Terpenes $C_{10}H_{16}$	
18 x Sesquiterpenes $C_{15}H_{24}$	

Furans	*Miscellaneous*
2-Ethylfuran	Phenol
2-n-Butylfuran	Methyl salicylate
2-n-Amylfuran	
2-Isoamylfuran	
Furfural	

3. Cocoa

Only one literature quotation describes the enrichment of
cocoa volatiles from cocoa mass by using a cooling trap prior to
GC (29).

A fascinating tool that could facilitate the gc resolution
problem raised by complex aroma mixtures after headspace enrichment - is multidimensional chromatography. If combined with intermediate trapping and selective detectors, extremely small traces
of volatile substances can be identified in the gc/ms-combination.

We used the headspace aroma of cocoa mass as an example to demonstrate the "heart cutting" technique (Fig. 7).
Partially resolved overlapping peaks in column 1 could be separated excellently on column 2. The large pool of interfering substances thus can be disintegrated stepwise by suitable cuts in
the eluate of the first column. As the substances never passed

heated valves, decomposition problems were minimized. The cocoa
mass used for our experiments was cocoa liquor of African origin
(Ghana).

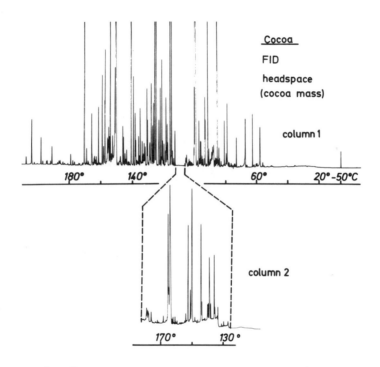

*Fig. 7. Chromatogram of enriched headspace aroma
from cocoa mass obtained by multidimensional GC.
GC-conditions: 100 m x 0.3 mm i.d. glass capillary
column coated with Ucon HB 5100 (column 1), and
Carbowax 20 M (column 2).*

4. Measurement of Coffee Staleness

A practical example for the application of headspace techniques with enrichment on the cooled gc capillary column is the
measurement of coffee staleness.

It is generally known that whole coffee beans packed in
common air packs - also called bag packs - will keep their freshness for a period of 8 to 10 weeks after roasting (30). Then the
aroma becomes stale and the taste becomes bitter. Roast and

ground coffee becomes stale even faster; it loses its freshness 8 to 10 days after grinding. In airtight packages or cans, however, i.e. sealed under vacuum, this coffee will keep its fresh aroma at least 12 months.

The process of staleness is accelerated by oxygen and humidity. Its chemical mechanism is not yet known. Typical staleness compounds have not been discovered.

Reymond et al. (31), however, demonstrated that the ratio of

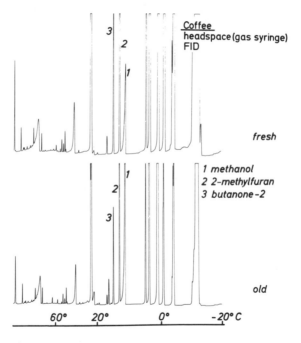

Fig. 8. Chromatograms of fresh and old roasted coffee. Sampling: 5 ml headspace gas from 30 gms. of fresh ground coffee stored at ambient temperature in 100 ml flask for 3 hours were injected into cooled column. GC-conditions: Carlo Erba 2101 AC gas chromatograph with splitless injection device and FID; 100 m x 0.3 mm i.d. glass capillary column coated with Ucon HB 5100; temperature program -45°C to +20°C with 3°/min.

the two coffee aroma compounds methylfuran and methylethylketone analysed from an aqueous suspension of ground coffee will decrease from 2.6 to 0.1 within 4 days. It is well known that aqueous suspensions become perceptibly stale in a few days.

We found that these compounds and the methanol values were good indicators to evaluate the freshness of roast coffee (Fig. 8). They can be easily measured by taking a headspace sample from fresh ground coffee and injecting it into a cooled glass capillary column. An injector for splitless injection should be used. Separation is performed by temperature programming between -45°C and $+20^{\circ}$C. As it is seen from the chromatogram the three indicator compounds are well separated to allow quantitative analysis. An aging coffee shows a significant increase of methanol and a decrease of butanone-2.

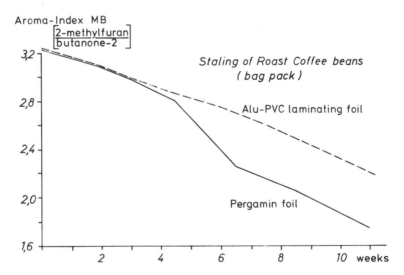

Fig. 9. Influence of packaging materials on the staling of whole beans in (air) bag packs.

Fig. 9 shows the changes in the ratio of 2-methylfuran to butanone-2 for a period of 10 weeks. We started with fresh roasted whole beans kept in common bag packs of different materials. Every week one pack was opened and the ratio - we call it "aroma index MB" - was analysed. A steady drop of the MB-values was observed. The less protective Pergamin foil tested in comparison to the Alu-PVC laminating foil as packaging material showed a steeper slope of the line. Starting with an MB-value of 3.2 the tasters characterized a loss of fresh coffee flavor below the index level of 2.4 - 2.5. This corresponds to a life of good coffee aroma for whole beans packed in Alu-PVC of 8 to 10 weeks versus 5 to 6 weeks for Pergamin foil.

If air is admitted also to roast and ground coffee the decrease of the MB-values with time is stronger than for whole beans (Fig. 10).

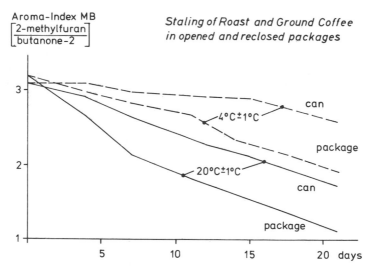

Fig. 10. Influence of temperature on staling of ground coffee in packages and cans in presence of air.

The storage time for open packages of ground coffee depends on the storage temperature. From our studies it can be concluded that opened packages or cans of ground coffee in households may keep their freshness two or three times longer if stored in a refrigerator.

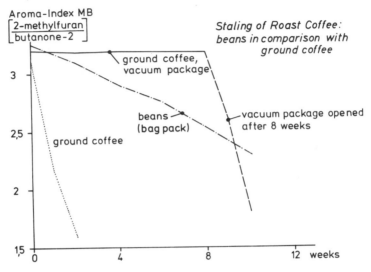

Fig. 11. Influence of kind of packaging on staling behavior of ground coffee in comparison to whole beans in bag packs.

Fig. 11 demonstrates that ground coffee packed in cans or packages under exclusion of oxygen will keep its freshness longer than coffee beans in bag packs. If those vacuum packages are opened, i.e. after 8 weeks, the subsequent decrease of the aroma index curve shows a similar fast staleness process as with fresh coffee ground immediately after roasting.

As the methanol content increases correspondingly to the staleness of coffee we will find a reverse direction of the curve if we observe the methanol/2-methylfuran ratio, - which we call "aroma index MM". Fig. 12 shows these curves for whole beans in bag packs with different packaging materials. The MM-values for the other examples mentioned before demonstrate a similar behavior, i.e. an increase with staleness.

We believe that these methods will give a useful tool to analyse sufficiently the freshness character of whole or ground
roast coffee beans.

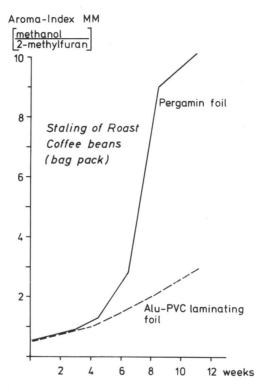

Fig. 12. Influence of packaging materials on
the staling of whole beans in bag packs.

REFERENCES

1. Rhoades, J.W., Food Res. 23 (3), 254 (1958).

2. Bailey, S.D., Mitchell, D.G., Bazinet, M.L., Weurman, C.,
   J. Food Sci. 27, 165 (1962).

3. Wickremasinghe, R.L., Swain, T., J. Sci.Food Agric. 16, 57
   (1965).

4. Gautschi, F., Winter, M., Flament, Y., Willhalm, B., Stoll, M., J. Agric. Food Chem. 15, 15 (1967).

5. Gianturco, M.A., in "The Chemistry and Physiology of Flavors" (H.W. Schultz, E.A. Day, L.M. Libbey, Eds.), p. 431. AVI Publ. Co. 1967.

6. Friedel, P., Krampl, V., Radford, T., Renner, J.A., Shephard, F.W., Gianturco, M.A., J. Agric. Food Chem. 19, 530 (1971).

7. Vitzthum, O.G., Werkhoff, P., Z. Lebensm. Unters.-Forsch.160, 277 (1976).

8. Reymond, D., Food Technol. 25, 1152 (1971).

9. Cazenave, P., Horman, I., Helv. Chim. Acta 57, 209 (1974).

10. Renold, W., Näf-Müller, R., Keller, U., Willhalm, B., Ohloff, G., Helv. Chim. Acta 57, 1301 (1974).

11. Vitzthum, O.G., Werkhoff, P., J. Agric. Food Chem. 23, 510 (1975).

12. Nguyen, T.T., Yamanishi, T., Agr. Biol. Chem. 39, 1263 (1975).

13. Marion, J.P., Müggler-Chavan, F., Viani, R., Bricout, J., Reymond, D., Egli, R.H., Helv. Chim. Acta 50, 1509 (1967).

14. Praag, M. van, Stein, H.S., Tibbetts, M.S., J. Agric. Food Chem. 16, 1005 (1968).

15. Wal, B. van der, Kettenes, D.K., Stoffelsma, J., Sipma, G., Semper, A.T.J., J. Agric. Food Chem. 19,276 (1971).

16. Vitzthum, O.G., Werkhoff, P., Hubert, P., J. Food Sci. 40, 911 (1975).

17. Zlatkis, A., Lichtenstein, A., Tishbee, A., Chromatographia 6, (2), 67 (1973).

18. Bergert, K.H., Betz, V., Pruggmayer, D., Chromatographia 7 (3), 115 (1974).

19. Deans, D.R., Chromatographia 1 (1-2), 18 (1968).

20. Bertsch, W., Hsu, F., Zlatkis, A., Analytical Chemistry 48, 928 (1976).

21. Schomburg, G., Husmann, H., Weeke, F., J. Chromatogr. 112, 2o5 (1975).

22. Withycombe, D.A., Walradt, J.P., Hruza, A., in "Phenolic, Sulfur, and Nitrogen Compounds in Food Flavors" (G. Charalambous, I. Katz, Eds.), 170th Meeting of the ACS, Chicago Aug. 25-26 (1975), ACS Symposium Series 26, p. 85. American Chemical Society - Washington, D.C. 1976.

23. Kaiser, R.E., 6th Intern. Colloqu. on Coffee Chemistry (Bogotá, 4-9 June 1973), ASIC-Paris, p. 73.

24. Tassan, C.G., Russell, G.F., J. Food Sci. 39, 64 (1974).

25. Heins, J.T., Maarse, H., ten Noever de Brauw, M.C., Weurman, C., J. Gas Chromatog. 4, 395 (1966).

26. Co, H., Sanderson, G.W., J. Food Sci. 35, 160 (1970).

27. Reymond, D., Flavour Industry 2, 575 (1971).

28. Central Institute for Nutrition and Food Research TNO, "Lists of Volatile Compounds in Food", (S. van Straten, J. C. de Beauveser, F. de Vrijer, Eds.), Suppl. 1 to 7, Rapport Nr. R 4030, p. 73. 8 May 1976.

29. Müggler-Chavan, F., Reymond, D., Mitt. Gebiete Lebensm.Hyg. 58, 466 (1967).

30. Vitzthum, O.G., in "Kaffee und Coffein" (O. Eichler, Ed.), p. 25. Springer-Verlag Berlin Heidelberg New York, 1976.

31. Reymond, D., Chavan, F., Egli, R.H., 1st Intern. Congr. Food Sci. Technol., p. 595, London 1962.

DETERMINATION OF CITRUS VOLATILES BY HEADSPACE ANALYSIS

Eric D. Lund
U. S. Citrus and Subtropical Products Laboratory

and

Howard L. Dinsmore
Florida Southern College, Department of Chemistry

Many citrus volatiles have been determined by both direct and indirect headspace analysis. The more concentrated components methanol, ethanol, acetaldehyde and limonene have been determined quantitatively by direct sampling methods. The more dilute volatiles require a preliminary concentration step. Compounds which contribute to flavor or off-flavor include acetaldehyde, ethyl vinyl ketone, ethyl butyrate, n-octanal, citral, α-terpineol, and 4-vinyl guaiacol. Limonene, furfural and diacetyl have been indirectly related to flavor quality and quantitative methods have been developed for these three. Limonene levels have been related to peel oil content and diacetyl determination has been used to indicate microbial contamination. Furfural concentrations have been correlated with storage abuse of orange and grapefruit juices. Concentrations of several other volatiles from citrus products have been related to cultivar, maturity, and product storage history. Several improved extraction and trapping methods were developed. These techniques could form the basis for more rapid and convenient quality control procedures.

Although quality of citrus products is currently assayed by classical methods of titration and colorimetry, a more thorough evaluation could be obtained by chromatographic methods based on headspace sampling or related techniques. The importance of volatile compounds to citrus flavor has been well established; and with the availability of less expensive gas chromatography (GC) instruments suitable for quality control, analysis of volatiles has become practical.

Four prominent volatile compounds have been quantitatively determined by direct headspace analysis of citrus products: methanol, ethanol, acetaldehyde, and limonene. Numerous other less prominent volatiles have been determined after concentration by distillation, extraction, or adsorption. Many of these latter compounds are important to citrus flavor and off-flavor and concentrated samples of these volatiles have provided much useful information for quality evaluation. Some volatiles, such as acetaldehyde, ethyl vinyl ketone, ethyl butyrate, *n*-octanal, citral, α-terpineol and 4-vinyl guaiacol, have been correlated directly with flavor or off-flavor. Other compounds, including ethanol, limonene, furfural, diacetyl, valencene and linalool, have been indirectly related to flavor quality. Limonene and diacetyl determinations have been particularly useful for quality control in processing plants. Furfural and α-terpineol concentrations have been closely correlated with storage abuse, but they are not yet routinely determined.

Relationships between varieties (or cultivars) and seasonal variations form the basis on which blending or adulteration can be detected. GC patterns of volatiles are often characteristic of the variety and degree of maturity. Analyses of headspace or concentrated volatiles are simple and convenient, and the application of these to detection of blending (or adulteration) and storage abuse seems to be a promising approach, as indicated by the preliminary studies reported in this chapter.

This chapter reviews the current status of headspace

analysis and enrichment techniques as applied to citrus volatiles. In the first section, techniques are discussed. Methods used in our laboratory are described in detail. The second section contains a discussion of results, both for commercial condensates and other juice or peel products. A review of pertinent literature is presented first, followed by a more detailed review of methods for furfural analysis and a discussion of some recent unpublished studies of juice volatiles from various citrus products.

I.   TECHNIQUES

Most of the usual methods for analysis of food volatiles have been applied to citrus products. Direct sampling of headspace gases, the simplest and easiest method, can only be applied to the most concentrated volatiles. Methanol, ethanol, acetaldehyde, and limonene are readily determined in this manner.

Other, more dilute volatiles require concentration before GC analysis. The most frequently used technique for citrus volatiles has been distillation, and the distillates are usually concentrated further by extraction (1). More recently, distilled volatiles have been adsorbed on porous polymeric adsorbents. A technique similar to distillation but less frequently used is stripping with a stream of inert gas. The same extraction, adsorption, and derivatization techniques have been used to concentrate the stripped volatiles. Finally, juice has been extracted directly (2). The gas chromatograph injection port then separates the volatile from non-volatile extracted material and effectively substitutes for the distillation or stripping step.

Adsorption on the porous polymer Porapak (Waters Associates) has been particularly useful at our laboratory for the analysis of certain types of commercial condensates. The volatiles were trapped on a Porapak column (3,4). The trap was then backflushed with an inert gas (5), which swept the volatiles to a cold trap or onto the upstream end of a cool GC column. Volatiles were then transferred by syringe onto a GC column; or the trap (or column) was heated and the volatiles carried rapidly onto a GC column by the carrier gas. These three steps are summarized in Fig. 1.

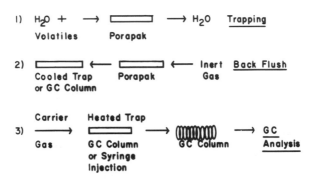

Fig. 1. Porapak trapping procedure.

A method was developed for the analysis of orange and grape-fruit juice volatiles. The juice (500 ml) was stripped with nitrogen (100 ml/min) at 55°C and the vapors swept into a 4-in. by 1/4-in. Porapak filled column held at 70°C (Fig. 2). After 1 hr, the sparging tube was replaced with a shorter tube so that the gas bypassed the juice and was blown through to expel water. After 15 min. the Porapak was heated to 180°C, the flow reversed, and volatiles eluted by the nitrogen stream for 1 hr. into a chilled glass capillary tube. Collected volatiles were transferred by syringe for GC analysis. By this method several chromatograms could be obtained from one stripping run.

By a suitable adjustment of the time allowed for the by-passing step, residual water, ethanol, acetaldehyde and methanol could be vented while the remaining relatively small amount of juice volatiles remains adsorbed. The resulting mixture of eluted compounds could be analysed by GC without interference from these relatively prominent components.

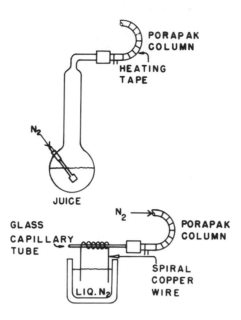

Fig. 2. Porapak trap for stripped volatiles.

A more rapid method for juice analysis is a simple
distillation-extraction procedure. Ten ml of distillate were
collected from 200 ml of juice distilled in a Scott-Veldhuis peel
oil determination apparatus (6). Condensate was transferred
directly to a microextractor tube (Fig. 3) attached to the
condenser outlet. The condenser was rinsed with an organic
solvent (0.2 to 2 ml) into the test tube. The tube was removed,
3.6 gm of NaCl added, the upper part of the extractor attached,
and the apparatus shaken vigorously with the sidearm plugged and
the stopcock closed. The phases were allowed to separate; then
saturated sodium chloride solution was slowly admitted through
the sidearm from a reservoir to displace the upper (organic)
layer through the open stopcock into the 10 cm length of
capillary tubing. The upper layer was sampled with a syringe for
GC analysis. In this manner a sample suitable for several chromatograms can be produced in a relatively short time (20 min vs.

1 hr for trapping and backflushing).

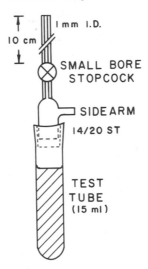

*Fig. 3.   Microextraction apparatus.   [From J. Food Sci. 42,
385 (1977).   Copyright by Institute of Food Technologists.]*

Efficiency of the distillation-extraction (D-E) method was
studied as a function of the extracting solvent. Diisopropyl
ether and cyclohexane were the extracting solvents (2 ml), and GC
traces were obtained on SP-1000 (Supelco, a polar liquid phase
similar to Carbowax 20M). A model citrus juice was formulated by
addition of an ethanolic solution of 5 typical citrus terpenes to
a 12°Brix aqueous solution of sucrose and citric acid (Table 1).
A sample prepared by direct extraction of 200 ml model juice with
4 ml of solvent and a sample prepared by the D-E method with the
same solvent were compared by quantitative GC analysis (Table 2).
Extraction coefficients and overall recoveries for the D-E method
were determined. Total recoveries ranged between 4 and 15%.
Although these were low, the improvement in concentration likewise ranged between 4- and 15-fold, and compensated for the low
recovery. Higher concentrations could be obtained by use of less
solvent. Extraction coefficients and recoveries were both
greater for diisopropyl ether than cyclohexane (Table 3), but

relative peak areas for the various components in the respective
solvents were very similar. Even though concentrations in cyclohexane were lower, tailing on polar columns is reduced in this
solvent so that more of the most volatile compounds can be distinguished.

TABLE 1
Composition of simulated juice.

Component	GC peak ID	mg/liter
Limonene	L	81
Linalool	LL	5
α-Terpineol[a]	T	2
Terpinyl acetate[a]	T	1
Valencene	V	10
Ethanol[b]		780

　　a. *Gave a single GC peak, no
resolution on SP-1000.*
　　　b. *Solvent.*

Comparisons were made of D-E and nitrogen stripping-Porapak
(N-P) methods. Volatiles from the same glass-packed orange juice
were analyzed by the two techniques. Diisopropyl ether was the
extraction solvent and GC traces were obtained on both OV-101
(non-polar silicone) and SP-1000. As Fig. 4 shows, the solvent
peak is absent from both N-P traces. Much of the less volatile
materials, whose peaks should appear in the latter part of the
OV-101 trace for N-P are lacking. On the other hand, as the SP-
1000 traces show, the N-P sample contained much larger quantities
of the more volatile components.

A principal advantage of porous polymer trapping over
extraction is the lack of an interferring solvent peak (7). For
compounds which are eluted well after the solvent, extraction
would probably be comparable to or better than trapping.
Extraction might be preferable for compounds with low steam

TABLE 2.
Recovery of terpenes from model juice.

Solvent[a]	L	LL	T	V
Diisopropyl ether				
Extraction coeff.[b]	2.2	4.5	3.7	3.7
D-E % recovery[c]	4.0	4.0	15.0	8.3
% Distilled (estimate)[d]	18.0	11.0	45.0	25.0
Conc. improvement[e]	4.0	4.0	15.0	8.3
Cyclohexane				
Extraction coeff.[b]	1.1	3.2	3.0	2.2
D-E % recovery[c]	3.5	3.9	13.0	6.7
% Distilled (estimate)[d]	27.0	13.0	45.0	29.0
Conc. improvement[e]	3.5	3.9	13.0	6.7

a. *L-limonene, LL-linalool, T-α-terpineol (terpenyl acetate), V-valencene.*
b. *Conc. in direct extract/conc. in model juice.*
c. *Percentage of component in model juice recovered in extract.*
d. *By indirect calculation.*
e. *Conc. in D-E extract/conc. in model juice.*

TABLE 3.
Comparison of chromatograms from direct extraction of model juice vs. D-E method.[a]

	L	LL	T	V
Original (diluted)[b]	85.3	2.1	2.3	8.6
Directly extracted (E)	79.1	3.8	3.2	13.2
D-E recovered (E)	71.0	2.0	6.8	15.0
Directly extracted (H)	72.0	6.1	4.9	15.2
D-E recovered (H)	73.7	2.2	6.9	14.6

a. *Peak area percent values. E-diisopropyl ether; H-cyclohexane.*
b. *By dilution of ethanolic solution to concentration of model solution.*

volatility because usually they are not eluted quantitatively
from the polymer. For determination of general groups of compounds, such as alcohols, aldehydes, and ketones, or specific
compounds such as limonene, derivatization is the preferred
technique.

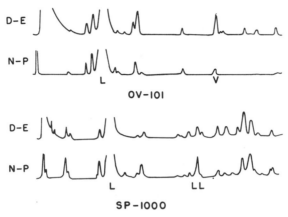

*Fig. 4. GC traces: D-E vs. N-P procedures. Peak identi-
ties: L-limonene, LL-linalool, V-valencene.*

II. RESULTS

Citrus volatiles can be obtained from two general product
types: commercial condensates and juice or peel products.

A.   Commercial Condensates

The commercial condensates include essence, which is the low-
boiling condensate from commercial juice evaporators, and peel
aroma, which is distilled from waste peel-oil emulsion.

Studies on citrus essence composition have recently been reviewed (8). Essence, derived from juice, has been a convenient
source of juice volatiles for identification. Over 140 components
have been identified in orange essence. Evaluation of the contribution of individual compounds to orange flavor or off-flavor has
been based largely on compounds found in orange essence or peel

oil (9). Volatiles from grapefruit, lemon, tangerine, and lime
have not been as extensively studied.

Other related commercial sources of citrus volatiles are the
higher-boiling fraction of condensate from commercial juice evaporators and the waste condensate from peel drying equipment. GC
analysis of the former, which has a pleasant, fruity aroma,
showed that a single unidentified component predominates. Presumably, this unidentified compound is volatile, but not enough
so to be entirely collected with the essence fraction. Waste peel
condensate from evaporation of lime-treated citrus peel pressings
contains about 1% alcohol (ethanol and methanol) and 200 to 400
ppm of a mixture of 3 components with a pronounced "rotten fruit"
aroma. The processing procedure must alter the volatile composition considerably, since it is different from the composition
of other peel-derived distillates directly distilled from peel.

Aroma solutions produced by distillation of aqueous discharge
from peel oil centrifugation contain many essence components, and
are similar to essence in flavor and aroma properties (8). The
aromas most studied have been from orange but grapefruit and lemon
peel aromas have also been prepared and analyzed by similar
techniques. Typical compositions of these products are shown in
Table 4.

Methanol, ethanol and acetaldehyde represent a separate class
of more concentrated compounds, although acetaldehyde concentration is apparently relatively low in grapefruit and lemon. Because of the high concentrations of these three, they could be
directly analyzed on Porapak. The others were generally much less
concentrated, and a preliminary extraction-concentration step was
required. Among the latter, linalool, α-terpineol, and *cis*-3-
hexene-1-ol predominate in orange aroma; α-terpineol, *n*-octanal,
linalool, 1-octanol, *trans*-2-hexenal and *trans*-linalool oxide in
grapefruit; and α-terpineol, terpinene-4-ol, geranial, neral,
linalool, and nerol in lemon. Thus, α-terpineol and linalool were
most prominent among the less concentrated volatiles in all three

aromas.

TABLE 4.
Peel aroma composition (10) concentration range, wt. % x 10^3.[a]

Compound	Orange	Grapefruit	Lemon[b]
Methanol	12-820	7.7-46	53
Acetaldehyde	3-74	0.33-2.16	1.2
Ethanol	24-1200	11.8-37	32
Linalool	0.9-4.6	0.49-1.11	1.7
α-Terpineol	0.18-1.8	0.53-1.15	8.3
cis-3-Hexen-1-ol	0.16-2.5	0.191-0.83	−
n-Octanal	0.06-0.65	0.69-1.33	−
1-Hexanol	0.06-1.18	0.032-0.51	−
1-Octanol	0.07-1.3	0.34-3.23	−
trans-2-Hexenal	0.02-0.8	0.32-1.07	−
Terpinen-4-ol	0.028-0.194	0.102-0.196	4.3
n-Hexanal	0.03-0.51	−	−
Nerol	0.05-0.24	−	1.6
Geraniol	0.02-0.4	−	−
Neral	0.10-0.27	0.029-0.040	1.4
Geranial	0.012-0.31	0.093-0.174	2.1
cis-Carveol	0.02-0.03	−	−
trans-Carveol	0.01-0.12	0.069-0.188	−
cis-Linalool oxide	0.02-0.04	0.095-0.33	−
trans-Linalool oxide	0.0006-0.076	0.30-0.94	−
1-Penten-3-ol	0.05-0.52	−	−
n-Amyl alcohol	0.03-0.56	−	−
n-Decanal	0.01-0.03	−	−
trans-2-Hexen-1-ol	0.02-0.75	0.04-0.167	−

TABLE 4 *continued*

Compound	Orange	Grapefruit	Lemon
Terpinyl formate	0.08[b]	-	-
Ethyl-3-hydroxyhexanoate	0.11-0.24	-	-
cis-2,8-p-Menthadien-1-ol	0.02-0.07	-	-
trans-2,8-p-Menthadien-1-ol	0.05-0.12	0.027-0.12	-
1,8-p-Menthadiene-9-ol	0.05-0.18		
$\Delta^{8(10)}$-p-Menthene-1,2-diol	0.12[b]	-	-
Citronellol	0.02-0.13	-	-
Perillaldehyde	0.02-0.13	-	-
Nootkatone	-	0.0102-0.0143	-

a. *Unpublished studies, E. D. Lund, C. J. Wagner, Jr. and W. L. Bryan.*
b. *Single determination.*

Many aroma components contribute to flavor quality. Acetaldehyde, *n*-octanal, neral, geranial and possibly ethyl-3-hydroxyhexanoate are important to orange flavor (12). Citral (geranial and neral) and possibly nerol contribute to lemon flavor. Nootkatone is the only aroma component known to be important to grapefruit flavor. Because of the low steam volatility of this compound, the bottoms (pot residue) fraction from grapefruit aroma preparation still contained more than 80% of the nootkatone. The 1-octanol concentration in grapefruit aromas varied over a wide range; this suggests a correlation between octanol content and some factor such as storage history, cultivar, or maturity.

A study showed that aroma from frozen, stored orange peel contained less aldehydes and more alcohols than aroma from fresh peel. For example, the octanol:octanal ratio changed from a maximum of 4.4 for aroma from fresh peel to 12.6 in aroma from stored peel, and the hexanol:hexanal ratio went from 3.7 to 9.6. Such reductive conversions under anaerobic storage conditions must be caused by the alcohol dehydrogenase in citrus (11). A change in the octanol:octanal ratio would have a particularly serious effect on flavor of orange aromas, since octanal is apparently one of the most important contributors to orange flavor (12).

Related studies on the influence of maturity on composition were carried out on Hamlin and Valencia orange aromas. The most pronounced variation was in the relative concentrations of the six carbon compounds in Hamlin aroma (Fig. 5). Of the two, Valencia

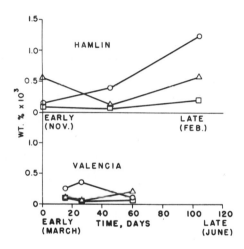

Fig. 5. Seasonal variation in the concentrations of cis-3-hexen-1-ol (o), 1-hexanol (△), n-hexanal (□) in orange peel aroma.

aroma did not change as much, and the general level of six-carbon compounds was much lower. The high concentrations and wide variability in levels of the six-carbon compounds probably have a considerable effect on the flavoring quality of Hamlin aromas, since most of these compounds have green, leafy, or immature odors which could be undesirable.

Another important variable is the content of ethyl vinyl ketone and 1-penten-3-ol. These two compounds have both been isolated from peel aroma; and since they have an oxidation reduction relationship, they could be influenced by storage history.

$$CH_2 = CH-\overset{\overset{\displaystyle O}{\displaystyle ||}}{C}-CH_2CH_3 \rightleftharpoons CH_2 = CH-\overset{\overset{\displaystyle OH}{\displaystyle |}}{C}-CH_2CH_3$$

ethyl vinyl ketone   *1-penten-3-ol*

The ketone has a low flavor threshold and contributes a green-beany off flavor to orange essence (12). The alcohol has a much **higher threshold.**

B.   Juice and Peel Products.

Analysis of citrus juice and peel is complicated by the presence of large amounts of nonvolatile materials not present in condensates. Distillation and derivatization of a specific component of the distillate has been the only method used for routine analysis of juice volatiles. Headspace analysis has not been adopted extensively by citrus juice processors. Ethanol and limonene have been quantitatively determined in orange juice and the necessary parameters established, but the method has not yet been widely applied.

1.   *Literature Review*
The first application of headspace determination to citrus products was made by Wolford *et al.* (13). GC analysis of a 4 ml sample of headspace vapor from the juice of each of 3 different orange cultivars showed a large limonene peak and a number of smaller peaks. The 3 chromatograms were qualitatively similar; but some quantitative differences suggested use of the technique to differentiate juices from different cultivars.

Most orange and other citrus juices contain added peel oil for flavoring. Since peel oil is largely limonene, the level of oil added is monitored by analysis of this compound. In 1966, Scott and Veldhuis (6) published an improved method for limonene, based on distillation-titration, which is now the standard procedure used by citrus processors. The method is rapid and simple and does not require expensive or complicated equipment.

Another volatile component of concern to processors of
frozen concentrated orange juice is diacetyl, a metabolite of
lactic acid bacteria. This compound can be determined conveniently by a distillation-colorimetric procedure (14) which is used
for quality control evaluation of microbial activity in various
process streams.

The stability of essence, added to frozen concentrated
orange juice by many processors, has been examined. Headspace
vapors above the diluted product (15) or juice which contained
added essence (16) were directly sampled (5 ml). Limonene,
ethanol, and acetaldehyde were the major components. The principal effect of storage on essence was a pronounced decline in
limonene. This change could not be consistently related to
sensory changes, however.

One of the above studies (16) showed that concentrated
orange juice with cutback (fresh juice) added (a standard industry practice) was lower in volatiles than concentrate with
oooonoo, and both concentrates had smaller amounts of volatiles
than fresh juice. Fresh juice contained larger quantities of
acetaldehyde, methanol, and several other unidentified volatiles
than the concentrates.

The first positive identifications of smaller peaks in orange
juice headspace chromatograms were made by Schultz et al. (4).
Volatiles trapped on Porapak from approximately 2 l of vapor were
analyzed. Twenty-nine compounds were identified by mass spectra
and retention times (Table 5). Many of the same compounds were
observed in the earlier headspace study (13), but the amounts were
too small for positive identification. Concentration by
adsorption on Porapak has been used for the identification of
trace components in several more recent studies as well (see below). Schultz et al. (4) also sampled headspace directly (20 ml
samples) and found a quantitative difference between traces of
normal and oil-free juices. Acetaldehyde, ethanol, and limonene

were the principal components of both juices, but normal juice
contained relatively larger limonene, α-pinene, myrcene γ-terpinene and terpinolene peaks. The increased amounts of these terpene hydrocarbons relative to amounts of other components suggest
that peel oil content might be determined from relative peak areas
in the headspace chromatogram.

TABLE 5.
Constituents of fresh orange juice vapor.

| Compound | Occurrence[a] | |
	Normal	Oil free
Acetaldehyde	L	L
Methanol	S	S
Ethanol	L	L
1-Propanol	S	S
Ethyl acetate	S	S
2-Methyl-3-buten-2-ol	S	S
Isobutyl alcohol	S	S
2-Pentanone	S	S
1-Butanol	–	–
Ethyl propionate	S	S
Methyl butyrate	S	S
Ethyl isobutyrate	–	–
3-Methylbutan-1-ol	–	–
2-Methylbutan-1-ol	–	–
Diethyl carbonate	–	–
Hexanal	–	–
Ethyl butyrate	M	M
Ethyl 2-methylbutyrate	S	S
trans-2-Hexenal	M	M
1-Hexanol	–	–
Methyl hexanoate	–	–
α-Thujene	S	S

TABLE 5 *continued*

| Compound | Occurrence[a] | |
	Normal	Oil free
α-Pinene	L	S
Benzaldehyde	-	-
Myrcene	L	S
Octanal	S	S
Limonene	L	L
γ-Terpinene	M	S
Terpinolene	M	S

a. *Relative peak size, L - large, M - medium, S - small. [Reprinted with permission from J. Agric. Food Chem. 19, 1060 (1971). Copyright by the American Chemical Society.]*

Ethanol is another interesting headspace component that may be useful in storage studies on citrus juice. Davis and Chase studied the parameters affecting ethanol determination (17). Two ml vapor samples were analyzed on a Porapak column. A temperature effect on alcohol concentration averaging about 7%/°C was observed. This effect demonstrated the importance of maintaining constant sample temperature. The ratio of total headspace volume to liquid volume was not critical as long as it was below 100-200. The most critical parameter was holding time before analysis: after 3 days at room temperature the alcohol concentration had increased more than twice. Accordingly, storage of samples in the refrigerator was recommended. Filtered juice was analyzed in preference to whole juice because limonene was removed along with insoluble solids; **analysis of the resulting limonene-free** samples was faster since the long retention time of limonene precludes rapid analysis. A number of juice samples from different citrus varieties and from individual fruits of the same variety and

maturity were analyzed. Large variations in alcohol content were
observed, but there was no attempt to correlate alcohol content
with juice source.

In related work, Roe and Bruemmer (18) determined acetaldehyde in orange juice. A headspace vapor analysis (1 ml, Porapak)
and an enzymatic assay were used. Acetaldehyde content increased
significantly in juice held at room temperature for 4 hr, but not
in juice that was heat treated or kept at 4°C (Fig. 6). This
surprisingly rapid change in acetaldehyde could affect flavor
quality since the aldehyde and compounds derived from it, such as
diacetyl, are known to be flavor related. The authors concluded
that juice should be held at low temperature if quality tests are
to be made before pasteurization.

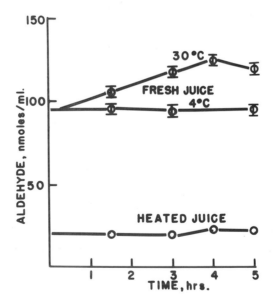

*Fig. 6. Change in aldehyde concentration of fresh orange
juice at 30° and at 4°, and change in aldehyde concentration of
heated juice. Mean ± SE from four experiments using enzyme assay;
concentration expressed in nmol of acetaldehyde/ml. [Reprinted
with permission from J. Agric. Food Chem. 19, 266 (1971). Copyright by the American Chemical Society.]*

Quantitative determination of relatively water-insoluble limonene in citrus juice requires knowledge of its distribution between pulp and serum. As we have seen (17), most of the limonene is associated with the pulp. More recently, Radford *et al* found the percentage distribution in orange juice to be 98% in pulp, 2% in serum (19). Massaldi and King (20) related the vapor pressure of limonene to solubility in the lipid phase; the latter is a component of the colloidal fraction (cloud) which is removed with the pulp in some centrifugal and filtration separations. These authors define a "lipid extraction parameter", $\lambda_F = K_F N_F/wb$. The distribution coefficient K_F is X_F/X_L, where X_F is the mole fraction of limonene in the lipid phase and X_L the mole fraction in the aqueous phase. The total moles of limonene in the lipid phase is N_F, w is the quantity of juice in gm, and b the fraction of dissolved solids. The lipid extraction parameter therefore represents the combined effects of the intrinsic solvent characteristics of the lipid phase and the total amount of lipid, per unit of soluble solids. By sampling the headspace vapors above diluted juice (7 or 11 gm juice diluted to 160 ml) to which limonene had been added and plotting the normalized limonene peak areas, A/A_O, against S, the volume of pure limonene added, Massaldi and King found the linear relationships shown in Fig. 7 and 8. From the slope and intercept, λ_F and the limonene concentration, respectively, were determined for 3 samples of orange juice (Table 6). For one of the samples (reconstituted frozen concentrate), two different juice concentrations were tested, and both gave values for limonene content and λ_F that agreed closely. The slopes (Fig. 8) were different, but when the concentration difference was taken into account, the lipid parameters were almost the same. This indicates that the juice concentration in the diluted sample used for headspace equilibration did not affect limonene solubility in the lipid phase relative to the aqueous phase. The approximate two-fold difference in λ_F between frozen concentrate and commercial single-strength or fresh juice reflects

the difference in dissolved solids content in the juice, b.   If b
is eliminated, the resultant quantity is about the same for the 3
juices, which would be consistent with the assumption that both
total lipids and lipid solvent strength are approximately the same
for all fresh juices and independent of dissolved solids levels in
the juice.   Measurement of a much larger number of juice samples
from various sources would be necessary to establish this point,
however.

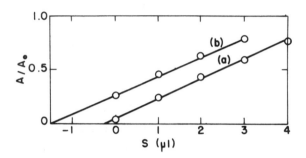

Fig. 7.   Normalized peak area vs volume of d-limonene added
to 7-gram samples of (a) fresh-squeezed (FS) Navel orange juice
and (b) commercial pasteurized (CP) orange juice (diluted to 160
ml).   [From J. Food Sci. 39, 434 (1974).   Copyright by Institute
of Food Technologists.]

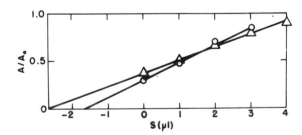

Fig. 8.   Normalized peak area vs. volume of d-limonene added
to 7-gram (o) and 11-gram (Δ) samples of CFC (frozen orange concentrate, reconstituted to 25 wt. % dissolved solids and diluted
to 160 ml).   [From J. Food Sci. 39, 434 (1974).   Copyright by
Institute of Food Technologists.]

TABLE 6.
Values of lipid parameter λ_F and d-limonene content
determined for different orange juices.

Type of juice[a]	Dissolved solids (wt %)	Sample weight used (w) (g)[b]	d-Limonene content (ppm, wt)	λ_F (g mol/g)
FS	12.7	7	30	9.9
CP	11.2	7	180	13.9
CFC	25.0	7	210	5.9
CFC	25.0	11	210	6.3

a. FS = fresh squeezed; CP = commercial pasteurized,
single-strength; CFC = reconstituted commercial frozen
conc.
   b. Diluted to 160 ml.
   [From J. Food Sci. 39, 434 (1974). Copyright by
Institute of Food Technologists.]

Other volatiles can also be quantitated by the method used
for limonene. As Tables 7, 8 and 9 show (19), the more polar compounds such as octanal and linalool are distributed mainly in the
serum, so the lipid extraction effect would not be as pronounced.

TABLE 7.
Flavor volatiles identified in orange juice and percentage
distribution of the more abundant compounds between pulp and
serum.

Peak no.	Assignment	Basis	% Distribution Pulp	Serum
1	Solvent			
2	Methyl butyrate	Ms, gc		
3	Unknown			
4	α-Pinene	Ms, gc	∿100	Not detected
5	Ethyl butyrate	Ms, gc	Trace	∿100
6	Hexanal	Ms, gc		
7	Sabinene	Ms, gc	∿100	Not detected
8	Myrcene	Ms, gc	∿100	Not detected
9	3-Methylbutan-1-ol	Ms, gc	Not detected	∿100

TABLE 7 *continued*

Peak no.	Assignment	Basis	% Distribution Pulp	Serum
11	Ethyl hexanoate	Ms, gc		
12	γ-Terpinene	Ms, gc		
13	Octanal	Ms, gc	12.5	87.5
14	Hexan-1-ol	Ms, gc		
15	*cis*-Hex-3-en-1-ol	Ms, gc		
16	Nonanal	Ms, gc		
17	Standard (ethyl octanoate)[a]			
18	Decanal	Ms, gc		
19	Linalool	Ms, gc	10.0	90.0
20	Octan-1-ol	Ms, gc		
21	β-Elemene	Ms		
22	β-Caryophyllene	Ms, gc		
23	Terpinen-4-ol	Ms, gc		
24	Methyl 3-hydroxyhexanoate	Ms, gc		
25	Ethyl 3-hydroxyhexanoate	Ms, gc	1.5	98.5
26	α-Terpineol	Ms, gc		
27	Sesquiterpene hydrocarbon	Ms		
28	Sesquiterpene hydrocarbon	Ms		
29	Sesquiterpene hydrocarbon	Ms		
30	Valencene	Ms, gc	99.0	1.0
31	δ-Cadinene	Ms, gc		
32	5β,7β,10β-Selina-3,11-diene	Ms		

    a. This compound has been reported in orange by several investigators but was not detected in this study. [Reprinted with permission from J. Agric. Food Chem. 22, 1066 (1974). Copyright by the American Chemical Society.]

TABLE 8.
Percentage distribution of the more abundant volatile flavor compounds between pulp and serum of grapefruit juice.

	% Distribution	
	Pulp	Serum
Pentan-1-ol	Not detected	∿100
Limonene	99.0	1.0
cis-Linalool oxide	Not detected	∿100
Caryophyllene	∿100	Not detected
Humulene	∿100	Not detected
Ethyl 3-hydroxyhexanoate	Not detected	∿100
Nootkatone	38.5	61.5

[*Reprinted with permission from J. Agric. Food Chem. 22, 1066 (1974). Copyright by the American Chemical Society.*]

TABLE 9.
Percentage distribution of selected volatile flavor compounds between pulp and serum of lemon juice[a]

	% Distribution	
	Pulp	Serum
β-Pinene	97.9	2.1
Limonene	93.4	6.6
γ-Terpinene	92.5	7.5
Terpinen-4-ol	4.6	95.4

a. Values were not determined for neral and geranial, as interference from neighboring peaks precluded accurate integration of the appropriate peak areas. However, it is obvious from the gas chromatograms that the greater proportion of these compounds is associated with the serum. [*Reprinted with permission from J. Agric. Food Chem. 22, 1066 (1974). Copyright by the American Chemical Society.*]

A study of off-flavor in stored *Citrus unshiu* (satsuma) juice by headspace analysis showed that ethanol and acetaldehyde were produced by both fresh and stored juice (21). A quantitative rather than qualitative difference in headspace composition was observed. The major component of storage off-flavor from the peel was assumed to be acetaldehyde.

In a related study of fresh and concentrated *Citrus unshiu* juice (22), a large number of volatile components were quantitatively analyzed by GC-MS of both aroma concentrate and headspace samples. The juice concentration process altered the levels of many volatiles. Prominent headspace components dimethyl sulfide, acetone and 2-methyl-3-buten-2-ol increased; and ethanol, γ-terpinene, and limonene decreased considerably as a result of the concentration process. Hydrogen sulfide was observed by derivative formation. The presence of hydrogen sulfide in orange and grapefruit (8) also suggests a possible role for it in the aroma of fresh citrus. The concentration process also increased the α-terpineol, terpinene-4-ol and several unidentified terpene carbonyls and decreased linalool. Aside from limonene, the most abundant compound in this group in concentrated juice was α-terpineol, which is a well known off-flavor component of processed orange juice.

The role of α-terpineol and a number of other off-flavor components was clarified in a study by Tatum *et al.* of canned single-strength orange juice (2). These authors found α-terpineol, 4-vinyl guaiacol, and 2,5-dimethyl-4-hydroxy-3(2H)-furanone to be the major off-flavor compounds among eleven isolated from stored, canned SSOJ by direct juice extraction (Table 10). Although α-terpineol, which contributes a stale, musty or piney odor, is relatively high in concentration (Table 11), its threshold is also high, compared to the other two major off-flavor compounds (Table 12). The most potent was 4-vinyl guaiacol, which imparted an aged or rotten aroma when added to unstored juice. The last of the 3 compounds is responsible for a pineapple-like odor. Although the compounds other than these three in Table 10 apparently do not contribute noticeably to the off-odor, one or more of them may be more convenient to determine. Since furfural is the most volatile it would probably be the most easily evaluated by headspace or similar enrichment techniques.

TABLE 10.
Degradation products in canned SSOJ after 12 wk at 35°C.

Compound	GLC retention time (min)[a]
Furfural	12.5
α-Terpineol	21.0
3-Hydroxy-2-pyrone[b]	41.0
2-Hydroxyacetyl furan[b]	41.0
2,5-Dimethyl-4-hydroxy-3(2H)-furanone[b]	43.0
Unidentified	43.0
cis-1,8-p-Menthanediol	47.5
trans-1,8-p-Menthanediol	52.0
4-Vinyl guaiacol	54.5
Benzoic acid	72.0
5-Hydroxymethyl furfural	75.0

a. *Retention times determined on 9-ft x 1/2-in. 20M column (20%).*
b. *Resolved on 9-ft x 1/4-in. UCW-98 column (20%).*
[*From J. Food Sci. 40, 707 (1975). Copyright by Institute of Food Technologists.*]

TABLE 11.
*Amounts of three degradation products in three
different samples of SSOJ after 12 wk at -18°
and 35°C.*

Sample	Temp (°C)	α-Terpineol	4-Vinyl guaiacol	cis-1,8-p-Menthanediol
		Degradation product (ppm)		
A	-18	0.1	Trace	Absent
	35	5.5	0.6	2.8
B	-18	0.8	0.07	Absent
	35	3.4	1.3	1.7
C	-18	0.1	Trace	Trace
	35	3.4	1.6	1.2

[*From J. Food Sci. 40, 707 (1975). Copyright
by Institute of Food Technologists.*]

TABLE 12.
*Concentration of degradation products causing
detectable flavor change when added to SSOJ[a].*

Compound	Conc (ppm)	Significance of difference
α-Terpineol	2.5	$p < 0.001$
	2.0	$p < 0.05$
4-Vinyl guaiacol	0.075	$p < 0.001$
	0.050	$p < 0.01$
2,5-Dimethyl-4-hydroxy-3(2H)-furanone	0.10	$p < 0.01$
	0.05	$p < 0.05$

a.   *Controls stored at -18°C.* [*From J.
Food Sci. 40, 707 (1975). Copyright by
Institute of Food Technologists.*]

2.   *Furfural Studies*
     Extensive furfural measurements have been made on citrus
juice. For these analyses, the juice is distilled and the
recovered furfural converted to a derivative which can be
evaluated colorimetrically. Correlations between off-flavor and
furfural are very good even though the compound itself does not

contribute to flavor change. A standard method for evaluation of the storage history of canned and bottled orange and grapefruit juices has been developed, based on furfural content in the distillate.

Dinsmore and Nagy (23) detected furfural in orange juice stored in bottles by stripping the juice in a nitrogen stream and capturing the volatile carbonyls as 2,4-dinitrophenylhydrazine (DNPH) derivatives. Furfural was the most prominent carbonyl in the stored juice. A 90-minute stripping period produced 35 to 50 mg DNPH derivatives from 500 ml of juice. The mixture of carbonyls was regenerated and analyzed by gas chromatography. Use of this procedure with a model juice containing C-4 to C-10 aldehydes showed that 0.1 ppm of aldehydes in this molecular weight range could be detected easily. Carbonyls detected in juice by GC and MS are shown in Table 13. Furfural was readily discernible in the stored juice.

A more extensive study of furfural in orange juice was made by the same authors using a refined version of a standard colorimetric reaction with aniline (24). Recovery was optimum (30%) in the first 5% by volume of distillate, based on total juice volume. This procedure enriched the sample about 6-fold relative to juice concentration. Distillation recoveries over a wide range of furfural concentrations were 30% $\pm$ 2 (95% confidence interval). The authors also stripped juice with nitrogen and found that only 10% of the furfural could be recovered from 500 ml juice in 1-1 1/2 hr at 68°C and a nitrogen flow rate of 40 ml/min. Since reproducibility was good and relatively high furfural concentrations could be rapidly obtained by distillation, the distillation procedure was considered adequate for routine determinations and superior to the stripping technique.

TABLE 13.
Identities of GLC peaks.

===

Peak No	Identity or MS data (major peaks)
1	CO and CO_2
2	Unidentified (m/e 87, 59, 45-43)
3	Acetaldehyde
4	Acetone
5	Unidentified (m/e 97, 44, 43, 15)
6	n-Butyraldehyde
7	Butanone
8	Unidentified (preceding peak still in ms)
9	Unidentified (m/e 84, 57, 44-41, 29)
10	C_5 Ketones (m/e 86-84, 72-69, 57, 43-41, 29-27, 15)
11	Furfural
12	Unidentified (m/e 122, 121, 107, 106, 105)
13	Unidentified (m/e 134, 133, 121, 120, 119, 91, 73)

In the same study, a taste panel detected off-flavor in orange juice when the furfural level reached about 30 µg per liter. Using this as the criterion, the authors determined the time for off-flavor development in a number of glass-packed orange juice samples stored at various temperatures (Tables 14 and 15). Since furfural could be detected in juices before development of noticeable off-flavor, the onset of deterioration could be monitored by furfural determination. Moreover, as compared to flavor testing, furfural levels could more accurately indicate the extent of deterioration from extreme storage abuse. The data in Tables 14 and 15 are based on glass-packed Valencia orange juice taken from a single processor late in the season. For these particular samples, storage temperature markedly

affected stability. It was apparent that storage at 40°F (5°C)
or below would be necessary to insure negligible flavor change
for extended periods. At storage temperatures above 70°F (21°C),
flavor quality deteriorated rapidly; for instance, at 86°F (30°C),
off-flavor was detected in less than 2 weeks.

TABLE 14.
*Stability of glass-packed orange
juice on the basis of minimum furfural
concentration associated with off-
flavor threshold.*

Storage °C	Onset of 30 µg/liter furfural
5	Well over 1 1/2 yr
10	Probably 6-9 months
16	9 wk
21	6 wk
30	Under 2 wk

[*From J. Food Sci. 37, 768 (1972).
Copyright by Institute of Food Technologists.*]

TABLE 15.
*Furfural levels in glass-packed orange juice:
relation to storage time, temperature and off-
flavor (furfural content in µg/liter).*

Storage °C	2 Wk	4 Wk	7 Wk	9 Wk	12 Wk
10	None	None	None	None	Possible trace
16	–	None	–	30	35^a
21	–	Trace	30^a	50^a	100^a
30	40^a	80^a	160^b	210^b	400^b

a. *Mild off-flavor*
b. *Considerable off-flavor*
[*From J. Food Sci. 37, 768 (1972). Copyright
by Institute of Food Technologists.*]

A similar, but more detailed study of grapefruit juice (25) revealed a similar pattern. Again, a minimum level of furfural could be correlated with the onset of off-flavor. In grapefruit, however, the level was much higher; approximately 175 µg per liter for canned and 150 µg per liter for glass-packed juice (Fig. 9 and 10). Off-flavor thresholds for 60, 70 and 85°F storage were similar for both types of juice. By extrapolation of furfural values, the extended lifetime of juice stored at 50°F (10°C) was predicted to be 30 to 80 weeks. At 85°F (30°C), the juice was stable only 2 to 3 weeks. At all temperatures, the relation between furfural content and storage time was nearly linear (Fig. 11 and 12).

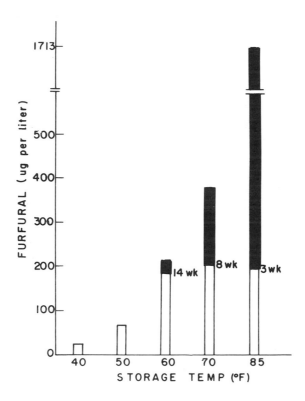

Fig. 9. Relationship of furfural content to flavor change (dark portion, p < 0.001) in canned single-strength grapefruit juice. [From Proc. Fla. State Hortic. Soc. 85, 222 (1972). Copyright by Fla. State Hortic. Soc.]

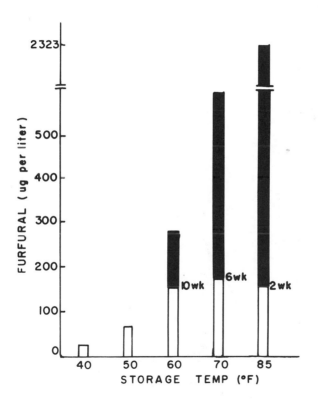

Fig. 10.   Relationship of furfural content to flavor change
(dark portion, p < 0.001) in glass-packed grapefruit juice.
[From Proc. Fla. State Hortic. Soc. 85, 222 (1972). Copyright
by Fla. State Hortic. Soc.]

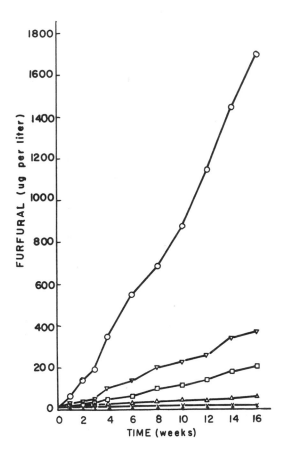

Fig. 11. Increase in furfural content in canned grapefruit juice during 16 weeks at 40°F (x), 50°F (△), 60°F (□), 70°F (▽), and 85°F (o). [From Proc. Fla. State Hortic. Soc. 85, 222 (1972). Copyright by Fla. State Hortic. Soc.]

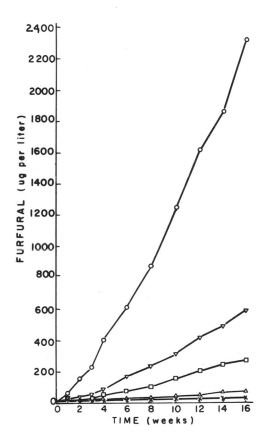

Fig. 12.   Increase in furfural content in glass-packed grapefruit juice during 16 weeks at 40°F (x), 50°F (△), 60°F (□), 70°F
(▽), and 85°F (o).   [From Proc. Fla. State Hortic. Soc. 85, 222
(1972).   Copyright by Fla. State Hortic. Soc.]

A subsequent study of canned and glass-packed orange juice
(26) based on the same approach revealed a very similar linear
relationship between time and furfural content. The minimum
furfural level was set at 55 µg per liter for both juices by a
taste panel rather than 30, as the earlier study on orange juice
had suggested. The earlier storage work was confirmed: either
juice stored at 50°F (5°C) was stable for 30-40 weeks and at 86°F
(30°C) for 1 to 2 weeks. Thresholds for 61, 70, and 86°F storage
were similar, varying from 47 to 64 µg per liter at a highly significant difference (p < 0.001), as shown in Table 16. In
general, orange juice seems to be less stable than grapefruit
when stored at elevated temperatures. The latter may have some
flavor characteristics which tend to mask off-flavors.

In a paper reviewing most of their earlier furfural studies,
Maraulja *et al.* (27) confirmed most of the results discussed so
far. Furfural was determined by a somewhat different analytical
procedure, which is not quite as sensitive and convenient as the
Dinsmore-Nagy method.

Dinsmore and Nagy subsequently refined their method even
further (28). Color stability and sensitivity were improved so
that lower furfural levels could be more reliably measured. Recovery efficiencies (RE) were improved to 34%, an increase of 4%.
The RE values for aqueous standards averaged 38%, which indicates
that there is some colorimetric interference in juice distillates.

The same authors used the improved method for a more extensive study of stored orange juice (29). They studied the influence of °Brix, °Brix/acid, pH, % citric acid, and vitamin C levels
on the furfural content of juice taken from 3 different processing plants at various times of the year and stored for 12 weeks at
95°F (Table 17). Significant correlations were found for pH
(citric acid) and vitamin C. The °Brix was not correlated significantly. Furfural and pH (citric acid) were exponentially related (Fig. 13). Regression analysis yielded the following
equation: mg furfural/liter = -2.343 + 4.266 (% citric acid).

TABLE 16.
Relationship of furfural content to extent of flavor changes in canned and glass-packed orange juice stored at 10, 16, 21 and 30°C.

Storage time, weeks	10°		16°		21°		30°	
	FF[a] ppb	Significance of difference	FF ppb	Significance of difference	FF ppb	Significance of difference	FF ppb	Significance of difference
				Canned orange juice				
1	12[b]	N.S.[c]	15	N.S.	18	N.S.	31	N.S.
2	17	N.S.	27	N.S.	32	N.S.	85	p < 0.001
3	21	N.S.	32	N.S.	39	N.S.	120	p < 0.001
4	24	N.S.	35	N.S.	47	p < 0.01	156	p < 0.001
6	24	N.S.	38	N.S.	54	p < 0.01	215	p < 0.001
8	25	N.S.	42	p < 0.05	62	p < 0.001	291	p < 0.001
10	27	N.S.	51	p < 0.001	77	p < 0.001	370	p < 0.001
12	29	N.S.	55	p < 0.001	94	p < 0.001	432	p < 0.001
14	31	N.S.	61	p < 0.001	115	p < 0.001	480	p < 0.001
16	32	N.S.	66	p < 0.001	131	p < 0.001	533	p < 0.001

TABLE 16 continued

Storage time, weeks	10°		16°		21°		30°	
	FF ppb	Significance of difference	FF ppb	Significance of difference	FF ppb	Significance of difference	FF ppb	Significance of difference
				Glass-packed orange juice				
1	9	N.S.	10	N.S.	14	N.S.	18	N.S.
2	9	N.S.	12	N.S.	24	N.S.	55	$p < 0.001$
3	11	N.S.	14	N.S.	27	$p < 0.05$	74	$p < 0.001$
4	11	N.S.	19	N.S.	37	$p < 0.01$	134	$p < 0.001$
6	12	N.S.	23	N.S.	48	$p < 0.01$	239	$p < 0.001$
8	13	N.S.	30	N.S.	64	$p < 0.001$	312	$p < 0.001$
10	13	N.S.	39	$p < 0.01$	81	$p < 0.001$	461	$p < 0.001$
12	15	N.S.	52	$p < 0.001$	105	$p < 0.001$	610	$p < 0.001$
14	19	N.S.	63	$p < 0.001$	145	$p < 0.001$	739	$p < 0.001$
16	25	N.S.	80	$p < 0.001$	173	$p < 0.001$	859	$p < 0.001$

a. FF – Furfural.
b. Furfural value represents the mean of three determinations.
c. Not significant at $p < 0.05$.
[Reprinted with permission from J. Agric. Food Chem. 21, 272 (1973). Copyright by the American Chemical Society.]

TABLE 17.
Chemical parameters of processed juice.

Season	Plant	pH	% Citric acid	°Brix	°Brix/ acid	Vit. C (mg %)	Furfural (μg/liter, 95°F-12 wk)
Early	A	3.54	0.98	10.43	10.64	53.85	2299
	B	3.67	0.80	10.67	13.34	51.19	1289
	C	3.69	0.77	10.16	13.19	47.72	1266
Mid-	A	3.68	0.92	11.64	12.65	57.62	1696
	B	3.67	0.96	12.59	13.11	62.09	1892
	C	3.52	1.11	11.94	10.76	52.45	2322
Early Valencia	A	3.63	0.88	10.66	12.11	43.75	1379
	C	3.64	0.95	10.99	11.57	41.58	1363
	D	3.58	1.01	11.07	10.96	50.22	1754
Late Valencia	A	3.78	0.80	12.15	15.19	42.64	874
	C	3.83	0.79	9.95	12.59	38.81	914
	D	3.88	0.77	12.39	16.09	33.99	652

[*From J. Food Sci. 39, 1116 (1974). Copyright by Institute of Food Technologists.*]

The sample correlation coefficient, r, was 0.882 and the test of significance, z, was 4.156. This correlation coefficient indicated that 78% of the variation was related to citric acid content. Vitamin C levels had an r of 0.794 and a z of 3.247; thus, furfural was also highly correlated to ascorbic acid. These results are consistent with an acid-catalyzed decomposition of ascorbic acid to produce furfural.

Also studied was the question of whether furfural levels are related to flavor change regardless of juice source (i.e., juices different in ascorbic acid and pH). Organoleptic tests were carried out on orange juices stored at 60, 70 and 95°F. They were taken from 3 plants (A, B and C) during early season (mostly Hamlin) and midseason (mostly Pineapple) and from plants A, C and

D during early and late Valencia seasons. Figures 14 and 15 show
a significant variation in mean flavor change threshold. Late
Valencia and midseason juice had mean threshold values of 29.8 and
52 µg/liter, respectively; these were the only significantly different values. The early season and early Valencia values were
38.6 and 38.1 µg/liter, respectively. It was speculated that the
difference between late Valencia and midseason was caused by
partial masking of off-flavor by the greater acidity of the
latter (see Table 17). Another conclusion from these data was
that the rate of furfural formation from late Valencia juice was
less than the others. Acidity differences, namely the low
acidity of this juice, could account for the rate reduction.

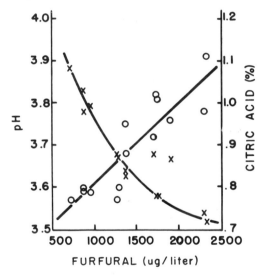

Fig. 13. pH (X) and % citric acid (o) vs furfural content
of 12 different processed juices after 12 wk storage at 95°F.
[From J. Food Sci. 39, 1116 (1974). Copyright by Institute of
Food Technologists.]

Relatively large variations among furfural-flavor threshold
levels for individual midseason and Valencia orange juices stored
at various temperatures were observed. These variations suggest
that for certain types of orange juice, some unpredictable
factor, such as the action of microorganisms, may be responsible

in part for the production of off-flavor compounds. Vinyl
guaiacol, for instance, can be derived from ferulic acid by loss
of CO_2. Although this is not an enzymatic reaction in most
foods, it might be under certain conditions.

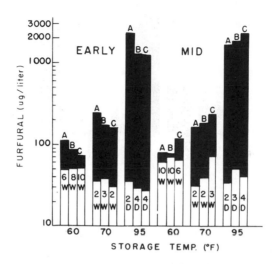

Fig. 14. *Relationship of furfural to flavor change (dark
area, p < 0.001) for early and midseason juices stored at 60, 70,
and 95°F taken from plants A, B, and C. Time of flavor change
shown in light portion of bar graph in weeks (W) or days (D).
The total height of each bar represents the furfural levels at 12
wk. [From J. Food Sci. 39, 1116 (1974). Copyright by Institute
of Food Technologists.]*

Threshold values determined in these studies of furfural-
flavor change relationships are not necessarily close to those
acceptable to consumers. Such values should be determined by
more comprehensive taste panel tests. Off-flavor detection is
related to many factors, and its threshold varies with the
sensivity of panelists. Grapefruit off-flavor, for instance, is
very likely related to bitterness. Milder flavored juices, such
as tangerine juice, may have much lower off-flavor thresholds
because of a lack of masking by acidity or bitter compounds.
A greater insight into the entire question of off-flavor
development could be obtained if more rapid and convenient

analytical methods were available for analysis of components directly responsible for off-flavors.

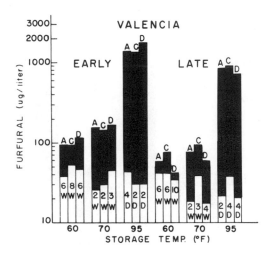

Fig. 15. Relationship of furfural to flavor change (dark area, p < 0.001) for early and late season Valencia juices stored at 60, 70, and 95°F taken from plants A, C, and D. Time of flavor change shown in light portion of bar graph in weeks (W) or days (D). The total height of each bar represents the furfural level at 12 wk. [From J. Food Sci. 39, 1116 (1974). Copyright by Institute of Food Technologists.]

3. *Recent Studies.*
A more detailed study of citrus volatiles has been carried out by use of the rapid and convenient distillation-extraction method referred to earlier in the Techniques Section. A large number of juice samples were analyzed by this method, and GC traces obtained on 10-ft x 1/4-in. columns packed with 10% SP-1000, or 5% OV-101 on Gas Chrom Q (Applied Science Laboratories). Helium flow was 60 ml/min, and the temperature was held for 4 min at 50°C, then programmed at 4°C/min. Peaks were identified by both retention times and mass spectra. Gas chromatographic profiles were obtained for orange and grapefruit juice blends, orange juice from different cultivars, from oranges of different maturity, and from juice stored at various temperatures. Finally, a study was made of volatile profiles from a number of different

citrus varieties and cultivars other than orange or grapefruit.

GC traces for canned orange juice stored 10 weeks at 40, 70, and 95°F are shown in Figs. 16 and 17. SP-1000 (Fig. 16) resolved the more volatile components better than the non-polar OV-101 (Fig. 17). On the other hand, OV-101 was better for the more polar, less volatile distillate components. The most pronounced changes resulting from storage among identified components were decreases in limonene, linalool, and valencene and an increase in α-terpineol. SP-1000 peaks 8, 12 and 18 also increased considerably.

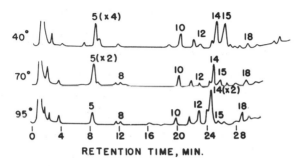

Fig. 16. Volatiles in canned orange juice distillate-extract (SP-1000). Peak identities: 5 - limonene, 8 - n-octanal (tentative), 10 - linalool, 14 - α-terpineol, 15 - valencene.

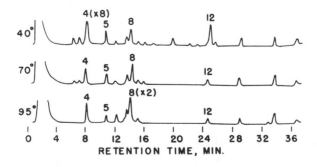

Fig. 17. Volatiles in canned orange juice distillate-extract (OV-101). Peak identities: 4 - limonene, 5 - linalool, 8 - α-terpineol, 12 - valencene.

An increase in α-terpineol was related to limonene hydration by several authors (2). In Fig. 16 and 17, however, the limonene peaks are too large to show the small decreases that would account for terpineol production. Recently it was found that linalool was converted to α-terpineol in stored juice (30); this finding is consistent with our observations. The increase in terpineol with storage time was found to be linear (31); thus terpineol content was suggested as an indicator of storage time.

The observed decrease in valencene is consistent with reported tin- or iron-catalyzed oxidation of valencene to nootkatone in orange juice stored in uncoated cans (32). Although we used coated cans in our study, the juice might have penetrated the coating in spots, and come into contact with the tin surface. In the previously mentioned study of stored canned orange juice (2), nootkatone was not formed; however the coating could have been intact and the required catalyst may not have been present. Since oxidation of valencene to nootkatone will produce a grapefruit-like off-flavor, valencene content could be a useful indicator of off-flavor development as well as a measure of the interior coating condition. Direct determination of nootkatone by headspace techniques is not practical because, like many off-flavor compounds, it is not very volatile.

In Fig. 16 some of the unidentified peaks shown to increase with storage temperature were probably due to other known off-flavor components, or related compounds. For example, unidentified peak 8 had a retention time similar to that of one of the major aldehydes, n-octanal. Since previous studies (31) had shown that aldehyde concentration changes considerably in stored orange juice, the observed increase in peak 8 could be evidence for a similar change. This increase in n-octanal contrasts with the decrease reported earlier in the chapter for stored, frozen orange peel. Apparently the same enzymatic reduction is not significant in stored juice.

The typical GC profile of volatiles from grapefruit is quite
unlike that from orange. Figures 18 and 19 represent OV-101 and
SP-1000 traces for glass-packed grapefruit juice stored 70 weeks
at 40 and 70°F. These traces again illustrate the better

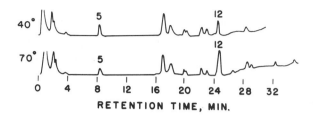

Fig. 18. Volatiles in grapefruit juice distillate-extract
(SP-1000). Peak identities: 5 - limonene, 12 - α-terpineol.

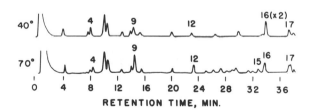

Fig. 19. Volatiles in grapefruit juice distillate-extract
(OV-101). Peak identities: 4 - limonene, 12 - β-caryophyllene.

resolution of the less volatile, more polar components by OV-101.
Limonene, α-terpineol and β-caryophyllene were the only identified components that changed markedly with juice deterioration.
The increase in terpineol was likely caused almost exclusively by
limonene hydration since linalool did not change sufficiently to
account for more than a small fraction of the terpineol increase.
Other peaks (OV-101) that changed were 9, 15 and 17 (increased)
and 16 (decreased).

In contrast to GC traces of orange volatiles, those of grapefruit show a large linalool oxide peak and a relatively small
amount of linalool. The difference between orange and grapefruit
with respect to these compounds can be used to determine percentage composition of orange-grapefruit juice blends. The relative
heights of linalool oxide (A) and linalool (B) peaks for a set of
duplicate D-E runs on various blends are compared in Table 18.
The ratio A/A+B was very close for both runs. The change in this
ratio is large enough to allow a good estimate of blend composition.

TABLE 18.
Orange-grapefruit juice blends.
===============================
Peak Heights for Duplicate Runs

| % | Peak A | | Peak B | | A/(A+B) | |
GFJ	#1	#2	#1	#2	#1	#2
0	0	0	87	121	0	0
20	43	42	77	74	36	36
40	80	84	47	47	63	64
60	150	140	56	47	73	75
80	238	246	35	43	86	85
100	276	260	30	25	91	91

A = Linalool oxide.
B = Linalool.

D-E traces can also be used for differentiation of different
cultivars and stages of maturity. Canned orange juice is produced from ruit picked in the fall (early season, mostly Hamlin),
winter (midseason, Pineapple), and spring (Valencia). The D-E
traces for canned early season, midseason, and Valencia juices
from 2 processors were obtained, and some limited correlations
observed. Portions of the SP-1000 traces shown in Fig. 20 include the region from 20 to 32 min retention time. This region
was the most useful for differentation. The patterns for early

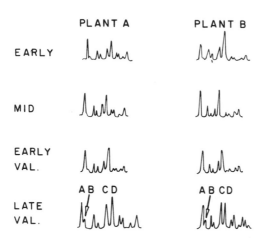

Fig. 20. Orange juices canned in different seasons. Peak identities: A - linalool, B - 1-octanol, C - α-terpineol, D - valencene.

for differentation. The patterns for early and midseason juices were very similar; but they differed slightly from the pattern for early Valencia, especially in the sizes of the last four peaks, and noticeably from the pattern for late Valencia. The trace for late Valencia showed greater amounts of 1-octanol (peak B), α-terpineol (peak C), and several of the smaller peaks in the latter part of the trace. These results suggest that D-E analysis may be useful in distinguishing juice from fruit at different stages of maturity. Differences between cultivars do not seem to be as pronounced.

A more thorough investigation of varietal differences was carried out on fresh juices from a number of commercial citrus varieties and cultivars. The D-E traces presented in Fig. 21 and 22 were obtained with SP-1000. The probable location, based on retention time, of some of the major peaks is shown in the capital letters over the top trace. Retention times varied somewhat, so comparisons were made of peak patterns rather than absolute retention times.

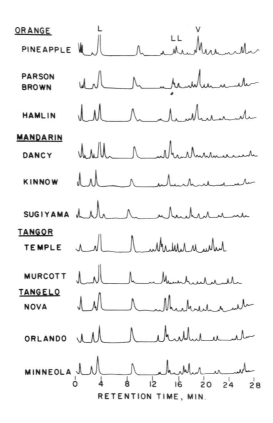

Fig. 21. D-E traces of citrus varieties. Peak identities: L - limonene, LL - linalool, V - valencene.

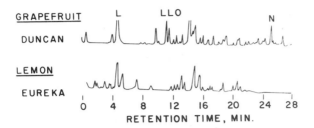

*Fig. 22. D-E traces of citrus varieties. Peak identities:
L - limonene, LLO - linalool oxide, LL - linalool, N - nootkatone.*

Patterns for the 2 early season orange cultivars, Hamlin ,and
Parson Brown, were similar, especially in the region from 22 to
28 min. Pineapple, a midseason fruit, differed quite a bit from
those two. Among the mandarins, Kinnow and Sugiyama (Satsuma-
type) had almost identical traces; Dancy differed considerably.
Traces for tangors (mandarin-orange hybrids) might be expected to
have features in the traces of both parents. The trace for
Temple, which is of unknown origin, does not resemble any of the
above, however. Murcott is thought to be a tangor, and its trace
resembles the Hamlin or Parson Brown orange in the 22 to 28 min
region and the Kinnow and Sugiyama mandarins in the region from
20 to 26 min. Another set of closely similar traces consists of
those for Orlando and Minneola tangelos, which are both Duncan
grapefruit-Dancy tangerine hybrids. The trace for the Nova
tangelo, which has a different parentage, is quite different from
the other two.

Duncan grapefruit and Eureka lemon have unique traces (Fig.
22) and can easily be distinguished from the others. Large
linalool oxide peaks in the grapefruit trace are especially
noticeable because they occur in an area that is usually relatively featureless. This fact, of course, was utilized in the
previously described study of grapefruit-orange blends.

Although the comparisons made seem to indicate possible correlations between different varieties or cultivars, more samples from various sources and from fruit at various stages of maturity need to be analyzed. More subtle differences in the patterns could then be examined in greater detail.

III. SUMMARY

To date, direct headspace analysis has only been used for quantitative analysis of the 4 most prominent citrus volatiles: methanol, ethanol, acetaldehyde and limonene. Determination of limonene, a non-polar terpene hydrocarbon, requires a correction for lipid solubility which is probably not necessary with the more water soluble headspace components. Among these 4 compounds, acetaldehyde was directly correlated with flavor: limonene and ethanol were indirectly related. The other, less concentrated volatiles have been isolated by indirect headspace techniques requiring a concentration step. This approach has not been used thus far for quantitative analysis because of the availability of better methods based on stripping or distillation.

Many of the less concentrated volatiles have been correlated with flavor quality. Examples of compounds directly correlated with flavor include ethyl vinyl ketone, ethyl butyrate, n-octanal, citral, α-terpineol, and 4-vinyl guaiacol. Furfural, diacetyl, valencene and linalool were indirectly correlated. Furfural is a particularly useful indirect indicator of off-flavor.

The compound that could best distinguish varieties is linalool oxide. It is abundant in grapefruit and appears in a region of the GC trace that contains few interferring peaks; thus, the percentage of grapefruit juice in blends with other citrus juices can be determined readily. Other, more subtle distinctions in GC patterns could distinguish between other varieties (or cultivars) or detect degree of maturity.

Headspace analysis of the less concentrated volatiles may be a simple, rapid way to detect storage abuse and blending (or adulteration) of certain citrus juices. The success of such analyses depends on their sensitivity since concentrations are quite low. Alternative methods based on distillation (or stripping) and extraction, adsorption, or derivative formation are more time consuming and complicated, but do not require such high sensitivities.

IV.   REFERENCES

1. Wolford, R. W., Alberding, G. E. and Attaway, J. W.   *J. Agric. Food Chem.* 10, 297 (1962).

2. Tatum, J. H., Nagy, S. and Berry, R. E.   *J. Food Sci.* 40, 707 (1975).

3. Moshonas, M. G. and Lund, E. D.   *J. Food Sci.* 36, 105 (1971).

4. Schultz, T. H., Flath, R. A. and Mon, T. R.   *J. Agric. Food Chem.* 19, 1060 (1971).

5. Dravnieks, A. and O'Donnell, A.   *J. Food Sci.* 36, 105 (1971).

6. Scott, W. C. and Veldhuis, M. K.   *J. Assoc. Offic. Anal. Chem.* 49, 628 (1966).

7. Lund, E. D. and Bryan, W. L.   *J. Food Sci.* 42, 385 (1977).

8. Shaw, P. E., in "Citrus Science and Technology" (S. Nagy, P. E. Shaw and M. K. Veldhuis, Eds.), Vol. I, p. 463.   Avi Publishing, Westport, Connecticut. (1977).

9. Shaw, P. E., in "Citrus Science and Technology" (S. Nagy, P. E. Shaw and M. K. Veldhuis, Eds.), Vol. I, p. 427.   Avi Publishing, Westport, Connecticut. (1977).

10. Lund, E. D. and Bryan, W. L.   *J. Food Sci.* 41, 1194 (1976).

11. Bruemmer, J. H. and Roe, B.   *J. Agric. Food Chem.* 19, 266 (1971).

12. Ahmed, E. M.   U. S. Department of Agriculture, Contract No. 12-14-100-10337(72) (1975).

13. Wolford, R. W., Attaway, J. A., Alberding, G. E. and Atkins, C. D.   *J. Food Sci.* 28, 320 (1963).

14. Murdock, D. I. *Proc. Fla. State Hortic. Soc.* 79, 312 (1966).

15. Guadagni, D. S., Bomben, J. L. and Mannheim, H. C. *J. Food Sci.* 35, 279 (1970).

16. Mannheim, H. C., Bomben, J. L., Guadagni, D. G. and Morgan, A. I., Jr. *Food Technol.* 21, 469 (1967).

17. Davis, P. L. and Chace, W. G., Jr. *Hortic. Sci.* 4, 117 (1969).

18. Roe, B. and Bruemmer, J. H. *J. Agric. Food Chem.* 22, 285 (1974).

19. Radford, T., Kawashima, K., Friedel, P. K., Pope, L. E. and Gianturco, M. A. *J. Agric. Food Chem.* 22, 1066 (1974).

20. Massaldi, H. A. and King, C. J. *J. Food Sci.* 39, 434 (1974).

21. Manabe, T. *Hiroshima Nagyo Tanki Daigaku Kenkyu Hokoku* 5, 59 (1974). CA 83:7506s (1975).

22. Imagawa, K., Yamanishi, T. and Koshika, M. *Nippon Nogei Kagaku Kaishi* 48, 561 (1974).

23. Dinsmore, H. L. and Nagy, S. *J. Agric. Food Chem.* 19, 517 (1971).

24. Dinsmore, H. L. and Nagy, S. *J. Food Sci.* 37, 768 (1972).

25. Nagy, S., Randall, V. and Dinsmore, H. L. *Proc. Fla. State Hortic. Soc.* 85, 222 (1972).

26. Nagy, S. and Randall, V. *J. Agric. Food Chem.* 21, 272 (1973).

27. Maraulja, M. D., Blair, J. S., Olsen, R. W. and Wenzel, F. W. *Proc. Fla. State Hortic. Soc.* 86, 270 (1973).

28. Dinsmore, H. L. and Nagy, S. *J. Assoc. Offic. Anal. Chem.* 57, 332 (1974).

29. Nagy, S. and Dinsmore, H. L. *J. Food Sci.* 39, 1116 (1974).

30. Askar, A., Bielig, H. J. and Treptow, H. *Deut. Lebensm. Rundschau.* 69, 360 (1973).

31. Askar, A., Bielig, H. J. and Treptow, H. *Deut. Lebensm. Rundschau.* 69, 162 (1973).

32. Bielig, H. J., Askar, A. and Treptow, H. *Deut. Lebensm. Rundschau.* 68, 173 (1972).

Mention of a trademark or proprietary product does not constitute a guarantee or warranty of the product by the U. S. Department of Agriculture, and does not imply its approval to the exclusion of other products that may also be suitable.

FLAVOR PROFILING OF BEER USING STATISTICAL
TREATMENTS OF G.L.C. HEADSPACE DATA

Joseph T. Hoff
Etzer Chicoye
William C. Herwig
J. Raymond Helbert

Miller Brewing Company

Using a salting-out concentration method, gas chromatographic headspace volatile profiling of beer was achieved on Porapak Q. The percent-of-total-peak-area (PTPA) data obtained were applied to beer flavor problems using several statistical treatments. Correlation of headspace profiles of 310 pairs of beers with corresponding triangular taste-panel results was found using t-statistics calculated from PTPA differences and pooled standard deviations obtained from a computerized database. Product uniformity was effectively evaluated with the aid of stepwise discriminant analysis. Regression analysis of acetaldehyde PTPA's and panel scores for staling flavor showed that acetaldehyde could be valuable as an index of beer staling.

I. INTRODUCTION

In the brewing industry, flavor and aroma impact are regarded as the main components of consumer preference although other properties such as foam and colloidal stability must also be considered. In this report, we confine our attention to flavor and aroma. We are all familiar with the fact that human taste buds are capable of differentiating only four basic stimuli while the nose is capable of discerning thousands of different odors. Therefore, it is not surprising that much research has been devoted to measuring headspace volatiles and attempting to use the data to solve flavor problems.

A survey of our qualified taste panel revealed that most members differentiated between two beers in a triangular taste test on the basis of aroma rather than taste 90-95% of the time. We inferred that consumer preferences may be based more on aroma than on taste. Therefore, the volatiles from a glass of beer would be the logical beer components to examine in order to differentiate beers or to discern a particular beer's flavor attributes.

Because of problems associated with other techniques for measuring volatiles (1), we felt the direct approach of salting-out and directly injecting headspace vapors into a gas chromatograph would be the way to attack flavor problems. Dravnieks and coworkers (2) suggested that accurate approximations of components relative to the entire aroma profile may be more important in differentiating between samples than absolute concentrations or estimations relative to an internal standard.

Hoff and Herwig (1) developed a headspace technique in our laboratories for measuring 12 volatiles in beer, expressed as percents of the total peak area (PTPA). They also introduced a statistical method for predicting triangular taste test results from the headspace data. Since the earlier publication, we have modified and improved the headspace method to measure 14 volatiles in beer and have verified the usefulness of the statistical method.

Because problems of differentiation and classification are more difficult, the use of high-speed computers and sophisticated statistical techniques, such as stepwise discriminant analysis (SDA), are mandatory. Recently, stepwise discriminant analyses of headspace volatile profiles have been utilized to study flavor and aroma.

Powers and Keith (3) showed that discriminant analysis of GLC peak ratios of potato chip headspace volatiles enabled them to successfully classify potato chips according to age. Dravnieks and coworkers (2,4) have successfully classified corn as good or bad in agreement with an organoleptic panel by discriminant analysis of headspace volatiles. Hoff and coworkers (5) have used stepwise discriminant analysis of headspace volatiles as an aid in solving practical brewing problems and demonstrated the utility of verifying the discriminant equations by classifying unknown samples of beer *a priori* using the BMD07M (6) program. A new, enhanced version--BMDP7M (7)--has been developed utilizing a "jackknife option" allowing derivation and verification of equations in a single run without losing information and has proven very useful in studying brewery problems, specifically branch-plant variation.

Numerous reports on regression analyses of aroma components and panel evaluations of flavor can be found in the literature, but the authors have found only one report of regression analysis of beer volatiles with panel evaluations of flavor (8). The problem may lie with taste-test evaluations. Stone, *et al.*, (9) have developed a taste-test technique called quantitative descriptive analysis (QDA) and have studied beer utilizing this technique. Using a modification of this technique, we have been able to correlate acetaldehyde concentration in beer with staling flavor.

II. EXPERIMENTAL

A. Headspace Technique - Modification of Hoff and Herwig (1)

1. Instrumental

Gas chromatograph: Hewlett Packard Series 7621A, with dual flame ionization detectors and glass-lined injector.

Temperatures: Detector: 270°C
Injector: 250°C

Sensitivities: Electrometer: Range: 10^3

Attenuator: 1

Recorder: 2 mv

Integrator: slopes: 0.01 mv/min

Columns: Dual 10 ft × 1/8 in stainless steel packed with Porapak Q (80-100 mesh)

Programming Steps: 1. Isothermal 1 min at 70°C.

2. 10°/min to 120°C.

3. 1°/min to 125°C.

4. 2°/min to 205°C.

5. Isothermal 30°min at 205°C.

Carrier gas: Nitrogen: Flow rate: 35 ml/min

Inlet pressure: 78 psi

2. *Preparation of Sample*

After chilling overnight at 0°C, 50 ml of beer are gently measured and poured into a 7 oz beer bottle containing 20 g of anhydrous sodium sulfate. A neoprene crown insert (Firestone Industrial Rubber Products, Chicago, IL) is placed over the top, and the bottle is crowned with a beer cap (insert removed) which has a small hole drilled in it for sampling purposes. The sample is warmed in a 50°C water bath for 10 min, shaken 30 sec, and kept at 50°C for 20 min. The bath is then cooled to ambient and the sample stored in the dark overnight at 25°C. Five microliters of a standard meta-xylene solution (1 ml diluted to 100 ml with absolute ethanol) is added, and the sample is shaken for 15 min. An 8 ml vapor sample is obtained (after gently pumping five times) using a 10 ml gas-tight syringe with a Teflon valve. The sample is then injected.

B. Organoleptic Testing

1. *Triangular Taste Testing*

For each triangular taste test, ten panelists were drawn from a pool of 40 qualified members. The average accuracy of panel members was approximately 80% on triangular tests significant at the 0.05 level of risk. From the binomial expansion, the β error was estimated at 0.12.

2. *Quantitation of Stale Flavor*

For each taste evaluation, 12 to 17 panelists were drawn from a pool of 40 members and asked to evaluate stale flavor (oxidation) using a 24-point modified QDA technique. After application of Dixon's test for outliers at an α of 0.05, the mean scores were calculated.

C. Statistical Analyses

1. *The Statistical Method of Hoff and Herwig (1)*

A chronologically updated database is used to calculate an unbiased estimate of the standard deviation for each peak. This approach minimizes problems associated with aberrant values sometimes obtained from duplicate determinations and problems associated with small changes occurring over the life of the chromatographic column. This database consisted of standard deviations for each peak of the 24 previous duplicate determinations plus the duplicate determination under investigation.

A two-tailed t-test is then performed on mean values from the duplicate determinations of the two beers to be tested, using the pooled standard deviations from the updated database. The following criteria are then used to predict triangular taste panel results.

   a. If no peaks are significantly different between samples at 0.005 risk, one predicts that panel results will be insignificant at 0.05 risk.

   b. If one or more peaks is significantly different between samples at 0.001 risk, one predicts that panel results will be significant at a risk of 0.05 or less.

   c. If one or more peaks is significantly different between samples at 0.005 risk but insignificant at 0.001 risk, no prediction is made. The sample number is increased, and the t-statistics are recalculated using actual standard deviations until the results are resolved by either of the first two criteria.

2. Stepwise Discriminant Analysis

The BMDP7M (7) program was used. From suitable data, this program generates a set of mathematical equations that efficiently differentiate and classify individual cases. After these equations were generated, their general validity was tested using the "jackknife" option: for each profile, functions are computed with that profile omitted. These functions are then used to classify the omitted profile. This is somewhat different than the methodology employed by Hoff, *et al.* (5).

III.   RESULTS AND DISCUSSION

A.   The Headspace Technique

A typical chromatogram is shown in Fig. 1.

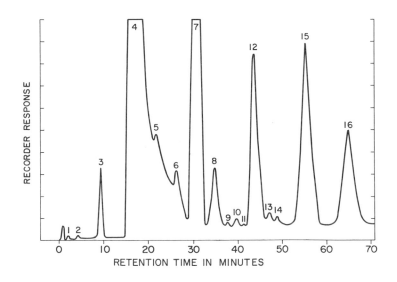

Fig. 1.   A typical headspace volatile profile.

The identities of the peaks were established by peak rein-
forcement and are given in Table 1. Of course, the possibility
that some peaks contain more than one compound should not be
ignored.

TABLE 1

Identities of Peaks in Fig. 1

Peak No.	Identification	Peak No.	Identification
1	Unidentified	9	Isopropyl acetate
2	Unidentified	10	Ethyl propanoate
3	Acetaldehyde	11	Unidentified
4	Ethanol	12	Isoamyl alcohols
5	2-Methyl butene-2	13	Isobutyl acetate
6	n-Propanol	14	Unidentified
7	Ethyl acetate	15	m-Xylene (I.S.)
8	Isobutanol	16	Isoamyl acetate

To quantify the results, the individual raw peak areas were
divided by the sum of all raw peak areas (exclusive of ethanol
and the internal standard) to give PTPA's.

Headspace analysis was performed on 16 samples of the same
beer. The means and standard deviations are given in Columns 2
and 3, respectively, in Table 2. Column 4 shows the pooled standard deviations obtained from the database. Column 5 shows the
F-values obtained from comparing these two variances. The low
F-values obtained indicate that the pooled standard deviations
are accurate approximations to the population standard deviations, thereby allowing comparisons using the statistical method
discussed earlier.

TABLE 2

Reproducibility of the Headspace Technique and Reliability of the Database

Peak No.	Mean	Actual Standard Deviation from 16 Replicates	Pooled Standard Deviation from Database	F-Value (0.05; 15, 25) = 2.09
1	0.198	0.021	0.021	1.00
2	0.026	0.009	0.009	1.00
3	1.051	0.036	0.031	1.35
5	0.187	0.013	0.011	1.40
6	0.957	0.049	0.037	1.75
7	64.730	0.636	0.508	1.57
8	3.901	0.152	0.120	1.60
9	0.037	0.009	0.008	1.27
10	0.421	0.012	0.012	1.00
11	0.053	0.012	0.014	1.36*
12	17.670	0.630	0.468	1.81
13	0.094	0.010	0.009	1.23
14	0.110	0.015	0.014	1.15
16	10.566	0.322	0.305	1.12

* $F(0.05; 25, 15) = 2.28$

B.   Correlation Between the Statistical Method of Hoff and Herwig
and Triangular Taste Test Results

Table 3 compares predictions by the statistical method with
actual panel results for 310 triangular taste tests. In only 6
of the 76 trials that the statistical method predicted insignificant did the panel succeed in differentiating the beers at 0.05
risk. This is equivalent to chance. However, the possibility of
the panel succeeding in some trials on the basis of factors un-
detected by the gas chromatographic procedure should not be over-
looked. Of equal importance is the possibility that the panel
cannot find a significant difference between beers when the
statistical method does. This could be due to a number of factors including panel size. The panel failed to find a difference
in 34 of 234 trials that the method predicted they would at α =
0.05 or less.

TABLE 3

Correlation of Statistical with Panel Results

Statistical Results		Panel Results (0.05)	
Category	*No. of Trials*	*Insignificant*	*Significant*
Insignificant	76	70	6
Significant	234	34	200

χ^2 = 1.64 χ^2(0.05; 1) = 3.84

A χ^2 test was performed using theoretical values of suc-
cesses and failures obtained from an α = 0.05 and β = 0.12. The
upper 5% point for χ^2 with one degree of freedom is 3.84. The

low experimental χ^2 value of 1.64 indicates good agreement between the statistical predictions and actual panel results.

C. Evaluation of Branch-Plant Beers

Let us now consider differences between branch-plant beers and the problem of interplant consistency. The statistical method consistently predicted that beers produced at three different branch plants (P, Q, and R) would be found different ($p \leq 0.05$) by the triangular taste test panel. The panel also consistently found them different and consistently preferred the beer produced at branch plant "P" over that produced at branch plant "Q". Table 4 summarizes the results of SDA of 10 headspace profiles from each branch plant utilizing the "jackknife" classification option of BMDP7M. All beers were correctly classified.

TABLE 4

Classification of Branch-Plant Beers Before Process Changes

Beers Tested	Classified As		
	P	Q	R
P	10	0	0
Q	0	10	0
R	0	0	10

A canonical plot is shown in Fig. 2, indicating excellent discrimination based on the five variables listed in Table 5 which were used in the analysis.

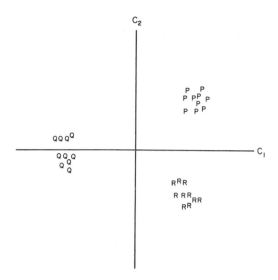

Fig. 2. Canonical plot of branch-plant beers before process changes.

TABLE 5

Selection of Variables

Step Number	Variable Selected	F-Value to Enter
1	Ethyl acetate	179.81
2	Isoamyl alcohols	64.61
3	n-Propanol	15.07
4	Ethyl propanoate	14.65
5	Isobutanol	4.39

Because of these differences, process changes were initiated at branch plant "Q" in an attempt to bring its beer into line with that produced at branch plant "P". Duplicate samples from branch plant "Q" after process changes and duplicate controls

from branch plant "P" were analyzed by the headspace method and
subjected to classification by the stepwise discriminant analysis. A canonical plot (Fig. 3) with capital letters signifying
the beers used to calculate the discriminant functions and lower
case letters indicating the newly classified samples shows that
both the sample and control beers were classified as branch plant
"P" beers.

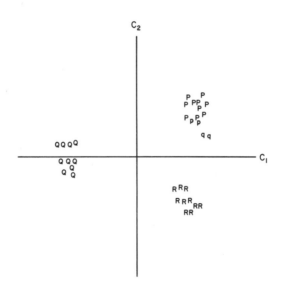

*Fig. 3.   Canonical plot of branch-plant beers after process
changes.*

Although some remaining differences are suggested by the
distance of the "q's" from the "p's", the method and the qualified panel were unable to differentiate the two beers.

D.   Correlation Between Acetaldehyde PTPA and Stale Flavor

Preliminary aging studies over time at elevated temperatures
resulted in the statistical method of Hoff and Herwig and SDA
finding significant differences at the same time the triangular
taste panel found differences between aged samples and controls

kept at 0°C. Both statistical methods indicated that increasing
acetaldehyde may be related in some manner to the increasing
staleness perceived by the taste panel.

To test this hypothesis, packages of the same beer were
stored at various elevated temperatures for various lengths of
time to determine effects on stale flavor as noted by a trained
panel utilizing the modified QDA method. Acetaldehyde was
monitored at the same time by analyzing the beer in duplicate
by the headspace method. Fig. 4 shows the linear relationship
between the PTPA of acetaldehyde and stale flavor to be quite
good (correlation coefficient = 0.90) for 98 observations.

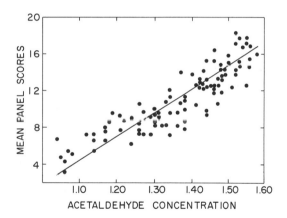

*Fig. 4. Regression line of PTPA of acetaldehyde vs. stale
flavor.*

Hoff and Herwig[1] showed that the formation of acetaldehyde
appeared to follow pseudo-first-order kinetics, the rate being
dependent upon air level and temperature. These findings, in
conjunction with the following regression equation for stale

---

[1]Hoff, J. T., and Herwig, W. C., Amer. Soc. Brew. Chem. 35(4),
        1977, in press.

flavor as a function of acetaldehyde PTPA,

$$\text{Stale Flavor} = 21.318 \text{ (acetaldehyde PTPA)} - 17.868,$$

led us to the conclusion that acetaldehyde formation could be used to indicate the staling potential of a beer. Although acetaldehyde, as such, does not contribute to staling flavor, our findings indicate it can be useful as an index of staling. This view is consistent with the suggestion of Hashimoto and Kuroiwa (10) that the alkenals responsible for stale flavor may come from the aldol condensation of increased concentrations of acetaldehyde and alkanals.

IV.   SUMMARY

A procedure was described for the routine gas chromatographic analysis of headspace volatiles. A method for predicting panel performance was discussed, and correlation between this method and actual triangular taste panel results was demonstrated. The problem of interplant variation was investigated with the aid of stepwise discriminant analysis of headspace volatiles. Utilizing the headspace technique, acetaldehyde PTPA was found to correlate quite well with panel evaluations of stale flavor, indicating its potential use as an index of staling.

V.   ACKNOWLEDGEMENTS

The authors wish to thank Vincent S. Bavisotto, Director of Brewing - Master Brewer, for his encouragement and interest in this work, and the Officers of the Miller Brewing Company for permission to publish it. We also wish to thank Deborah Schmitt and Ronald Wagener for their technical assistance.

VI.   REFERENCES

1. Hoff, J. T. and Herwig, W. C., J. Amer. Soc. Brew. Chem. 34, 1 (1976).

2. Dravnieks, A., Reilich, H. G., Whitfield, J., and Watson,
       C. A., J. Food Sci. 38, 34 (1973).

3. Powers, J. J. and Keith, E. S., J. Food Sci. 33, 207
       (1968).

4. Dravnieks, A. and Watson, C. A., J. Food Sci. 38, 1024
       (1973).

5. Hoff, J. T., Helbert, J. R., and Chicoye, E., M.B.A.A. Tech.
       Quart. 12, (4)213 (1975).

6. Dixon, W. J. (Ed.) in "BMD: Biomedical Computer Programs",
       p. 214a. University of California Press, Berkeley,
       1968.

7. Dixon, W. J. (Ed.) in "BMDP: Biomedical Computer Programs",
       p. 441. University of California Press, Berkeley,
       1975.

8. Anderson, R. J., Clapperton, J. F., Crabb, D., and Hudson,
       J. R., J. Inst. Brew., 81, 208 (1975).

9. Stone, H., Sidel, J., Oliver, S., Woolsey, A., and Single-
       ton, R. C., Food Tech. 28, (10)24 (1974).

10. Hashimoto, N. and Kuroiwa, Y., Rept. Res. Lab., Kirin
       Brewery Co., Ltd., 18, 1 (1975).

SENSORY AND INSTRUMENTAL EVALUATION OF WINE AROMA

A. C. Noble
Department of Viticulture and Enology
University of California, Davis

Aromas of a series of wines were evaluated by headspace (HS) analysis and sensorially by descriptive analysis. Trained judges scored the wines on specified aroma attributes. Volatiles from the same wines were collected in triplicate on a tenax GC trap from 500 ml wine HS by displacement. After ethanol and water were flushed from the trap, volatiles were eluted from the adsorbent and introduced through a closed system to the gas chromatograph (GC). Using a displacement collection system, the GC effluent was split and the eluted components were evaluated by panelists in one case, and by mass spectrometer in a second case.

GC peaks were eliminated from further statistical analyses which were not reproducibly recovered, were very highly correlated, or had no appreciable aroma upon GC-sniff evaluation. With 2 or 3 GC peaks, significant regression equations were developed which predicted the intensities of the aroma attributes within the data set. Using different wines to derive the equations, however, generally resulted in selection of different GC peaks as variables. The number of wines studied was too small to generate predictive equations to apply to wines outside of the data set.

I.   INTRODUCTION

     Cabernet Sauvignon is often considered to be the premium
red grape variety of California primarily because of its complex
yet distinctive aroma. Wines produced from Ruby Cabernet (a
cross between Carignane and Cabernet Şauvignon), Merlot and
Malbec grapes have similar, but less distinctive aromas. The
characteristic aroma of these wines has been described as green-
olive, green-pepper, herbaceous, asparagus, vegetative, or more
generally as "Cabernet" or "Cabernet-like".

     Volatiles of wines and grapes have been investigated by
many workers. Most of the components identified in Cabernet
Sauvignon are also reported in other Vitis vinifera wines (1,2,
3). Recently, Bayonove et al. (4) identified 2-methoxy-3-
isobutylpyrazine in Cabernet Sauvignon wine. This component has
a threshold of 0.003 ppb in water and the distinct odor of green
peppers (5), and no doubt contributes to the distinctive Cabernet
aroma. However, aromas are usually the result of a pattern of
components rather than a specific impact compound, such as the
pyrazine. Therefore, quantification of a representative composition of headspace volatiles is necessary, in addition to the
volatile identifications reported in past studies, to evaluate
the aroma of Cabernet Sauvignon wines. No quantitative data has
been published for Cabernet volatiles other than one report in
which relative concentrations of major components were reported
in Cabernet Sauvignon and Merlot (6).

     Correlation between sensory and instrument flavor data has
recently been attempted by several multivariate statistical
techniques. Multiple regression analyses have been used to
develop equations to predict the intensities of beef aroma (7),
beef fat (8), onion oil (9), and ginger oil (10) using gas
chromatographic (GC) peaks as the independent variables. Using
one or two components, predictions of aroma intensity have been

obtained with correlation coefficients of 0.90 or higher (7,9). The technique of discriminant analysis (DA) has been applied to GC data to discriminate between separate flavor categories (11, 12,13,14). Peaks are selected on the basis of their ability to discriminate between groups, and functions derived to correctly classify the aroma. In the investigation of blends of Pepsi and Coca-Cola, discriminant analysis of GC data was able to classify the blends more accurately than sensory analysis of the same beverages (15).

Other multivariate techniques, factor and principal component analyses, have been used to reduce large numbers of sensory or instrumental variables to a smaller number of factors, or to look at underlying patterns in the variables (16,17,18,19,20).

To investigate the aroma of Cabernet Sauvignon wines, we have evaluated the volatiles of Cabernet Sauvignon and Ruby Cabernet wines and of one blend by instrumental and by sensory methods. In this paper, the results of these analyses will be presented and correlation between the two sets of data discussed.

II. EXPERIMENTAL SECTION

A. Methods

1. Instrumental Headspace Analysis
    a. Headspace collection. Headspace volatiles were collected from 200 ml of wine by displacement of the headspace at 20 ml/min by 500 ml of the same wine and the volatiles adsorbed on 20 mg of Tenax GC. To remove ethanol and water, the tenax trap was flushed with nitrogen for 20 min at 50 ml/min at room temperature. The trap was then connected to a closed system for the transfer of the volatiles to the gas chromatograph using

Carle micro-switching valves. The trap was heated to 130°C and
the desorbed volatiles swept by nitrogen (50 ml/min) to a coiled
stainless steel (s.s.) spiral trap, chilled in dry-ice ethanol.
After 25 min, the trap was heated and the volatiles flashed onto
the GC column through a heated inlet line.

   b. Gas chromatography. Volatiles were analyzed on a 152.5
M x 7.5 mm i.d. coiled s.s. capillary column coated with SF-96
(50) and 5% Ipegal CO-880, in a Hewlett-Packard 7620A Research
Gas Chromatograph. Carrier and make up nitrogen flow rates were
7.0 ml/min and 23 ml/min respectively. FID temperature was 200°
with a hydrogen flow rate of 25 ml/min and air flow of 500 ml/
min. Runs were temperature programmed from 40 to 160°C. Further
details on the headspace and gas chromatography procedures used
in this study are described elsewhere (21).

   Peak areas were integrated using an Autolab Minigrator.
Peak numbers were assigned on the basis of pattern similarity
rather than absolute correspondence of retention times, although
coefficients of variation for the Retention time (R_t) of any
peak across the 11 triplicate analyses (which were done over a
2.5 month interval) were $\leq$ 0.01. Coefficients of variation for
R_t data on triplicate analysis of one wine were generally
< 0.005 (manuscript in preparation).

   For GC-Sniff evaluation, volatiles were collected as described previously, the effluent was split 1:1 and the aromas
of the eluting components sniffed. The intensities were rated
on a 0 (no odor) to 9 (very intense odor) scale and aromas
described by two individuals.

   For Gas Chromatography-Mass Spectrometry (GC-MS), 4.2
liters of headspace were collected from wine 4 in six 700 ml
increments by mechanical displacement using a motor driven
syringe at 20 ml/min on Tenax GC (22). Volatiles were as described previously and separated on a 205M x 7.5 mm i.d. coiled

s.s. capillary column coated as above in a temperature programmed to run from 50 to 185°. The column was mounted in a modified
Beckman Thermotrac oven fitted with a Carle thermistor detector.
The Detector effluent was passed through a 0.001 in methyl silicone membrane into an Electronic Associates Quad 300 quadrupole
mass spectrometer. Scans were recorded at scan rates of 1 or
1.5 sec as described by Flath and Forrey (23).

2. *Sensory Evaluation Methods*

  a. Judge selection and training. The wines were evaluated
by descriptive sensory analysis as reviewed by Amerine et al.
(24). Thirteen judges were selected on the basis of their reproducible performance in preliminary rating tests. The male
judges, most of whom had participated in food or wine sensory
panels previously, were students in the Department of Viticulture
and Enology or Food Science, University of California, Davis.
In two groups (of 6 and 7), the panelists met with a panel moderator for four round table discussions held either at 12:00 or
1:00 p.m. Tuesday through Friday in week one. In the first and
second sessions, one wine was presented to each judge and they
were encouraged to discuss any descriptors which they felt adequately described the wine's aroma. The moderator focused the
discussion on agreement on specific terms such as herbaceous,
vegetative, weedy or green pepper. For the first session, a
list of terms developed in a previous study (Melchor, thesis
in preparation) was used. After each session, these terms were
modified and an updated scorecard was prepared for the following meeting. Where possible, reference standards were prepared
in 10% ethanol to anchor the descriptive terms and were available during the discussion or prior to scoring.

  During the third and fourth round table sessions,   two
wines were introduced. The judges scored them for intensity of

the attributes specified on the scorecard before discussing the
wines.

   b.   Testing procedures.   The ten wines were evaluated in
quadruplicate in two groups of five wines.   The sequence in
which the groups were tasted was randomized over the 8 days of
testing.   In each session, one group of 5 wines was scored.
The judges were presented with a glass containing the reference
wine and one test wine.   When they were through scoring the
attributes of the first wine, a second wine was presented.   The
order of presentation of the wines within each group of five
was randomized for each judge.   Judges tasted between noon and
3 p.m. Tuesday through Friday in isolated booths provided with
a spittoon and incandescent light.   Standard tulip shaped clear
wine glasses were used.

   Intensity of each aroma attribute was rated using an un-
structured category scale on a scorecard similar to that shown
in Figure 1.   (In the actual testing, both taste and appearance
attributes were also rated.)   The results were converted to
numbers by measuring from the left end of the 10 cm scale to
the marked intensity.

   Sensory results were analyzed by analysis of variance (AOV)
for each judge for each term.   Three-way AOV's were then run
for each attribute across the 10 wines.   Four judges were eliminated who showed poor reproducibility or misuse of terms.   Final
results were calculated using only the third and fourth tastings
to avoid significant interactions.

3.   *Correlation of Sensory and Instrumental Data*

   Two-way AOV's were run across all wines for peaks which had
coefficients of variation above 0.35 in more than two wines.
Peaks with significant F ratios for replication were not used
for further statistical analyses.   (Specifically, peaks 9/10,
51, 67, 68, 70, and 72 were eliminated.)   Peaks with correlations

Fig. 1.

SCORECARD FOR DESCRIPTIVE ANALYSIS OF CABERNET
SAUVIGNON WINE AROMA

Name _____   Code ------

PLEASE EVALUATE THE AROMA ATTRIBUTES OF THIS
WINE IN THE SEQUENCE GIVEN BELOW. PLACE A
SLASH MARK ON THE SCALE TO RATE THE INTENSITY
OF THE ATTRIBUTE IN THIS WINE RELATIVE TO THAT
OF THE REFERENCE WINE.

ATTRIBUTE   INTENSITY

VEGETATIVE

(green pepper,
 asparagus)   less   reference   more

PEPPERY

(black pepper)   less   reference   more

SHARPNESS

(ethanol)   less   reference   more

WOODY CHARACTER
                  less   reference   more

RAISIN/CARAMEL
                  less   reference   more

ARTIFICIAL FRUIT
                  less   reference   more

VARIETAL CHARACTER
                  less   reference   more

above 0.85 and components without perceptible aroma on elution from the GC were also excluded.

The remaining GC peaks were used as independent variables in multivariate analyses. Stepwise multiple regression for each aroma term was done using the U.C.L.A. Biomed program. To look at underlying relationships in the GC peaks and possibly reduce the data further, Principal Component Analysis (PCA) was performed on unstandardized data also using a Biomed program. PCA is a technique which linearly transforms many variables into components or factors which explain most of the variance in only a few factors.

B. Materials

Ten commercial California wines were selected for evaluation. All of the bottles used were from the same bottling lot. Wines 1-9 were Cabernet Sauvignons and wine 10, Ruby Cabernet. To provide a reference wine to serve as a standard for sensory analysis, a blend of a commercial non-varietal, non-vintage red wine and of Pinot noir wine, produced by standard procedures in the University of California winery in the Department of Viticulture and Enology was made. Details about the wines are shown in Table 1.

Reference standards to define the descriptive terms used in rating of the wines were prepared by adding food products or extracts to the reference wine or by obtaining wines which were high in a specific attribute.

III. RESULTS

A. Gas Chromatographic Analyses

About 80 separate peaks were detected in the wine headspaces, although in many peaks more than one component was

TABLE 1

Description of Wines Used in the Study
==

Code	Year of Vintage	Grape Variety
1	1973	90% Cabernet Sauvignon; 10% Merlot
2	1970	97% Cabernet Sauvignon; 3% Merlot
3	1972	90% Cabernet Sauvignon; 10% Pinot noir
4	1971	60% Cabernet Sauvignon; 40% Cabernet Franc
5	1973	75% Cabernet Sauvignon; 5% Merlot
6	1973	75% Cabernet Sauvignon; 25% Merlot
7	1972	100% Cabernet Sauvignon
8	1971	55% Cabernet Sauvignon; 45% Zinfandel
9	nv[a]	100% Cabernet Sauvignon
10	nv	100% Ruby Cabernet
11 (Reference)	nv	27% Ruby Cabernet; 22% Petite Sirah; 16% Barbera, 25% Carignane and Zinfandel; 10% Pinot noir

a. *nv = nonvintage*

present. A typical headspace profile is shown in Figure 2 with
aroma descriptions obtained by sniffing the effluent. Tentative
identification of components based on GC-MS data is shown in
Table 2.

Despite the rigorous standardization of the headspace collection procedure, many peaks had coefficients of variation
greater than 0.40 (across three replicate analyses of an individual wine). Two profiles for the analyses of wine 4 (Figure
3) are typical of the variation observed in all wines. As can

TABLE 2

Tentative Identification[a] of Components in
Cabernet Sauvignon Headspace

Peak #	Tentative Identity
A	Acetaldehyde
B	Ethanol
C	Ethyl acetate
1	3-methyl butanal
	2-Methyl propanol
2	
4	Ethyl propanoate
	Propyl acetate
9,10	3-Methyl-1-butanol
	2-Methyl-1-butanol
13	Ethyl butyrate
19	Ethyl-2-methyl butyrate
	Ethyl-3-methyl butyrate
20	Ethyl benzene
22	2-Methylbutyl acetate
	3-Methylbutyl acetate
24	Hexanol
38	Ethyl hexanoate
39	Hexyl acetate
58	Ethyl octanoate
65	B-phenylethyl acetate
75	1,5,8-Trimethyl-1,2,-dihydronapthalene
77	Ethyl decanoate

a. Based on correspondence of mass spectral data to
    authentic components.

be seen from Table 3, the poorest reproducibility is associated
with the smallest peaks. Mean values for the headspace analyses
for the 11 wines are reported in Table 4.

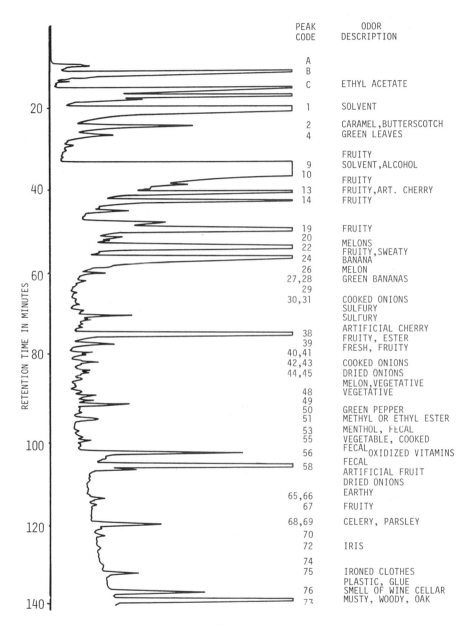

Fig. 2.   GC Headspace profile and effluent odor descriptions.

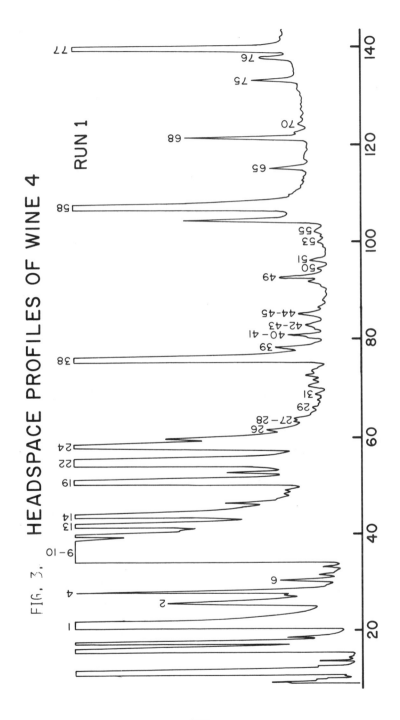

FIG. 3. HEADSPACE PROFILES OF WINE 4

RUN 1

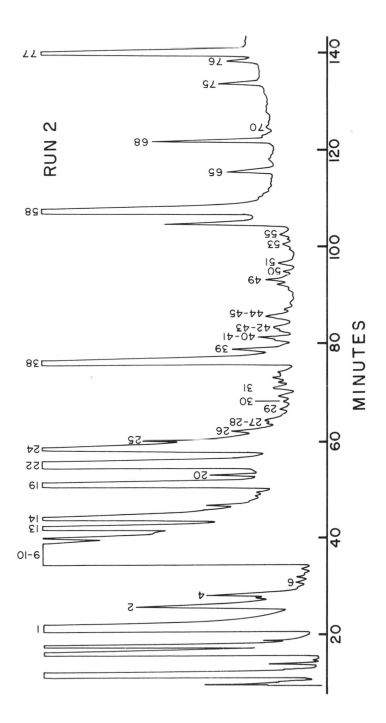

TABLE 3

Wine 4.   Peak Area Means and Coefficients of Variation

Peak	Mean Area[a]	Coeff. of var.[b]
1	62.08	0.05
2	10.48	0.23
9/10	129.32	0.03
13	16.25	0.15
14	18.95	0.40
19	34.20	0.16
22	42.19	0.06
24	29.02	0.06
26	0.79	0.32
27	0.55	0.62
29	0.18	0.74
30	0.13	0.51
31	0.40	0.11
38	42.37	0.09
39	1.45	0.40
40/41	1.66	0.23
42/43	0.68	0.03
44/45	1.66	0.35
48	0.49	0.75
49	2.24	0.10
50	0.27	0.13
53	0.46	0.15
55	0.49	0.16
58	37.51	0.15
65	2.52	0.39
66	0.05	0.47
67	0.04	0.48
68	5.29	0.31
70	0.60	0.02
72	0.01	0.87
74	0.02	1.32
75	2.00	0.37
76	0.91	0.38
77	20.78	0.21

a.   *n = 3*
b.   *Coefficient of variation = std. dev./mean*

TABLE 4

Mean Peak Areas[a] for Wines 1 to 11[b]

Peak Number	Wine				
	1	2	3	4	5
1	56.53	64.50	56.43	62.08	53.69
2	8.23	11.21	6.46	10.48	8.64
4	21.32	22.50	2.81	5.75	1.33
9/10	124.77	126.56	111.80	129.32	105.81
13	16.10	6.20	17.77	16.25	18.5
14	12.87	27.49	17.18	18.95	16.02
19	35.03	36.68	27.96	34.20	25.01
22	37.07	35.12	32.47	42.19	30.35
24	29.97	34.89	31.27	29.02	24.24
26	1.22	0.83	0.96	0.79	0.71
27	0.50	0.57	0.34	0.55	0.24
29	0.42	0.31	0.30	0.18	0.20
30	0.22	0.19	0.16	0.13	0.25
31	0.68	0.45	0.43	0.40	0.49
38	30.16	43.06	32.76	42.37	24.63
39	2.94	2.14	2.57	1.45	2.12
40/41	0.52	0.92	0.85	1.66	0.41
42/43	0.89	0.79	0.97	0.68	1.63
44/45	1.60	2.57	1.10	1.66	0.37
48	0.76	0.80	0.51	0.49	0.57
49	2.31	2.07	1.57	2.24	1.69
50	0.33	0.22	0.12	0.27	0.15
51	0.76	0.81	1.08	0.72	0.50
53	0.30	0.42	0.57	0.46	0.16
55	0.06	0.36	0.37	0.49	0.08
58	31.81	42.33	31.43	37.51	23.25
65	1.61	2.77	0.66	2.52	0.22
66	0.42	0.00	0.14	0.05	0.08
67	0.27	0.32	0.00	0.04	0.10
68	3.20	6.89	3.17	5.29	2.49
69	0.28	0.17	0.11	0.13	0.07
70	0.34	0.34	0.23	0.60	0.33
72	0.17	0.08	0.12	0.01	0.17
74	0.13	0.12	0.15	0.02	0.08
75	0.56	4.91	1.84	2.00	0.30
76	0.71	2.86	3.85	0.91	0.23
77	17.31	27.19	23.00	20.78	17.6

a. n = 3
b. Wine codes described in Table 1.

TABLE 4 (continued)

Mean Peak Areas[a] for Wines 1 to 11[b]

| Number | Wine | | | | | |
	6	7	8	9	10	Ref.
1	68.28	47.24	65.21	66.79	59.67	67.41
2	11.57	10.83	11.92	9.28	9.24	12.96
4	4.14	---	4.26	5.01	10.11	2.08
9/10	131.98	94.31	126.40	122.10	125.94	118.76
13	15.58	16.13	19.40	16.52	17.77	15.98
14	22.79	19.80	17.16	24.90	4.77	4.96
19	33.60	53.51	32.36	36.86	35.26	21.84
22	34.69	32.76	31.96	32.76	34.19	47.79
24	28.38	28.76	42.05	42.70	34.37	25.16
26	1.70	1.38	1.05	0.73	0.75	1.01
27	0.36	0.28	0.37	0.39	0.38	0.69
29	0.28	0.25	0.27	0.23	0.23	0.28
30	0.15	0.20	0.23	0.13	0.20	0.33
31	0.58	0.23	0.51	0.24	0.45	0.63
38	33.18	26.97	36.61	39.59	38.21	37.71
39	2.43	4.42	2.62	1.90	2.98	9.89
40/41	0.56	0.68	0.73	0.84	0.37	0.70
42/43	0.98	2.21	0.99	1.65	0.75	1.00
44/45	2.38	0.71	2.42	2.40	2.08	1.39
48	0.92	1.06	0.66	0.99	0.61	0.66
49	1.16	1.48	1.09	1.87	15.91	8.35
50	0.21	0.30	0.28	0.253	0.12	0.14
51	0.68	0.35	0.79	0.84	0.89	0.80
53	0.42	0	0.25	0.31	0.50	0.29
55	0.24	0	0.34	0.28	0.24	0.40
58	37.35	24.40	34.41	37.66	38.76	41.41
65	2.49	0.35	1.59	1.87	1.95	2.48
66	0.45	0.37	0	4.79	0	0.77
67	0.26	0	0	0.43	0.12	0.22
68	1.64	3.69	3.47	4.79	9.12	1.85
69	0.26	0.10	0.11	0.56	0.07	0.21
70	0.16	0.23	0.17	0.24	0.07	0.15
72	0.11	0	0.14	0.11	0.10	0.04
74	0.13	0	0	0.07	0.09	0.14
75	0.42	2.22	0.91	2.70	2.82	1.58
76	0.36	0.59	0.22	1.46	0.71	0.85
77	20.91	17.43	19.22	27.58	20.77	23.97

a.   n = 3
b.   Wine codes described in Table 1.

B. Descriptive Analyses

Analyses of Variance for each of the 7 terms rated are shown in Table 5. Both "Peppery" and "Sharp" attributes were not significantly different among the wines. The "Vegetative", "Raisin", "Fruity" and "Varietal Character" attributes were significantly different across the wines, with no significant interactions.

The term "Woody", although rated significantly different among the wines, had a significant wine X judge interaction indicating that the term was being used differently by the judges, and results for the "Woody" term are of dubious value.

To show the profiles of the wine aromas, deviations of the mean intensity ratings for each attribute from the reference rating are plotted (with their standard deviations) in Figure 4. Generally speaking, all wines were higher in "Vegetative", "Woody", "Raisiny" and "Varietal Character" than the reference wine, and lower in fruitiness. The overall term, "Varietal Character", was not significantly correlated with any of the other aroma terms for the 10 wines.

C. Correlation of Sensory and Instrumental Data

Twenty peaks were used to develop regression equations for each of the significant aroma terms. Equations were developed using all 11 wines (Table 6) and excluding the reference wine, using only wines 1-10 (Table 7). Better fitting equations were developed using 11 wines which is somewhat unexpected, since the reference wine (Wine 11) was an outlier, both sensorially and with respect to 3 components used in the regression equations: Peak 19, 22 and 39.

In only two cases, Steps 1 to 4 of the prediction of "Vegetative" aroma and Step 1 of the "Fruity" prediction, were the

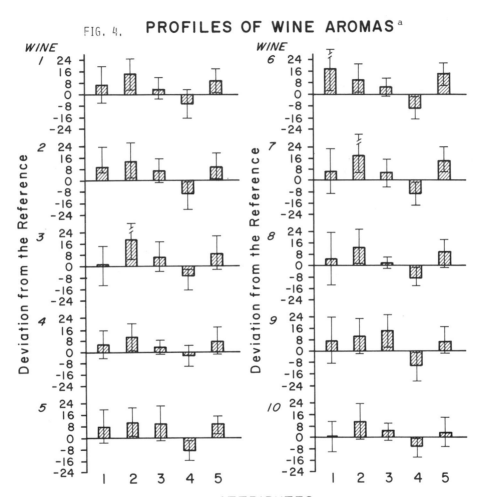

FIG. 4. PROFILES OF WINE AROMAS[a]

[a]Means (n=16) shown in cross-hatch with standard deviations.

ATTRIBUTES
1 - Vegetative
2 - Woody
3 - Raisiny
4 - Artificial fruit
5 - Varietal

TABLE 5

AOV Summary

Vegetative

Source of Variation	df	MS	F	sig
Wine (W)	9	393.44	3.36	**
Judge (J)	8	1419.88	12.14	***
Reps (R)	1	4.05	0.035	NS
W X J	72	121.34	1.04	NS
R X J	8	135.19	1.16	NS
R X W	9	91.89	0.78	NS
Error (E)	72	116.98		

Peppery

Source of Variation	df	MS	F	sig
W	9	26.41	0.71	NS
J	8	1442.04	38.76	***
R	1	5.34	0.14	NS
W X J	72	42.73	1.15	NS
R X J	8	12.86	0.35	NS
R X W	9	46.62	1.25	NS
E	72	37.20		

Sharp

Source of Variation	df	MS	F	sig
W	9	78.27	1.36	NS
J	8	589.92	10.28	***
R	1	118.42	2.06	NS
W X J	72	42.37	0.74	NS
R X J	8	28.10	0.49	NS
R X W	9	55.19	0.96	NS
E	72	57.38		

Woody

Source of Variation	df	MS	F	sig
W	9	144.20	3.30	**
J	8	1817.11	41.55	***
R	1	18.05	0.41	NS
W X J	72	73.14	1.67	*
R X J	8	25.72	0.59	NS
R X W	9	18.99	0.43	NS
E	72	43.73		

TABLE 5 (continued)

AOV Summary
===

Raisiny

Source of Variation	df	MS	F	sig
W	9	260.70	7.76	***
J	8	641.11	19.08	***
R	1	28.00	0.83	NS
W X J	72	50.56	1.50	NS
R X J	8	13.77	0.41	NS
R X W	9	29.77	0.89	NS
E	72	33.60		

Artificial Fruity

Source of Variation	df	MS	F	sig
W	9	87.82	3.42	**
J	8	874.40	34.11	***
R	1	51.20	2.00	NS
W X J	72	37.94	1.48	NS
R X J	8	20.25	0.79	NS
R X W	9	20.10	0.78	NS
E	72	25.64		

Varietal

Source of Variation	df	MS	F	sig
W	9	165.58	2.64	*
J	8	318.75	5.07	***
R	1	147.60	2.35	NS
W X J	72	81.38	1.30	NS
R X J	8	67.50	1.07	NS
R X W	9	55.01	0.88	NS
E	72	62.80		

```
  * = p<0.05
 ** = p<0.01
*** = p<0.001
 NS = Not significant
```

TABLE 6

Summary of Multiple Regression Equations Developed to Predict
Intensity of Aroma Attributes in 11 Wines

Aroma Attribute	Step	GC Peak Entered	Multiple Correlation Coefficient (R)	Std. Error of the Estimate	F^a
"Vegetative"	1	14	0.714	3.57	9.35*b
	2	76	0.842	2.91	9.77**
	3	31	0.928	2.16	14.4 **
"Wood"	1	48	0.822	2.86	18.80**
	2	39	0.905	2.27	17.99**
	3	76	0.982	1.08	63.05***
Raisin	1	22	0.593	3.35	4.87NS
	2	69	0.780	2.65	7.10*
	3	26	0.893	2.10	9.46**
	4	24	0.965	1.34	20.10**
Fruit	1	22	0.905	1.45	40.94***
	2	13	0.981	0.71	99.81***
Varietal Character	1	14	0.755	2.77	11.92**
	2	38	0.918	1.77	21.44***
	3	19	0.950	1.49	21.76***

a. $F = MS$ regression/MS residual
b. The level of significance where $*$ = $p<0.05$; $**$ = $p<0.01$;
    $***$ = $p<0.001$; NS = non-significant

same GC peaks used as independent variables when the equations
were derived using either 10 or 11 wines. However, for the
prediction of "vegetative" aroma, virtually the same equation
was generated from either data set.

Since the selections of wines so drastically altered the
resulting equations, with the above exceptions, it is obvious
that a larger sample size is needed. Despite the high multiple
correlation coefficients and significant F statistics, the
equations have predictive power only within the data set, and
are of limited value in predicting the aroma intensity of a
new wine, unless it is similar to those in the present study.

Further, even within the data set, because of the inter-
correlation (multicollinearity) of the GC peaks, the regression
coefficient of any peak depends on the other peaks included in
the equation. Thus it is not possible to conclude from the size
of the regression coefficient the magnitude of the effect the
GC peak has on an aroma attribute.

As a first attempt at reducing the data further, Principal
Component Analysis was applied to 20 unstandardized GC peaks
using wines 1-11. Results are summarized in Table 8. Eighty-
two percent of the variance is accounted for by the first five
components. However, none of the principal components can be
readily identified. Most GC peaks have a low correlation with
more than one component. No systematic loading of the fruity
GC peaks (13,14,19,22,24,26,38,39), of the "vegetative or
sulfury" peaks (31,42,44,48,55,69), or of ethyl esters or
acetate esters onto a component is evident. Principal components derived using just the 14 "fruity" and "vegetative-
sulfury" GC peaks for either 10 or 11 wines similarly lacked
a clear weighting pattern.

TABLE 7

Summary of Multiple Regression Equations Developed to Predict
Intensity of Aroma Attributes using Wines 1-10

Aroma Attribute	Step	GC Peak Entered	Multiple Correlation Coefficient (R)	Std. Error of the Estimate	F^a
"Vegetative"	1	14	.646	3.79	5.74NS[b]
	2	76	.811	3.11	6.71*
	3	31	.914	2.33	10.08**
"Wood"	1	39	.601	2.40	4.52NS
	2	76	.926	1.21	21.14**
Raisin	1	69	.591	3.15	4.28NS
	2	50	.750	2.76	4.49NS
	3	53	.881	2.13	6.96*
	4	27	.979	1.01	28.50**
Fruit	1	22	.765	1.51	11.26*
	2	48	.965	0.65	47.97***
Varietal Character	1	26	.736	2.18	9.43**
	2	49	.898	1.51	14.61**
	3	42	.950	1.10	18.46**

a. F = MS regression/MS residual
b. The level of significance where * = $p<0.05$; ** = $p<0.01$;
    *** = $p<0.001$; N.S. = non-significant.

TABLE 8

Summary of Principal Component Analysis of 20 Gas Chromatographic Peaks. Correlation of GC Peaks within Principal Components[a] (n=11)

==

	Principal Components				
GC PEAK	1	2	3	4	5
13			-0.429		
14	0.224	0.324	0.154		
19	0.275		0.210		
22	-0.355		0.274		
24		0.334		0.306	-0.358
26			0.277	0.221	0.401
27	-0.281		0.379		
31	-0.230	-0.201		0.292	0.423
38	-0.274	0.329			-0.165
39	-0.221	-0.301	0.211		-0.256
40		0.297	0.162	-0.402	
42	0.325		0.154	-0.154	-0.352
44		0.323		0.479	
48	-0.286	-0.231	0.213		-0.258
49	-0.200	-0.162	-0.206	0.259	-0.292
50	0.181		0.353		
53	-0.255	0.225	-0.248		0.225
55	-0.324	0.250		-0.167	
69		0.199	0.244	0.278	-0.235
76		0.217		-0.341	
% of Total Variance	27	22	16	9	8
Cumulative Total Variance	27	49	65	74	82

a. *Correlations of < 0.150 have been omitted to simplify the table.*

IV. CONCLUSION

Correlation of GC headspace components with quantitative descriptive analyses of 9 Cabernet Sauvignon, one Ruby Cabernet and one blend resulted in the developmment of predictive equations for 5 attributes: "Vegetative", "Woody", "Raisin", "Fruity", and "Varietal Character or Cabernet-like". Although significant equations were derived within the data set, the equations cannot be used for prediction of wines outside of it. Further investigation of a larger number of wines must be done for development of equations which can validly predict intensity values in untested wines.

V. REFERENCES

1. Webb, A. D., Kepner, R., and Maggiora, L., Am. J. Enol. Vitic. 20, 16 (1969).

2. Webb, A. D., and Muller, C. J., Adv. Appl. Micro. 15, 77 (1972).

3. Schreier, P., Drawert, F., and Junker, A., J. Agric. Food Chem. 24, 331 (1976).

4. Bayonove, C., Cordonnier, R., and Dubois, P., C. R. Acad. Sci. Paris 281(1), 75 (1975).

5. Seifert, T. M., Buttery, R., Guadagni, D., Black, D., and Harris, J., J. Agric. Food Chem. 18, 246 (1970.

6. Ribereau-Gayon, J., Connaissance de la Vigne et du Vin 7(2), 79 (1973).

7. Persson, T., von Sydow, E., and Akesson, C., J. Food Sci. 38, 682 (1973).

8. Kosaric, N., Duong, T., and Svrcek, W., J. Food Sci. 38, 369 (1973).

9. Galetto, W., and Bednarczyk, A., J. Food Sci. 40, 1165 (1975).

10. Bednarczyk, A., and Kramer, A., Chem. Senses Flavor 1, 377 (1975).

11. Powers, J., and Keith, E., J. Food Sci. 33, 207 (1968).

12. Dravnieks, A., Reilich, H., and Whitfield, J., J. Food Sci. 38, 34 (1973).

13. Milutinovic, L., Bargmann, R., Chang, K., Chastain, M., and Powers, J., J. Food Sci. 35, 224 (1970).

14. Hoff, J., Helbert, J., and Chicoye, E., M.B.A.A. Tech. Quart. 12, 209 (1975).

15. Young, L., Bargmann, R., and Powers, J., J. Food Sci. 35, 219 (1970).

16. Baker, G., Amerine, M., and Pangborn, R., J. Food Sci. 26 644 (1961).

17. Vuatez, L., Sotek, J., and Rahim, H., Proc. 4th Intl. Congr. Food Sci. Technol. (Madrid, Spain) Ia, 25 (1974).

18. Palmer, D., J. Sci. Food Agric. 25, 153 (1974).

19. Martens, H., Solberg, Y., Roer, L., and Vold, E., Potato Res. 18, 515 (1975).

20. Wu, L., Bargmann, R., and Powers, J., J. Food Sci. 42, 944 (1977).

21. Coope, G. C., M.S. Thesis submitted to University of California, Davis (1977).

22. Forrey, R., M.S. Thesis submitted to University of California, Davis (1977).

23. Flath, R. A., Forrey, R., J. Agric. Food Chem. 18, 306 (1970).

24. Amerine, M. A., Pangborn, R. M., and Roessler, E. B., "Principles of Sensory Evaluation of Food," p. 377, Academic Press, New York, 1965.

SAKE FLAVOR AND ITS IMPROVEMENT USING METABOLIC MUTANTS OF YEAST

Hiroichi Akiyama, Kiyoshi Yoshizawa, and Kozo Ouchi

National Research Institute of Brewing, Japan

Sake, *the native alcoholic beverage of Japan, is brewed from rice and water using* sake *yeast and* koji. *About one hundred flavor compounds of which higher alcohols and esters are the principal components have been detected. To determine several important* sake *flavor compounds, a headspace gas chromatography was established as follows. A 200 ml Erlenmeyer flask containing 20 ml of* sake *is sealed tightly and kept at 50°C for 30 min. Then 3 ml of the headspace gas is withdrawn and submitted to gas chromatography (column 1 m, 10% DNP, temperature 75°C, N_2 gas flow 40 ml/min, HFI detector). Isobutanol, isoamyl alcohol, isoamyl acetate and ethyl caproate in* sake *and various alcoholic beverages are rapidly determined using n-amyl alcohol and methyl caproate as inner standards. The composition of these components is characteristically different in each type of* sake *and in various spirits. Most of the* sake *flavor compounds are formed by yeast during the fermentation process and the production of these compounds is affected by the yeast strain used and by the fermentation conditions such as contents of nitrogenous compounds and lipids and temperature. To improve* sake *flavor, some yeast mutants of the related metabolic pathway were examined for use.*

I.   CHARACTERISTICS OF *SAKE* BREWING

Sake has long been a traditional alcoholic beverage in Japan, and is still one of the most popular drinks of the Japanese. The annual consumption of *sake* was estimated at 1,700 thousand kiloliters in 1976.

It is made from rice and water. The mash is fermented in an open tank without any special sterilization and the alcohol content reaches as high as 20% after 20 days fermentation. Fig. 1 shows an outline of *sake* brewing process (1, 2). The main process can be divided into three parts; (a) preparation of *"koji"*, a 2 day culture of *Aspergillus oryzae* on steamed rice grains, (b) preparation of *"moto"*, seed mash, and (c) fermentation of *"moromi"*, main mash. *Koji* is used for saccharification of starch in *sake* brewing in contrast with the prevalent use of malt in beer brewing. *Moto* is prepared by mixing *koji*, steamed rice and cold water, followed by inoculation of pure yeast culture. To prevent harmful bacterial contamination, lactic acid is added to 0.5% by volume. *Moromi* is prepared by adding *koji*, steamed rice and water to *moto* containing 200 million cells/g of *sake* yeast. In *moromi*, yeast ferments sugars which are formed from rice starch by the amylase action of *koji*. *Sake* brewing differs markedly in this respect from beer brewing in which fermentation starts after saccharification finishes. Proteolipids from *koji* mold is a factor for producing such a high concentration of alcohol (3).

The composition of flavor components characteristically differs in each type of alcoholic beverages owing to various factors, especially yeast strains, fermentation temperature, contents of nitrogen compounds and lipids in the raw materials. Since *sake* is made from highly polished rice grains which have no characteristic aroma or taste, the formation of flavors of *sake* is mainly due to *koji* and yeast fermentation.

Studies on the flavor compounds of *sake* have been undertaken from the beginning of this century. Higher alcohols and esters,

TABLE 1
Flavor Compounds in Sake
===

Alcohols
   Methanol
   Ethanol
   n-Propanol
   n-Butanol
   Isobutanol
   n-Amyl alcohol
   Isoamyl alcohol
   Active amyl alcohol
   n-Hexanol
   β-Phenethyl alcohol

Esters
   Ethyl formate
   Ethyl acetate
   Ethyl lactate
   Ethyl Butyrate
   Ethyl caproate
   Ethyl caprylate
   Ethyl caprate
   Ethyl laurate
   Ethyl myristate
   Ethyl pyruvate
   Ethyl isovalerate
   Ethyl isocaproate
   Ethyl oxoisovalerate
   Ethyl oxoisocaproate
   Ethyl oxyisovalerate
   Ethyl oxyisocaproate
   Ethyl phenylacetate
   Ethyl *p*-oxybenzoate
   Ethyl *p*-oxycinnamate
   Ethyl vanillate
   Ethyl ferulate
   Monoethyl malate
   Monoethyl succinate
   Propyl acetate
   Butyl acetate
   Isobutyl acetate
   n-Amyl acetate
   Isoamyl acetate
   Phenethyl acetate

Acids
   Formic
   Acetic
   Propionic
   Butyric

Caproic
Caprylic
Capric
Lauric
Myristic
Palmitic
Palmitoleic
Oleic
Isobutyric
Isovaleric
Isocaproic
Isocaprylic
Isocapric
Pyruvic
Oxobutyric
p-Oxycinnamic
Vanillic
Phenylpyruvic

Carbonyl compounds
   Formaldehyde
   Acetaldehyde
   Propionaldehyde
   Isovaleraldehyde
   Caproaldehyde
   Benzaldehyde
   p-Oxybenzaldehyde
   Cinnamaldehyde
   Vanillin
   Furfural
   Diacetyl
   Acetoin
   Aceton

Amines
   Ethanolamine
   Isobutylamine
   Putrescine
   Cadaverine
   Phenethylamine

S-Compounds
   Hydrogen sulfide
   Methyl mercaptan
   Dimethyl disulfide

Miscellaneous
   3-Oxy-4,5-dimethyl-2(5H)-
      furanon

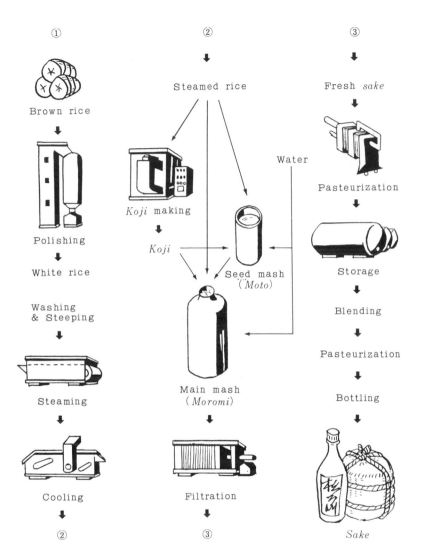

Fig. 1. Diagram of sake *making process.*

and aldehydes in aged *sake* were analyzed (4,5). With the development of gas chromatography, the flavor chemistry of *sake* has
also been practised widely and about one hundred compounds shown
in Table 1 were detected (4 - 10). Higher alcohols and esters
are very important flavor components of *sake*. *Sake* contains

about 400 ppm of higher alcohols consisting mainly of isoamyl alcohol, *active* amyl alcohol, isobutanol, *n*-propanol and phenethyl
alcohol (7,11). *Sake* contains about 100 ppm of volatile esters,
in which ethyl acetate, isoamyl acetate, ethyl esters of fatty
acids C_6 - C_{18} and phenethyl acetate are found in a fairly large
amount (7,9).

A rapid method to determine the main flavor compounds of
sake by headspace gas chromatography was designed and the composition of some of those compounds is used to estimate the type
and quality of not only *sake* but also of various alcoholic beverages.

Higher alcohols are formed mainly through biosynthetic pathways of amino acids as well as by Ehrlich mechanism. Several
yeast mutants auxotrophic for amino acids are used to brew *sake*
characteristic in flavor.

II. DETERMINATION OF FLAVOR COMPOUNDS IN *SAKE* USING HEADSPACE
GAS CHROMATOGRAPHY

Method of determination of flavor compounds in *sake* using
headspace gas chromatography is as follows (12). Using this
method, flavor compounds such as higher alcohols and volatile esters are determined rapidly and an accurate result (with 3% error)
can be obtained.

1. Apparatus and Reagent
     a. Gas chromatograph. A gas chromatograph with flame ioni-
zation detector. Column 1 m × 3 mm inner diameter SUS packed
with 100 to 120 mesh 10% dinonyl phthalate at 75°C. Detector and
inlet temperature 150°C. N_2 flow rate 40 ml/min.
     b. Alcohol stock solution. Dilute 1 g of isoamyl alcohol
and 0.5 g of isobutanol with 30% ethanol solution to 100 ml respectively. Keep in refrigerator within 2 weeks.

c. *Ester stock solution.* Dilute 0.1 g of isoamyl acetate with 30% ethanol solution to 200 ml.

d. *Inner standard solution.* Dilute 2 g of *n*-amyl alcohol and 0.1 g of methyl caproate with 30% ethanol solution to 1,000 ml.

e. *Standard solution.* Mix each 0.5, 1.0, 1.5 and 2.0 ml of isobutanol stock solution, isoamyl alcohol stock solution and isoamyl acetate stock solution respectively. Fill up each mixture with 15% ethanol solution to 100 ml.

2. *Determination*

Pipet 20 ml of each standard solution into 200 ml Erlenmeyer flask and add 2 ml of inner standard solution respectively. Cap immediately with rubber stoppers having a hollow in center as shown in Fig. 2. Shake the mixture lightly, and let stand at 50°C in a water bath. After 30 min, pull out 3 ml gas from headspace through the hollow of a rubber stopper using a syringe, and inject it immediately into gas chromatograph. Fig. 3 shows the gas chromatogram usually obtained from *sake* analysis.

Determine peak areas and calculate the ratio of areas of isobutanol and isoamyl alcohol to *n*-amyl alcohol respectively and those of isoamyl acetate to methyl caproate. Plot content of each alcohol and ester (ppm) as abscisca against each ratio as ordinate to prepare calibration curves.

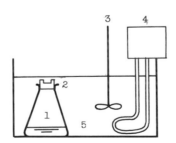

Fig. 2. *Erlenmeyer flask in water bath.*
1) *Erlenmeyer flask, 2) Rubber stopper, 3) Stirrer, 4) Heater,*
5) *Water bath*

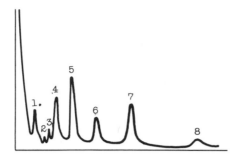

Fig. 3. *Gas chromatogram obtained from headspace analysis of* sake.
1) Isobutanol, 2) Isobutyl acetate, 3) Ethyl butyrate, 4) Isoamyl alcohol, 5) n-Amyl alcohol (Inner standard), 6) Isoamyl acetate, 7) Methyl caproate (Inner standard), 8) Ethyl caproate

Perform determination on *sake* sample as above and calculate content of isobutanol, isoamyl alcohol and isoamyl acetate using calibration curves. It takes about 25 minutes for gas chromatography. Changes of warming temperature and warming time of the flask affect slightly the analytical value, but changes of ethanol concentration from 15 to 20% had no effect on the analytical value.

Other flavor components such as *n*-propanol, *active* amyl alcohol and isobutyl acetate are determined using columns of carbowax 550 (2 m × 3 mm, temp. 90°C, N_2 gas 25 ml/min) and diglycerol (3 m × 3 mm, temp. 70°C, N_2 gas 40 ml/ min).

III. THE FEATURE OF FLAVOR COMPOUNDS IN *SAKE* AND VARIOUS ALCO-
HOLIC BEVERAGES

Various flavor compounds are detected in alcoholic beverages. Since yeast produces the greater part of them during fermentation, they are found widely in all alcoholic beverages. But the compositions differ in every alcoholic beverage. This fact is one of the essential factors of making characteristic flavor in each al-

coholic beverage. For example, volatile esters and higher alcohols are very important flavor compounds, the composition of
which characteristically differs among alcoholic beverages. Some
of them are determined quantitatively and the data are used to
estimate the type and quality of the tested alcoholic beverages.

1.   *Esters*

   a. *The feature of ester composition of* sake *and various alcoholic beverages*. As shown in Table 2, alcoholic beverages contain various volatile esters, among which ethyl acetate, isoamyl
acetate, ethyl caproate, ethyl caprylate, ethyl caprate, ethyl
pelargonate, ethyl laurate and phenethyl acetate are found in a
fairly large amount (9). Spirits generally contain more esters
than wines. Generally speaking, the alcoholic beverage made from
grain contains a large amount of isoamyl acetate, but its total
ester content is less than that found in alcoholic beverage made
from fruit, in which ethyl esters of C_2 to C_8 acids are dominant.

   Sake contains a fairly large amount of various esters. Table 3 shows ester composition of *sake* of different quality and
the concentrate of gas evaporated from *moromi* mash during fermentation. "*Ginzyo*", specially refined *sake* having high aroma,
contains a fairly large amount of esters, especially ethyl esters
of C_2, C_4 and C_8 fatty acids and isoamyl acetate whereas these
esters are found in every grade of *sake*. Flavor components of
the concentrate of evaporated gas from mash consist of large a-
mounts of volatile esters such as isoamyl acetate, ethyl caproate,
ethyl caprylate, ethyl acetate, ethyl caprate and ethyl butyrate
whereas the flavor compounds having higher boiling points, such
as ethyl laurate, are scarcely found (13). Addition of an adequate amount of the concentrate to *sake* markedly enhances its
flavor, especially "top note", though an excessive addition of
this solution spoils the quality of *sake* as shown in Table 4.

   Sometimes this concentrate is added to *ginzyo* when put on a
contest which prohibits any addition of artificial substances to

TABLE 2
Volatile Ester Content in Various Alcoholic Beverages (ppm)

	Cognac	Whisky		Wine	Beer
		Scotch	Bourbon		
Ethyl acetate	55	13	60	15	25
Isobutyl acetate	2	0.3			0.1
Ethyl butyrate	1	1	3		0.5
Isoamyl acetate	2	7	3	0.1	1.5
Ethyl caproate	15	1	5	4	
Ethyl caprylate	20	10	10	1	0.3
Ethyl caprate	45	20	10	0.5	
Ethyl pelargonate	5	5	5	0.5	0.2
Ethyl laurate	5	15	4		
Phenethyl acetate	5	3	1	0.5	0.3
Ethyl myristate	1	1	3		

TABLE 3
Volatile Ester Content in Various Sake *and the Concentrate of Gas Evaporated from Fermenting Mash (ppm)*

	Sake			Vapor Concentrate
	Ginzyo[a]	Refined	Ordinary	
Ethyl acetate	60	30	20	480
Isobutyl acetate	0.5	0.3	0.2	50
Ethyl butyrate	0.5	0.3	0.2	60
Isoamyl acetate	6	3	2	1,600
Ethyl caproate	5	3	2	640
Ethyl caprylate	5	2	2	520
Ethyl caprate	5	5	5	320
Ethyl pelargonate	3		3	100
Ethyl laurate	5	5	2	5
Phenethyl acetate	5	4	4	2

a) *Specially refined*

·the exhibited *sake*. To exclude such faulty action, every exhib-
ted *sake* is examined whether there may be any faulty addition of
flavor substances by headspace gas chromatography described in

TABLE 4
*Effect of Addition of the Concentrate on the Quality
of* Sake

Volume of the Added Concentrate (ml/100 ml)	E/A Ratio (× 100)	Sensory Evaluation[a]
0	2.9	2.0
0.2	4.1	1.9
0.5	6.1	1.5
1.0	9.1	2.5
1.2	10.3	3.2

a) Best 1 - 5 Worst

TABLE 5
Composition of Sake *Exhibited in the Contest in 1975
and 1976*

		1976 Total	1976 Good	1975 Total	1975 Good
Ethanol	Ave	17.6	17.5	17.7	17.7
(%)	Max	20.7	19,1	20.6	19.8
	Min	15.8	16.5	15.8	16.0
Acidity	Ave	1.4	1.5	1.3	1.4
	Max	2.8	2.3	2.3	1.9
	Min	1.0	0.6	0.8	1.0
Isoamyl alcohol	Ave	129	131	122	129
(ppm)	Max	206	175	200	173
	Min	34	92	27	90
Isoamyl acetate	Ave	3.2	3.6	1.9	2.6
(ppm)	Max	14.0	5.1	9.0	5.4
	Min	0.0	2.0	0.0	0.9
E/A Ratio	Ave	2.5	2.7	1.6	2.0
(× 100)	Max	9.9	3.9	7.5	3.8
	Min	0.0	1.5	0.0	0.9

the former chapter. Since the concentrate contains an extraordi-
narily large amount of isoamyl acetate, the *sake* in which the concentrate is added shows a very high ratio of the amount of isoamyl acetate to the amount of isoamyl alcohol (E/A ratio) compared with naturally prepared *sake*. The content of isoamyl acetate
and isoamyl alcohol and E/A ratio are used to judge if the *sake*
has been naturally prepared or not. Table 5 shows the analytical
data of the *sake* exhibited in the contests in 1975 and 1976 (14).

   b. Formation of flavor compounds during moromi *fermentation.*
As shown in Figs. 4 and 5, in *moromi*, main mash fermentation,
higher alcohols and volatile esters increase their amounts according to ethanol production (9,15). When fermentation subsides and
ethanol production ceases, these flavor compounds gradually decrease their amounts (13).

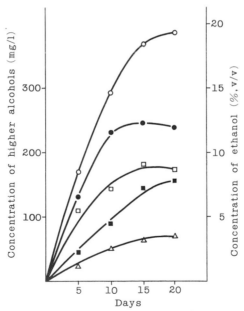

   Fig. 4. Changes in the amounts of various alcohols during
sake *fermentation.*
(○) Ethanol, (●) Isoamyl alcohol, (□) Isobutanol, (■) n-Propanol,
(△) Active amyl alcohol

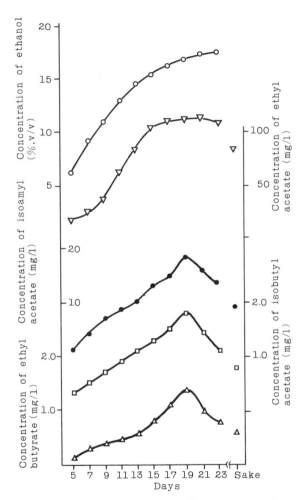

Fig. 5.   *Changes in the amounts of esters during* sake *fermentation.   For comparison, change in the content of ethanol* (○) *is also indicated.*
(▽) *Ethyl acetate,* (●) *Isoamyl acetate,* (□) *Isobutyl acetate,*
(△) *Ethyl butyrate*

Moromi contains about 10 mM of lipids consisting mainly of linoleic, palmitic, oleic and stearic acid.   While ester formation by yeast is promoted in the presence of saturated fatty acids and their derivatives, unsaturated fatty acids such as linol-

eic acid and oleic acid strongly suppress the ester formation
(16). Low fermentation temperature also favors ester formation.
These facts support the rationality of the procedure of *ginzyo*,
i. e., low fermentation temperature, selection of yeast strain
producing a large amount of flavor compounds, and highly polished
rice grain which contains little lipids as raw material.

The formed flavor compounds, especially volatile esters decrease their amounts by decomposition and evaporation during fermentation, filtration, pasteurization and aging. Some nonvolatile components such as ethyl palmitate restrain some of these
esters such as isoamyl acetate from decrease, and thus they contribute to maintain a good flavor in *sake* (10).

2. *Higher Alcohols*

Higher alcohols, one of the most popular flavor compounds,
are composed mainly of isoamyl alcohol, *active* amyl alcohol, isobutanol, *n*-propanol and phenethyl alcohol. As shown in Table 6,
every alcoholic beverage, especially every type of whisky has its
own higher alcohol composition (11). Generally speaking, the alcoholic beverage made from grain contains less higher alcohols,
especially isoamyl alcohol compared to that made from fruit, and
the ratio of the content of isoamyl alcohol to that of isobutan-
ol(A/B ratio) of the former is lower than the latter. These
characteristic differences are caused mainly by the differences
in their raw materials, especially in their nitrogen contents.

When mash contains little amino acids such as valine, leucine as in the case of grape juice, which contains 0.71 mM/l valine, 0.07 mM/l leucine and 15.57 mM/l total amino acids, yeast
forms much isoamyl alcohol as a by-product of amino acid synthesis. In *moromi*, which contains 1.54 mM/l valine, 2.82 mM/l leucine and 29.58 mM/l total amino acids, yeast produces much isobutanol and isoamyl alcohol mainly from valine and leucine in the
medium. In this case, A/B ratio is similar to the ratio of the
content of leucine to that of valine in the medium. The value is

TABLE 6
Higher Alcohol Content in Various Alcoholic Beverages

| Alcoholic Beverage | mg/100 ml | | | | Phenethyl alcohol | A/B Ratio | |
| | Isobutanol | | Isoamyl alcohol[a] | | | | |
	Ave[b]	SD[c]	Ave	SD	Ave	Ave	SD
Sake	6.4	2.1	17	4.7	7.5	2.7	0.3
Beer	1.7	0.4	6.8	1.4	2.0	4.0	0.5
Wine	7	2.9	34	13.8	2.5	4.8	0.6
Whisky Scotch	29	8.5	34	9.5	1.5	1.2	0.2
Irish	137	6.0	217	12.5		1.6	0.1
Japanese(special class)	23	3.1	56	9.2		2.5	0.2
American(straight)	48	17.7	241	20.4	1.7	5.4	1.3
Canadian	9	1.1	33	7.1		3.7	0.0
Brandy Cognac	53	6.2	157	17	3.0	3.0	0.3
German	28	4.5	89	16		3.2	0.2
Japanese(special class)	20	11.7	67	31		3.8	0.8

a) It includes active amyl alcohol.
b) Average value
c) Standard deviation

usually about 2, which is lower than that found in the case of fruit (11). *Sake* contains characteristically large amounts of *n*-propanol and phenethyl alcohol.

Distillation procedure largely affects the composition of higher alcohols of the product (17). The composition of higher alcohols, especially A/B ratio differs characteristically in each type of whisky, i. e. Scotch 1.2, American 5.4, Canadian 3.7, Irish 1.6 and Japanese special class 2.5. Scotch type and the whisky produced by the procedure similar to Scotch type, such as Irish and Japanese, show lower A/B ratios compared with American and Canadian whiskies. A/B ratio is considered as one of the most useful signs in distinguishing one type of whisky from another. Among various factors such as yeast strain and mashing procedure, blending of malt whisky with grain whisky largely contributes to give the lowest A/B ratio to Scotch whisky. Since grain whisky contains isobutanol but only a trace of isoamyl alcohol, its mixture with malt whisky shows lower A/B ratio than the original malt whisky (18).

IV. YEAST MUTANTS AS A METHOD TO CONTROL *SAKE* FLAVOR

Table 7 shows the ability of representative *sake* yeasts (all belong to *Saccharomyces cerevisiae*) to produce main higher alcohols (19). A 1.5-fold variation in the higher alcohol formation can be found among the strains which include choice *sake* yeasts (strains A and B) and typical wild yeasts (strains C and D) isolated as contaminants from *sake* mashes. The proportion of the higher alcohols formed, however, is about the same for all *sake* yeasts.

Application of metabolic mutants is under a plan in order to give much more variety of flavor to *sake*. Since the main components of higher alcohols, i. e. isoamyl alcohol, isobutanol, *n*-propanol and *active* amyl alcohol are all the by-products of leu-

TABLE 7
Ability of Sake *Yeasts to Produce Higher Alcohols*

| | Strain | | | |
	A	B	C	D
n-Propanol	22.1	22.1	23.5	12.4
Isobutanol	61.3	61.5	45.7	40.0
Active amyl alcohol	36.6	33.5	26.8	24.4
Isoamyl alcohol	127.6	108.5	100.2	92.2

The amount (ppm) of higher alcohols produced was analyzed after fermentation in koji-*extract medium (Bllg. 10) at 25°C for 10 days.*

cine, valine and isoleucine metabolism, as illustrated in Fig. 6, the relevant mutants will produce *sake* with a modified composition of flavor. Fig. 7 shows the profiles of the four higher alcohols in *sake* produced by a leucine-, an isoleucine- or an isoleucine and valine-requiring mutant, and by a usual *sake* yeast as a reference (20). The *sake* produced by the *leu2* mutant defective in Step 8 in Fig. 6, contained a less proportion of isoamyl alcohol but, on the other hand, a more proportion of isobutanol. These findings are rational because the mutant lacking the ability to synthesize isoamyl alcohol from carbohydrate formed the alcohol only from exogenous leucine by Ehrlich mechanism but it could form isobutanol from exogenous valine and also from α-keto-isovalerate (KV) which was accumulated by blockage of the pathway to leucine. The *ilv1* mutant defective in Step 1 in Fig. 6, can not synthesize either *n*-propanol or *active* amyl alcohol from carbohydrate, although it can form the latter alcohol from exogenous isoleucine. The *sake* produced by this mutant clearly presented these characteristics. The *ilv3* mutant defective in Step 4 in Fig. 6 can not form *active* amyl alcohol, isobutanol or isoamyl alcohol by synthetic pathways, while it can form these alcohols from exogenous isoleucine, valine and leucine by Ehrlich mechanism. Therfore, the *sake* produced by this mutant had a signifi-

cantly reduced proportion of isobutanol, though the proportion of
active amyl alcohol was similar to, and that of isoamyl alcohol
was rather greater than the reference.

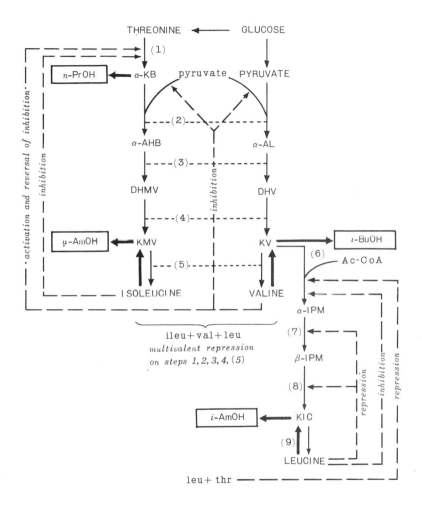

*Fig. 6. Pathway of the formation of main higher alcohols
(after Robichon-Szulmajster and Surdin-Kerjan (21)).*

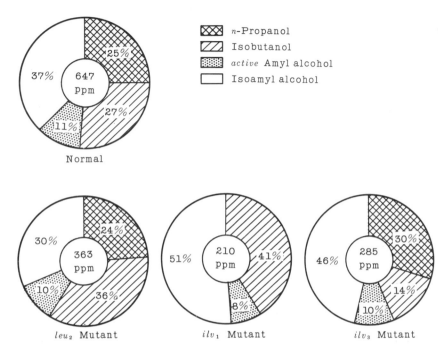

n-Propanol
Isobutanol
active Amyl alcohol
Isoamyl alcohol

Fig. 7. *Profiles of the main higher alcohols in* sake *produced by a* sake *yeast and the metabolic mutants.*
Values in the inner circles are the total amount of the four higher alcohols.

Thus, each mutant tested here could produce *sake* with a specific flavor or taste, but these mutants are probably not useful as such for *sake* brewing, especially because they grew and fermented much more slowly than usual sake yeast. However, this experiment serves to show the possibility that, if suitable mutants are available, the fermentation process can be controlled in such a way that desired amounts of compounds affecting flavor and aroma of *sake* are formed. We are attempting to breed useful mutants of *sake* yeast including regulatory mutants insensitive to feedback inhibition or repression by exogenous amino acids.

V. REFERENCES

1. Nunokawa, Y., in "Rice, Chemistry and Technology" (D.F. Hou-
    Ston, Ed.), p. 449. American Association of Cereal Chemists,
    Inc., St. Paul, Minnesota, 1972.

2. Kodama, K., in "The yeasts" (A.H. Rose, and J.S. Harrison,
    Eds.), Vol. 3, p. 225. Academic Press, London and New York,
    1970.

3. Hayashida, S., Feng, D. D., Ohta, K., Chaitiumvong, S., and
    Hongo, M., Agr. Biol. Chem. 40, 73 (1976).

4. Yamada, M., Ishida, A., and Kobayashi, T., J. Agr. Chem.
    Soc., Japan. 4, 544 (1928).

5. Higashi, K., Reports of Rikagaku Kenkyusho. 4, pp. 506, 763
    (1928).

6. Yamamoto, J., J. Agr. Chem. Soc., Japan. 35, pp. 617, 711,
    819, 1028 (1961). idem., ibid. 38, 231 (1964).

7. Komoda, H., Mano, F., and Yamada, M., J. Agr. Chem. Soc.,
    Japan. 40, 127 (1966).

8. Takahashi, K., and Sato, S., Agr. Biol. Chem. 40, 325 (1976).

9. Yoshizawa, K., J. Brew. Soc., Japan. 61, 629 (1966).

10. Yoshikawa, K., Okumura, Y., and Teramoto, S., J. Ferment.
    Technol. Japan. 41, 357 (1963).

11. Yoshizawa, K., Agr. Biol. Chem. 30, 634 (1966).

12. Yoshizawa, K., J. Brew. Soc., Japan. 68, 59 (1973).

13. Yoshizawa, K., Koshiba, M., and Otsuka, K., J. Brew. Soc.,
    Japan. 61, 824 (1966).

14. Yoshizawa, K., Akiyama, H., and Murakami, H., Report of Na-
    tional Research Institute of Brewing, Japan. 147, 16 (1975).

15. Ouchi, K., and Akiyama, H., J. Ferment. Technol. Japan. 54,
    615 (1976)

16. Yoshizawa, K., J. Agr. Chem. Soc., Japan. 50, 115 (1976).

17. Yoshizawa, K., Hara, S., and Otsuka, K., J. Brew. Soc., Ja-
    pan. 61, 355 (1966).

18. Yoshizawa, K., J. Brew. Soc., Japan. 60, 240 (1965).

19. Koizumi, T., and Takeishi, M., <u>J. Brew. Soc., Japan</u>. 66, 251 (1971).

20. Ouchi, K., Takagishi, M., and Akiyama, H., <u>Abstracts of Papers, Annual Meeting of Society of Fermentation Technology, Japan</u>, 1976, p.35.

21. Robichon-Szulmajster, H.D., and Surdin-Kerjan, Y., in "The Yeasts" (A.H. Rose, and J.S. Harrison, Eds.), Vol. 2, p. 335. Academic Press, London and New York, 1971.

CONCENTRATION AND IDENTIFICATION OF TRACE
CONSTITUENTS IN ALCOHOLIC BEVERAGES

R. ter Heide, P.J. de Valois, J.Visser,
P.P.Jaegers, R.Timmer,
NAARDEN International N.V.

I. ABSTRACT

*Components contributing to the characteristic flavor of alco-
holic beverages are present in very low concentrations. Their
identification implied concentration to a level at which they can
be studied by spectroscopic methods. To balance the volatiles
lost during the extraction and distillation process, headspace
concentration techniques applied to the whole beverage were developed. As an example the analysis of COGNAC is discussed. Continuous liquid-liquid extraction of the beverage succeeded in the
isolation of the characteristic flavor almost free from ethanol
and water. The greater part of the amyl alcohols was distilled
off by rapid distillation. Distillation was continued using a
molecular still operating at low pressure. The distillate still
had all the characteristic organoleptic properties of the original beverage. Large scale liquid chromatography and subsequent
high pressure liquid chromatography were employed to achieve
fractions of graduated polarity. The most essential fractions
were analyzed by combination GC-MS. Individual components were
isolated by means of gas chromatography on packed and SCOT*

*columns followed by spectroscopic identification and final
confirmation by synthesis. Concentration of the headspace resulted in various fractions with reduced amounts of water, ethanol
and amyl alcohols. These fractions were subjected to combined
GC-MS. Over 300 components were found in cognac.*

II. INTRODUCTION

The purpose of our study was to develop a general method, including concentration and separation steps, which should be appli-
cable to every alcoholic beverage. It should lead to fractions of
desired organoleptic quality containing the characteristic components in concentrations high enough for spectrometric investigations. Usually, as is the case with most complex mixtures, components contributing to the characteristic flavor are present in
very minute quantities. It is therefore required to start with a
large amount of beverage.

To study the most volatile constituents headspace concentration techniques were developed.

As an example the analysis of cognac will be described. A
search of the literature concerning the analysis of cognac revealed that, with the exception of recent work of Tsantalis (1),
Schaefer and Timmer (2) and of Marche et al.(3), the reported investigations dealt with a limited number of constituents (4-53).
Direct headspace analysis was used by Dellweg et al.(54) to
characterize the volatiles of cognac.

III. EXPERIMENTAL

A. Sample

    A genuine French cognac, selected by a panel of experts and containing 40 vol % of ethanol was investigated.

B. Extraction

    465 l of cognac was diluted with an equal volume of water, that was purified over active carbon. The diluted cognac was continuously extracted during 24 hrs in a nitrogen atmosphere with pentane-dichloromethane 2:1 (v/v). The extraction was carried out in an extractor of 70 l capacity. The solvent evaporated at a rate of 18 l/hr and the bath temperature was 43°. After each extraction of 70 l of diluted cognac, the solvent was removed by careful distillation, using a 2-meter column containing Raschig rings of glass, at a reflux ratio of 1:5.
The distillate was adjusted to the ratio pentane-dichloromethane 2:1 by refractive index measurement and was used again for the extraction of a subsequent batch of 70 l of diluted cognac.
The residues from the packed column distillation were combined, dried over magnesium sulphate and freed from residual solvent by careful distillation through a Vigreux column.
As a result 690 g of extract was obtained.
The organoleptic quality was determined by dilution of an aliquot of the extract to its original volume with water and alcohol. With the exception of some lack in the top flavor, the extract appeared to be of good organoleptic quality.

C. Isolation of Acids and Phenols from the Extract

The procedure applied for the isolation and separation of the acids and phenols from the extract of cognac is depicted in Fig.1.

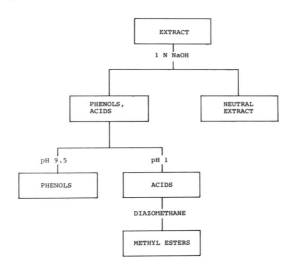

Fig. 1. *The isolation and separation of acids and phenols from the extract of cognac.*

The extract (600 g) was dissolved in 2 l of pentane and shaken at $0°$ with 5 x 100-ml portions of a 4 % sodium hydroxide solution, followed by 3 washings with 250 ml of water. The combined alkali layers were extracted with 5 x 100-ml portions of dichloromethane and the combined aqueous washings with 100 ml of dichloromethane. The dichloromethane extracts were added to the pentane solution whereafter the solvent was distilled off through a 2-meter column packed with Raschig rings of glass using a reflux ratio of 1:5, leaving 557 g of a neutral residue.

The combined aqueous phases were brought to pH 9.5 with dilute hydrochloric acid to liberate the phenols. They were extracted 5 times with dichloromethane. After drying the combined organic layers with magnesium sulphate the solvent was removed by distillation leaving 15 g of a phenolic fraction. This fraction was subjected to GC-MS analysis. The compounds identified are summarized in Table 1.

The acids were liberated from the remaining aqueous phase after addition of hydrochloric acid to pH 1. They were extracted 5 times with ether. The combined ether phases were dried over magnesium sulphate and concentrated by distillation. There remained 27.8 g of an acid fraction. After methylation with diazomethane the methyl esters were analyzed by GC-MS combination. The acids identified are mentioned in Table 1.

D. Distillation of the Neutral Extract

To concentrate the characteristic compounds of the neutral extract two distillation steps were employed. Firstly the greater part of the fusel alcohols was distilled off. In the second step the non-volatiles were removed by molecular distillation. A schematic representation is given in Fig.2.

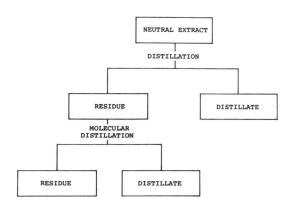

Fig.2. Concentration of the neutral extract by distillation.

1. Removal of the Fusel Alcohols

The neutral extract (557 g) was divided into 6 equal portions. Each portion was distilled through a Vigreux column of 25 cm length at a pressure of 2-3 mm Hg and a bath temperature of 18°. The distillate was collected in a flask cooled with CO_2-isopropanol, followed by 2 traps cooled with liquid nitrogen. The distillation was continued until most of the alcohols were collected. About 4.3% of the intake (24.3 g) remained as a residue.

The distillate was not further investigated because it appeared to be organoleptically of limited value.

2. Molecular Distillation of the Residue

The non-volatile constituents of 23.0 g of the distillation residue were removed by distillation in a molecular still operating at a pressure of 10^{-5} Torr. The distillation was carried out during 48 hrs at room temperature and continued for 16 hrs at 35°. About 79% (18.4 g) of distillate was collected in a flask cooled in liquid nitrogen.

The residue appeared to be less important with respect to the flavor and was therefore not further investigated.

The molecular distillate was diluted to its original volume with appropriate amounts of water, ethanol, isoamyl alcohol, acids and phenols. The beverage obtained was compared with the cognac investigated. The organoleptic properties were comparable as well as the strength of the flavor.

E. Liquid Chromatography of the Molecular Distillate

Because of its complexity the distillate obtained after molecular distillation was fractionated by two-steps liquid chromatography over silica gel. In the first step a crude separation was pursued, using large scale liquid chromatography. In a second

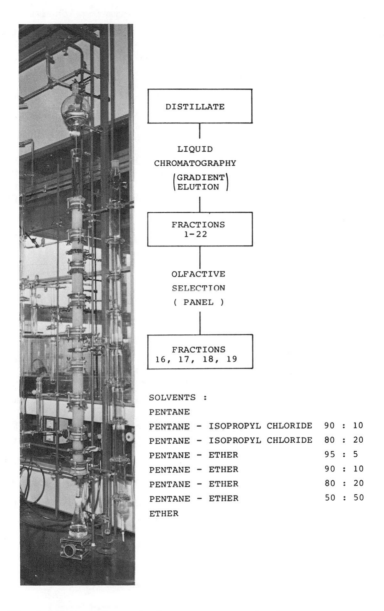

DISTILLATE

|
LIQUID
CHROMATOGRAPHY
(GRADIENT
ELUTION)

FRACTIONS
1-22

OLFACTIVE
SELECTION
(PANEL)

FRACTIONS
16, 17, 18, 19

SOLVENTS :
PENTANE
PENTANE - ISOPROPYL CHLORIDE   90 : 10
PENTANE - ISOPROPYL CHLORIDE   80 : 20
PENTANE - ETHER   95 : 5
PENTANE - ETHER   90 : 10
PENTANE - ETHER   80 : 20
PENTANE - ETHER   50 : 50
ETHER

Fig.3. Separation of the molecular distillate fraction of cognac by large scale liquid chromatography using stepwise gradient elution. A picture of the segmented column is shown as well as the solvents used for development.

step selected essential fractions were rechromatographed by high
pressure liquid chromatography.

Both methods will now be described separately.

1. *Large Scale Liquid Chromatography*

A crude separation of the distillate into fractions of different polarity was achieved by large scale liquid chromatography
using silica gel as an adsorbent. The apparatus used and a scheme
of the procedure, including the solvents used, are shown in Fig.3.

a. Preparation of the column. The column was built up with
8 segments of QVF glass parts (7" x 2"). It was completed with a
solvent containing segment and a collecting segment provided with
a Fischer and Porter PTFE needle valve. The segments were leak-
free connected with the aid of a PTFE-ring and tightened with
screws (see Fig.3). Silica gel (Merck, type 60, code 7754) was
sieved into fractions of 120–140, 100–120 and 80–100 mesh. Of each
size a 450 g portion was thoroughly mixed with 1 l of ether and
stored overnight. Starting with the smallest particle fraction
each portion was put into the column as a slurry in ether. After
settling, the ether in the column was displaced by elution with
4 l of pentane with a flow rate of 10 ml per min. The column was
now ready for use. The free volume is about 2 l.

b. Development. The molecular distillate (18.4 g) was dissolved in a few ml of pentane and divided homogeneously over the
top of the column. The column was developed with solvents of increasing solvent strength, differing by about 0.05 ε^o units. The
solvents are mentioned in Fig.3. Of each solvent 660 ml was used.
Collection was done as follows:

- the first 1980 ml was discarded (free volume of the column).

- 14 fractions of 230 ml were collected.

Subsequently each segment of the column was continuously extracted
with ether in a Soxhlet extraction apparatus during 16 hrs. Totally 22 fractions were obtained. Each fraction was tested olfacti-
vely by a panel of experts. Combined fractions numbered 16–19

resulted in a product which contained all the characteristic flavor elements of cognac. It was decided to select these fractions for further analysis. These fractions, weighting 9.18 g, accounted for about 20 ppm in the original cognac sample. They were concentrated by careful distillation before subsequent separation.

2. High Pressure Liquid Chromatography

The 4 selected fractions were separated further by high pressure liquid chromatography, using a 50 cm x 0.375" o.d. column, filled with 10 micron particles of silica gel (Micropak column, Varian Ass.). The column was installed in a liquid chromatograph, type ALC-201 (Waters, Ass.), provided with a differential refractometer and a Model 6000 solvent delivery system. The eluting solvents were mixtures of pentane and ether. The lower fraction number (No.16) required the least amount of ether to effect separation. The solvent mixtures were saturated for 50% with water. The flow rate was in all cases 1.5 ml per min. A scheme is given in Fig.4.

HIGH PRESSURE LIQUID CHROMATOGRAPHY

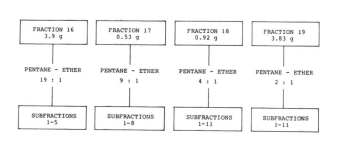

Fig.4. High Pressure Liquid Chromatography of 4 selected cognac fractions.

Totally 35 subfractions were collected.

F. Analysis of the 35 Subfractions

The subfractions were analyzed by combination GC-MS. The gas chromatograph, a Varian Aerograph Model 1220, was equipped with a 50 m x 0.75 mm i.d. glass SCOT column. This column was coated with suspension of 3 g of Ucon 50 LB-550X, 15 mg of Aerosil, Type R-972 (Degussa) and 3 g of ANM rice powder (Neckar Chemie) in 29 g of CCl_4 using the dynamic coating method with a constant flow of 2 cm per sec. The column temperature was programmed from 70 to 170° at a rate of 1° per min and held at upper limit. The helium flow was adjusted at 3.5 ml per min. The SCOT column was coupled by means of an all glass restriction (55) allowing a helium flow rate of 0.5-1 ml per min to the inlet of a single focusing 90° magnetic sector field mass spectrometer (Varian-MAT, CH-5, Bremen, W.Germany). The ionization chamber operated at 70 eV electron beam energy.

Components, which could not be identified by mass spectrometric analysis, were trapped from SCOT columns of 0.75 mm i.d., coated with different liquid phases. They were subjected to infrared analysis using a Perkin Elmer 457 grating spectrometer. Trace components were measured in ultramicrocavity cells (Barnes Engineering Co.), thickness 0.5 mm.

NMR spectra were determined on a Varian A 60 A instrument in CCl_4 solution using tetramethylsilane as an internal standard.

The compounds identified are summarized in Table 1.

G. Concentration of 1000 l of Headspace of Cognac

It was investigated whether concentration of large quantities of headspace (1000 l) would lead to identification of characteristic components which escaped notice during the extract analysis.

TABLE 1

Compounds identified in the Extract of Cognac

==

Compound	*Lit.*	Compound	*Lit.*

ACETALS

1-Ethoxy-1-(2-methylbutoxy)ethane	+
1-Ethoxy-1-(3-methylbutoxy)ethane	+
1-Ethoxy-1-hexoxyethane	−
1-Ethoxy-1-(3-hexenoxy)ethane	−
1-Benzyloxy-1-ethoxyethane	−
1-Ethoxy-1-(2-phenylethoxy)ethane	−
1,1-Di-(2-methylbutoxy)ethane	−
1-(2-Methylbutoxy)-1-(3-methylbutoxy)ethane	−
1,1-Di-(3-methylbutoxy)ethane	+
1,1,2-Triethoxyethane	−
1,1,3-Triethoxypropane	+
1,3-Diethoxy-1-(3-methylbutoxy)-propane	−
1,1,3-Triethoxy-2-methylpropane	−
1,1,3-Triethoxybutane	−
1,1,-Diethoxy-3-methylbutane	+
1,1,-Dimethoxyhexane	−
1,1,-Diethoxyhexane	−
1,1,-Diethoxyphenylethane	−

ACIDS

Acetic acid	+
Propanoic acid	+
2-Methylpropanoic acid	+
Butanoic acid	+
2-Methylbutanoic acid	−
3-Methylbutanoic acid	+
Pentanoic acid	+
Hexanoic acid	+
2-Methylhexanoic acid	−
Heptanoic acid	+
Octanoic acid	+
Nonanoic acid	+
Decanoic acid	+
Dodecanoic acid	+
Tridecanoic acid	+
Tetradecanoic acid	+
Hexadecanoic acid	+
(Z)-9-Hexadecenoic acid	+
Heptadecanoic acid	+
Octadecanoic acid	+
(Z)-9-Octadecenoic acid	+
(Z,Z)-9,12-Octadecadienoic acid	+
Benzoic acid	+
Phenylacetic acid	−
3-Phenylpropanoic acid	−
Salicylic acid	−
Lactic acid	+

ALCOHOLS

Ethanol	+
2-Methyl-1-propanol	+
2-Methyl-1-butanol	+
3-Methyl-1-butanol	+
1-Pentanol	+
2-Pentanol	+
3-Pentanol	+
3-Methyl-1-pentanol	−
4-Methyl-1-pentanol	−
1-Hexanol	+
3-Hexanol	−
1-Heptanol	+
2-Heptanol	−
3-Heptanol	−
4-Heptanol	−
2-Ethyl-1-hexanol	−
1-Octanol	+
2-Octanol	−
3-Octanol	+
2,6,-Dimethyl-4-heptanol	−
1-Nonanol	+
2-Nonanol	I
1-Decanol	+
2-Undecanol	+
1-Dodecanol	−
1-Tetradecanol	−
(E)-2-Hexen-1-ol	+
(Z)-2-Hexen-1-ol	−
(E)-3-Hexen-1-ol	+
(Z)-3-Hexen-1-ol	+
(E)-2-Hepten-1-ol	−
(E)-2-Octen-1-ol	−
1-Octen-3-ol	−
(E)-2-Nonen-1-ol	−
9-Decen-1-ol	−
(E)-6-Undecen-2-ol	−
(Z)-6-Undecen-2-ol	−
Linalool	+
Myrcenol	−
Citronellol	+
Nerol	+
Geraniol	+
3-Terpinen-1-ol	−
trans-β-Terpineol	−
γ-Terpineol	−
cis-Carvotanacetol	−
trans-1(7),8-p-Menthadien-2-ol	−
Isopulegol	−
1-Terpinen-4-ol	−

TABLE 1 (Continued)

===

Compound	Lit.	Compound	Lit.

ALCOHOLS (Continued)

		ESTERS (Continued)	
α-Terpineol	–	2-Phenylethyl formate	–
1-p-Menthen-9-ol	–	Ethyl acetate	+
Borneol	–	3-Methylbutyl acetate	+
Isoborneol	–	Hexyl acetate	+
trans-Pinocarveol	–	(E)-3-Hexenyl acetate	–
Myrtenol	–	(Z)-3-Hexenyl acetate	–
endo-Fenchol	–	Octyl acetate	+
Nerolidol	–	Decyl acetate	+
α-Cadinol	–	Linalyl acetate	–
m-Cymen-8-ol	–	Benzyl acetate	+
p-Cymen-8-ol	–	2-Phenylethyl acetate	+
α-Methylbenzyl alcohol	–	2-Phenylethyl 2-methylpropanoate	–
2-Phenylethyl alcohol	+	Butyl butanoate	+
Cuminyl alcohol	–	2-Methylbutyl butanoate	–
		3-Methylbutyl butanoate	+
ALDEHYDES		2-Phenylethyl butanoate	–
Hexanal	+	Ethyl 2-methylbutanoate	–
Heptanal	+	Ethyl 3-methylbutanoate	+
Octanal	+	2-Phenylethyl 3-methylbutanoate	–
Nonanal	+	Ethyl pentanoate	+
Decanal	+	Ethyl hexanoate	+
Undecanal	+	Propyl hexanoate	+
(Z)-2-Methyl-2-buten-1-al	–	2-Methylpropyl hexanoate	+
3-Methyl-2-buten-1-al	–	3-Methylbutyl hexanoate	+
(E)-2-Penten-1-al	+	2-Phenylethyl hexanoate	+
(E)-2-Methyl-2-penten-1-al	–	(E)-Ethyl 2-hexenoate	–
(E)-2-Hexen-1-al	–	(E,E)-Ethyl 2,4-hexadienoate	–
(E)-2-Hepten-1-al	–	Ethyl heptanoate	+
(E,E)-2,4-Heptadien-1-al	–	Methyl octanoate	+
(E)-2-Octen-1-al	–	Ethyl octanoate	+
(E)-2-Nonen-1-al	–	Propyl octanoate	+
(E,E)-2,4-Nonadien-1-al	–	2-Methylpropyl octanoate	+
(E,E)-2,4-Decadien-1-al	–	2-Methylbutyl octanoate	–
1-Cyclohexene-1-carboxaldehyde	–	3-Methylbutyl octanoate	+
2,2,3-Trimethyl-3-cyclopentenyl-		Ethyl nonanoate	+
1-acetaldehyde	–	Methyl decanoate	+
Phellandral	–	Ethyl decanoate	+
Benzaldehyde	+	Propyl decanoate	+
2-Methylbenzaldehyde	–	2-Methylpropyl decanoate	+
3-Methylbenzaldehyde	–	2-Methylbutyl decanoate	–
2,4-dimethylbenzaldehyde	–	3-Methylbutyl decanoate	+
Phenylacetaldehyde	–	Ethyl 9-decenoate	–
Cuminaldehyde	–	Methyl dodecanoate	+
Cinnamaldehyde	+	Ethyl dodecanoate	+
p-Anisaldehyde	–	Ethyl tetradecanoate	+
		Methyl benzoate	–
ESTERS		Ethyl benzoate	+
Ethyl formate	+	Methyl phenylacetate	–
3-Methylbutyl formate	+	Ethyl phenylacetate	–
Pentyl formate	–	Ethyl 2-phenylpropanoate	–

TABLE 1 (Continued)

Compound	Lit.	Compound	Lit.
ESTERS (Continued)		**KETONES** (Continued)	
Ethyl cinnamate	+	2-Tridecanone	+
Diethyl malonate	–	(E)-3-Penten-2-one	–
Ethyl methyl succinate	–	6-Methyl-5-hepten-2-one	–
Diethyl succinate	+	(E)-6-Methyl-3,5-heptadien-2-one	–
Ethyl propyl succinate	–	(Z)-6-Methyl-3,5-heptadien-2-one	–
Ethyl 2-Methylpropyl succinate	–	(E)-3-Nonen-2-one	–
Butyl ethyl succinate	–	(E)-2-Nonen-4-one	–
Ethyl 3-methylbutyl succinate	–	(E)-2-Undecen-4-one	–
Ethyl pentyl succinate	–	α-Ionone	+
Ethyl hexyl succinate	–	β-Ionone	+
Diethyl methylsuccinate	–	(E)-1-(6,6-Dimethyl-2-methylene-	
Diethyl glutarate	–	3-cyclohexenyl)-1-buten-3-one	–
Diethyl suberate	–	(E)-1-(2,3,6-Trimethylphenyl)-	
Diethyl azelate	–	1-buten-3-one	–
Dimethyl phtalate	–	(E)-β-Damascenone	+
Diethyl phtalate	–	(Z)-β-Damascenone	–
		(Z)-1-(2,3,6-Trimethylphenyl)-	
ETHERS		2-buten-1-one	–
1,4-Cineole	–	Acetophenone	+
1,8-Cineole	–	3-Phenyl-2-propanone	–
Pinol	–	4-Methylacetophenone	–
2-Methyltetrahydrofuran	–	2-Acetyl-p-cymene	–
cis-Rose oxide	–	Carvone	–
trans-Rose oxide	–	Carvenone	–
2-Isopropenyl-5-methyl-5-vinyl-		Pinocarvone	–
tetrahydrofuran	–	Geranylacetone	–
Nerol oxide	–	Camphor	–
Ethyl furfuryl ether	–	Fenchone	–
Ethyl geranyl ether	–	1-Indanone	–
Anisyl ethyl ether	–	3,5,5,-Trimethyl-	
1-Ethoxy-1-(4-methoxyphenyl)ethane	–	2-cyclohexene-1,4-dione	–
o-Dimethoxybenzene	–		
m-Dimethoxybenzene	–	**LACTONES**	
(E)-1-(2,3,6-Trimethylphenyl)-		cis-β-Methyl-γ-octalactone	+
3-ethoxy-1-butene	+	trans-β-Methyl-γ-octalactone	+
Methyleugenol	–	β-Methyl-γ-nonalactone	–
trans-Edulan	–		
4,4a-Epoxyedulan	–	**PHENOLS**	
6,7,8,8a-Tetrahydro-2,5,5,8a-		Phenol	+
tetramethyl-5H-1-benzopyran	–	4-Ethylphenol	–
		4-Ethylguaiacol	+
KETONES		4-Propylguaiacol	+
4-Methyl-2-pentanone	–	Carvacrol	–
2-Heptanone	+	Eugenol	–
2-Octanone	+	Vanillin	+
3-Octanone	+	Ethyl vanillyl ether	–
2-Nonanone	+		
2-Decanone	+	**MISCELLANEOUS**	
2-Undecanone	+	2-Furancarboxylic acid	–
2-Dodecanone	+	Methyl 2-furoate	–

TABLE 1 (Continued)

===

Compound	Lit.	Compound	Lit.

MISCELLANEOUS (Continued)

MISCELLANEOUS (Continued)

Compound	Lit.	Compound	Lit.
Ethyl 2-furoate	+	5-Methyl-2-thiophenecarbox-	
2-Methylpropyl 2-furoate	−	aldehyde	−
3-Methylbutyl 2-furoate	−	Ethyl 2-thiophenecarboxylate	−
(E)-Ethyl 3-(2-furyl)-2-propenoate	−	2-(Methylthio)benzothiazole	−
2-Acetylfuran	−	3-Ethoxy-1-propanal	−
2-Propionylfuran	−	2-Ethoxybenzaldehyde	−
5-Methyl-2-acetylfuran	−	1,1-Diethoxy-2-propanone	−
2-Acetyl-5-ethylfuran	−	1-(2,6,6-Trimethyl-1,3-cyclo-	
2-Acetyl-4,5-dimethylfuran	−	hexadien-1-yl)-3-ethoxy-	
1-(2-Furyl)-2-buten-1-one	−	butan-1-one	−
1-(2-Furyl)-1-penten-3-one	−	4-Hydroxy-4-methyl-2-pentanone	−
2-Furaldehyde	+	Phenylacetonitrile	−
3-Methyl-2-furaldehyde	−	Ethyl lactate	+
5-Methyl-2-furaldehyde	+	2-Methylpropyl lactate	+
cis-Linalool oxide	+	Butyl lactate	+
trans-Linalool oxide	+	3-Methylbutyl lactate	+
3-Acetyl-4-hydroxy-6-methyl-		Hexyl lactate	−
2H-pyran-2-one	−	(Z)-3-Hexenyl lactate	−
1-Methylpyrrole-2-carboxaldehyde	−	Ethyl 2-hydroxybutanoate	−
1-Ethylpyrrole-2-carboxaldehyde	−	Ethyl 2-hydroxy-4-methyl-	
1-(3-Methylbutyl)pyrrole-		pentanoate	+
2-carboxaldehyde	−	Ethyl 3-ethoxypropanoate	−
2,5-Dimethyl-3-propylpyrazine	−	Methyl salicylate	+
2-Thiophenecarboxaldehyde	−	Ethyl salicylate	+

Lit.: + *previously reported as a cognac component*
       − *first report in cognac*

The applied 3-steps concentration procedure is schematically depicted in Fig.5.

Because of its high temperature stability Tenax GC was chosen as
an adsorbent.

In a cylindrical sample container 1000 l of nitrogen at a flow
of 1 l/min was passed over 2 l of cognac into a glass tube of
15 cm length and 17 mm o.d., packed with 4.3 g of Tenax GC and
held at room temperature. All polar compounds like water, ethanol
and amyl alcohols were not adsorbed under these conditions. Ethyl
butyrate having a retention volume of 250 l/g of Tenax will just
not leave the column.

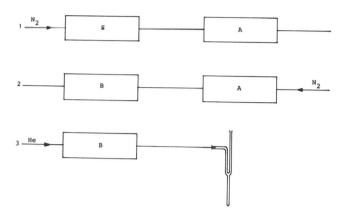

Fig. 5. Concentration of 1000 l of headspace of cognac by a 3-steps adsorption-desorption procedure.

S. *Cylindrical sample container of 60 cm length and i.d. of 10 cm.*

A. *Glass tube (length 15 cm, i.d. 15 mm) packed with 4.3 g of Tenax GC.*

B. *Glass tube (length 15 cm, i.d. 8 mm) packed with 0.46 g of Tenax GC.*

1. *Passage of 1000 l of N_2 (flow: 1 l/min) over 2 l of cognac, contained in sample tube S. Collection of the components on column A. A and S are at room temperature.*

2. *Backflush from tube A at 200° with 1 l of N_2 (flow: 100 ml/min) into tube B, kept at room temperature.*

3. *Transfer of enriched components in reverse direction from tube B at 200° with 60 ml He (flow: 5 ml/min) into a wide bore glass capillary trap (i.d.2 mm), partly immersed in liquid N_2.*

To concentrate the components as a small plug the contents of column A were backflushed at 200° into column B (length 15 cm, i.d. 8 mm), packed with 0.46 g of Tenax GC, which is held at room temperature (see also Fig.5).
From this tube the headspace components were transported in

reverse direction at 200° with 60 ml of dried helium (flow: 5
ml/min) into a wide bore glass capillary trap (i.d. 2 mm),
partly immersed in liquid nitrogen. The condensate was subjected
to GC-MS analysis.

Compounds having up to 16 carbon atoms were present in the concentrate. 65 components were identified from their mass spectra. The
headspace concentrate revealed no characteristic constituents,
which were not found before in the extract.

H. Concentration of 90 l of Headspace of Cognac

   The extraction and separation procedures described before
accounted for the loss of some of the very volatile flavor compounds. To balance the whole flavor they were separately collected by headspace concentration, which avoid the necessity of
using solvents.

The principal problem with headspace concentration of beverages
is the presence of relatively large amounts of water and ethanol
vapor. Water vapor was eliminated by application of a tandem-wise
arrangement of adsorption tubes, containing different amounts of
Chromosorb 102, thereby taking advantage of the low retention
volume of water. Ethanol vapor was retained by a diglycerol
column. In all 90 l of headspace was concentrated in batches of
10 l. Fig.6 shows a scheme of the 7-steps arrangement used for
the collection of headspace.

   A stream of 10 l of pure nitrogen (flow: 100 ml/min) was
passed over 2 l of cognac in a cylindrical container S of 60 cm
length and an i.d. of 10 cm, held at room temperature. The vapors
were collected on 45 g of Chromosorb 102, being freshly conditioned overnight at 180° in a nitrogen flow of 300 ml/min.
The adsorbent was contained in a spiralized glass column A of
3 m x 8 mm i.d., held at room temperature.

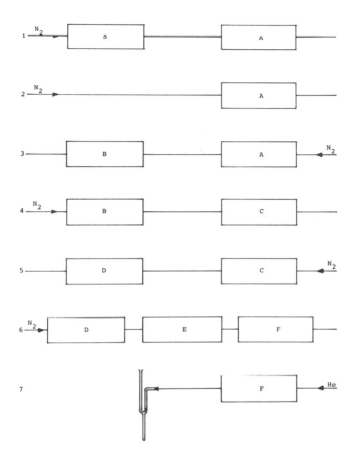

Fig.6. Block diagrams of a 7-steps system for the concentration of 90 l of headspace of cognac with removal of water and
ethanol.

S. Cylindrical sample container of 60 cm length and i.d. of
10 cm.

A,B. Spiralized glass column (3 m x 8 mm i.d.), packed with
45 g of Chromosorb 102.

C,D. Adsorption tube (15 cm x 15 mm i.d.), packed with 8 g of
Chromosorb 102.

Fig.6. Continued.

   E. Spiralized glass column (2 m x 4 mm i.d.), filled with 5 g
   of Diglycerol coated on 15 g of 60-80 mesh Embacel support.
   F. Adsorption tube (15 cm x 8 mm i.d.), containing 1.7 g of
   Chromosorb 102.

   1. Passage of 10 l of N$_2$ (flow: 100 ml/min) over 2 l of cognac
in container S into adsorption tube A. A and S are at room
temperature.

   2. Elution of water by passage of 10 l of N$_2$ through column A
at room temperature.

   3. Backflush from column A at 150° with 2 l of N$_2$ (flow: 100
ml/min) into adsorption tube B at room temperature.
Procedures 1 to 3 were carried out 9 times so 9 x 10 l of head-
space volatiles were collected in column B.

   4. Elution of enriched components from column B at 150° in re-
verse direction with 2 l of N$_2$ (flow: 100 ml/min) into adsorption
tube C, kept at room temperature.

   5. Concentration of the headspace volatiles in a relatively
small plug by transporting them at 150° from tube C in reverse
direction with 360 ml of N$_2$ (flow: 20 ml/min) into tube D, kept
at room temperature.

   6. Backflush from tube D at 60° with 360 ml N$_2$ (flow: 20 ml/min)
into the diglycerol column E, also held at 60°. The almost ethanol
free concentrate is collected in tube F at room temperature.

   7. Transfer of headspace concentrate in reverse direction at
150° with 50 ml of He (flow: 5 ml/min) from tube F into a wide
bore glass capillary tube (i.d. 2 mm), partly immersed in liquid
nitrogen.

In the same direction 10 l of pure nitrogen was passed through
column A, which resulted in elution of most of the adsorbed
water.
The retention volume of water is about 110 ml, of ethanal 540 ml,
of methanol 590 ml and of ethanol 2400 ml per gram Chromosorb 102

at 25°. The retention volume of ethanal was chosen as a limiting value. For safety reasons only 20 l of nitrogen was passed through 45 g of Chromosorb.

It was found that due to tailing effects not all of the water was removed by a single passing through column A. Therefore also the other adsorption tubes were eluted with a calculated surplus of nitrogen in order to remove residual water.

Subsequently the volatiles of column A were backflushed at 150° in an air thermostate with 2 l of nitrogen (flow: 100 ml/min) into adsorption column B (at room temperature). This column has the same dimensions and contents as column A.

Ethanal was eluted from column A at 150° with 1.5 l of nitrogen. Thus the surplus of nitrogen was 0.5 l.

Column B was used for the collection of 9 batches of 10 l of headspace of cognac by application of steps 1 to 3.

After this enrichment the volatiles were eluted from column B in reverse direction (step 4, Fig.6.) at 150° with 2 l of nitrogen into adsorption tube C, packed with 8 g of Chromosorb 102 and kept at room temperature.

To concentrate the volatiles as a small plug and to remove possible last traces of water column C was fitted in an aluminum block provided with 4 cartridge heaters and the volatile material was backflushed at 150° with 360 ml of nitrogen and a flow of 20 ml/min. The vapors were collected on an identical column D, held at room temperature.

In the next step a diglycerol column E (2 m x 4 mm i.d. spiralized, glass), filled with 5 g of diglycerol coated on 15 g 60-80 mesh Embacel support was introduced to retain ethanol.

Taken into account the retention volume of ethanol on diglycerol, being 380 ml at 60°, backflushing of the volatiles from column D at 60° with 360 ml of nitrogen (flow: 20 ml/min) through column E (60°) into column F, containing 1.7 g of Chromosorb 102 (room temperature) resulted in a concentrate, which contained only minute amounts of ethanol.

In the last step the volatiles were condensed in a wide bore capillary tube (i.d. 2 mm and at -196°), by passing 50 ml of super-dry helium with a flow of 5 ml/min in reverse direction at 150° through column F. It was found that the helium gas from the cylinder could be dried effectively by leading it through an U-shaped tube, filled with 2 g of gelatin powder (Bacto gelatin, Difco certified) and cooled at -196°.

The headspace concentrate was analyzed by combined GC-MS as described earlier. The compounds identified are summarized in Table 2.

TABLE 2

Headspace Volatiles of Cognac

Compound	Lit.	Compound	Lit.
1,1-Diethoxymethane	−	3-Methylbutyl formate	+
1,1-Diethoxyethane	+	Methyl acetate	+
1-Ethoxy-1-propoxyethane	−	Ethyl acetate	+
1-Ethoxy-1-(2-methylpropoxy)ethane	−	Propyl acetate	+
1,1-Diethoxypropane	+	2-Methylpropyl acetate	+
1,1-Diethoxy-2-methylpropane	+	3-Methylbutyl acetate	+
Ethanol	+	Ethyl propanoate	+
Ethanal	+	Ethyl 2-methylpropanoate	+
Propanal	+	Ethyl butanoate	+
2-Methyl-1-propanal	−	Ethyl 2-methylbutanoate	−
2-Methyl-2-propen-1-al	−	Ethyl 3-methylbutanoate	+
2-Methyl-1-butanal	+	Acetone	+
3-Methyl-1-butanal	+	Butanone	+
Methyl formate	+	3-Methyl-2-butanone	−
Ethyl formate	+	2-Pentanone	+
2-Methylpropyl formate	−	2-Hexanone	+

Lit.: + previously reported as a cognac component
        - first report in cognac

IV. RESULTS AND DISCUSSION

To concentrate characteristic volatiles of alcoholic beverages at first it is necessary to remove water and ethanol selectively from the sample. In our experience this can be successfully achieved by extraction with volatile solvents. Optimum
conditions were determined using model experiments in a reduced
scale extraction apparatus. A mixture of pentane and dichloromethane (2 : 1) distilling as an azeotrope at 31-32° was preferred as an extraction solvent since it gives high flavor yield.
It appeared that extraction with 6 times the volume of diluted
cognac was necessary to obtain an extract almost free from water
and ethanol having good organoleptic properties.

Because of the relatively high concentration of acids the
extract was neutralized prior to fractionation. The alkali
treatment of the extract did not damage the flavor as was established by organoleptic evaluation of the combined acid-
phenolic fraction and the neutral extract.

The neutral extract contained considerable amounts of methyl-
butanols. Distilling the neutral extract from 4.3% of a residu
had as a result that the concentration of the characteristic
flavor compounds was markedly increased. A further concentration
of the flavor was achieved by removal of the non-volatiles (about
20% of the intake) from the residue by molecular distillation,
giving a distillate that served as a basic material for fractionation by liquid chromatography. In view of its complexity and the
large range of polarities involved, it was necessary to utilize
gradient elution. Solvents were used exhibiting an increase of
solvent strength by 0.05 ε° units. The crude liquid
chromatographic separation was carried out in a segmented column
to avoid a prolonged elution procedure. It appeared that the
non-polar fraction and the fractions containing the very polar
compounds gave only minimal contribution to the cognac aroma and
they were for that reason not examined. The fractions numbered

16-19, present in a concentration of about 20 ppm in the cognac sample, contained according to our experts all the characteristic features. Due to the complexity of these fractions further separation was needed. Application of high pressure liquid chromatography using 10 micron particles of silica gel resulted in a subfractionation into 35 fractions. They were all subjected to GC-MS analysis.

By utilizing the aforementioned separation steps and by the use of glass capillary SCOT columns for the gas chromatographic separations confusion due to peak overlap in the GC-MS system was reduced to a minimum.

The components identified in the extract of cognac are listed in Table 1. Many of these compounds have not been reported before as cognac constituents. These compounds include 13 acetals, 5 acids, 38 alcohols, 19 aldehydes, 33 esters, 18 ethers, 23 ketones, 1 lactone, 4 phenols and 32 miscellaneous compounds. The identification of the components was based on comparison of their respective mass spectral data and retention times with those of authentic reference compounds, which were obtained from reliable commercial sources or were synthesized for the purpose of this investigation. The structures of the synthesized products were substantiated by spectral analysis.

20 Components were isolated from appropriate fractions utilizing SCOT columns, analogous to those used in the combination GC-MS in order to make their location easier. They were analyzed by infrared and/or NMR spectroscopy.

In our experience, in particular when dealing with products hard to extract the concentration of 1000 l of headspace on Tenax GC adsorbent can give valuable information about the vapor composition of the sample in a relatively short time hereby eliminating the use of solvents. Application of this procedure being schematically shown in Fig. 5, to cognac did not reveal any components that were not found already in the extract of cognac.

65 Components were identified from their mass spectra. Major

compounds were ethyl butanoate, 3-methylbutyl acetate, ethyl
lactate, 2-furaldehyde, ethyl hexanoate, ethyl octanoate, ethyl
decanoate and ethyl dodecanoate.

During the extraction-distillation steps some of the most
volatile constituents of cognac got lost by evaporation. For
their identification a headspace concentration technique was
developed. The presence of water in the condensate results in
much lower detection limits of other compounds and sometimes in a
two-layer condensate. Because insertion of drying tubes between
the adsorption columns may lead to adsorption of flavor compounds
(56) water was removed by making use of its low retention volume
on Chromosorb 102. Using a tandem-wise arrangement of tubes with
different amounts of adsorbent and by using a surplus of nitrogen
in the elution steps water could be completely removed. Ethanol
was retained, due to its high retention volume, on diglycerol.
Volatiles of interest passed the diglycerol column as was checked
with synthetic mixtures.

In the last step of the procedure (see Fig. 6) superdry helium
gas must be used as a carrier gas at a low flow rate in order to
obtain a dry condensate in a high yield. In accordance with ex-
periences of Szymanski and Amabile (57) gelatin was found to be
a powerful desiccant, especially when used at low temperature.
GC-MS analysis of the condensate revealed 32 components being
identified from the mass spectra by comparison with those of authentic reference samples followed by verification of GC retention times on capillary columns. The constituents are listed
in Table 2. Seven of the listed compounds were also found in the
extract mainly because of their high concentrations in the cognac
sample.

Totally the analysis of both extract and headspace resulted
in the identification of 339 constituents of which 193 were newly
found in cognac.

The chemical groups will now be discussed separately (see Table 1
and 2).

The 24 acetals found in cognac are for the greater part derived from ethanal. The unsaturated 1-ethoxy-1-(3-hexenoxy)-
ethane was tentatively identified on the basis of the mass
spectrum. No reference substance was available. Its presence is
not surprising because of the relatively high concentration of
3-hexen-1-ol. The isomeric 1-ethoxy-1-(2-hexenoxy)ethane reported
by Marche et al. (3) was not found in the fractions analyzed. The
structures of 1-benzyloxy-1-ethoxy-ethane, 1,1,3-triethoxy-
propane, 1,1,3-triethoxy-2-methylpropane and 1,1,3-triethoxy-
butane were derived from their MS and infrared spectra.

Most of the 27 acids, identified as methyl esters by GC-MS
were already reported as cognac constituents (2,3,12,21,22,27,39,
42). Most abundant acids are the homologous acids with an even
number of carbon atoms C_2-C_{12}. Also 2-methylpropanoic acid,
2-methylbutanoic acid and 3-methylbutanoic acid are present in
relatively high concentrations. The higher fatty acids from
tetradecanoic acid were identified on the basis of their GC-
retention times by comparison with authentic reference samples.

As was expected the 63 alcohols characterized were almost
exclusively present in the most polar fraction 19. Of the 11
straight chain unsaturated alcohols only 2-hexen-1-ol (3) and
3-hexen-1-ol (3,45) were reported earlier as cognac components.
Of these, the unsaturated alcohols (Z)-3-hexen-1-ol, (E)-2-hexen-
1-ol and 1-octen-3-ol are predominant constituents. The 6-undecen-
2-ol isomers were isolated from fraction 19. Their structures
were elucidated by infrared analysis and confirmed by synthesis.
With the exception of linalool, citronellol, α-terpineol and
nerolidol the 21 terpenic alcohols occur in very small quantities
in cognac (below 0.01 ppm).

An interesting group of compounds are the aldehydes of which
28 were found in the extract and 6 by headspace analysis. Table 1
and 2 show that 21 of these were newly found in cognac. Many
unsaturated straight chain aldehydes are included. Because of
their powerful odors they are indispensible constituents of

cognac, in spite of the fact that they occur in rather low
concentrations.

There were 77 esters found in our sample of cognac, the most
volatile ones being identified in the headspace concentrate
(Table 2).

Ethyl 9-decenoate was isolated by preparative GC. The structure
was confirmed by synthesis. It is reported for the first time in
cognac, but already known as a component of whisky (58,59), wine
(60) and of beer (61). It has a pleasant and strong, somewhat
fatty odor. Noteworthy is also the presence of ethyl 2-hexenoate
and ethyl 2,4-hexadienoate. The first of these has recently been
detected in wine (62).

Of the nine succinic esters diethyl succinate occurs by far the
highest concentration.

The presence of traces of phtalates often assigned as artefacts
may not be surprising since the report of phtalic acid in cognac
(3). In our acid fraction phtalic acid could not be detected.
The methyl and ethyl ester were reported as components of whisky
(63,64).

Except the recently reported presence in cognac of (E)-1-
(2,3,6-trimethylphenyl)-3-ethoxy-1-butene (53) the 19 ethers
listed in table 1 were found for the first time in cognac. The
presence of the reported ether (53) could be confirmed by
spectroscopic analysis and by synthesis. In addition to GC-MS
analysis the structures of pinol and trans-edulan were elucidated
by infrared spectroscopy and by synthesis. A compound isolated
from fraction 18 having a molecular weight of 208 (from mass
spectrum) was investigated by infrared spectroscopy. The spectrum
showed great resemblance with that of edulan. Additional bands in
the 800-950 cm^{-1} region indicate an ether group. An epoxy group
was very likely. A 2-3 epoxy function would result in a ketal
group which is not likely from the IR spectrum. An epoxy in 4-4a
position was suggested by comparison with the spectrum of edulan
and was based on the absence of a band at 770 cm^{-1}, which is very

likely resulting from the 4-4a double bond in edulan and moreover on the presence of the (Z)-7-8-double bond at 727 cm^{-1}. Characteristic bands in the IR spectrum are at (CCl_4): 3068, 3025, 2835, 1661, 1475, 1436, 1426, 1395, 1385, 1373, 1365, 1327, 1166, 926, 864 cm^{-1} and in CS_2 at: 825, 748, and 727 cm^{-1}. On the basis of these data 4,4a-epoxyedulan was the proposed structure.

The rose oxides and neroloxide, a dihydropyran derivative, have recently been reported as constituents of wine (65).

The ketones represent another group of components with interesting organoleptic properties. Twenty-three of them were newly found in cognac.

Apart from the well known compounds α- and β-ionone, reported earlier (3,43), two analogous components were isolated from the extract. They were analyzed by MS and IR spectrometry. One of them appeared to be (E)-1-(6,6-dimethyl-2-methylene-3-cyclohexenyl)-1-buten-3-one (γ-dehydroionone), the structure of which was confirmed by synthesis. The other compound was found to be (E)-1-(2,3,6-trimethylphenyl)-1-buten-3-one, an aromatic ionone derivative. Also in this case synthesis of the product confirmed the structure.

Additionally an aromatic isomer of damascenone was isolated by preparative gas chromatography. The proposed structure (Z)-1-(2,3,6-trimethylphenyl)-2-buten-1-one was based on careful interpretation of mass and infrared spectrum. The mass spectrum showed strong resemblance with the (E)-isomer of which an authentic reference sample was available. Relevant IR wavelengths are at (CCl_4): 1704, 1673, 1616, 1418, 1381, 1358, 1265, 1209, 1171, and in CS_2 at: 812, 806, 766, and 724 cm^{-1}.

(E)-Damascenone was recently detected in cognac (3) and also in rum (66). On account of the great resemblance of the mass spectrum with the (E)-isomer and the expected GC retention time it is assumed that also the isomeric (Z)-damascenone may be present in cognac. This is supported by literature data (3,66). A reference sample was not yet available.

Apart from 3-penten-2-one, being reported as a rum constituent (67), and acetophenone (3) the remaining aliphatic unsaturated ketones, the terpenic ketones and also indanone and 3,5,5-tri-methyl-2-cyclohexene-1,4-dione were to our best knowledge newly found in alcoholic beverages.

Three lactones were found. The isomeric β-methyl-γ-octa-lactones were reported by various authors (3,48,52). Some investigators are of the opinion that the cis-isomer is eluted first from the gas chromatographic column (48,68,69). We have studied the NMR-spectra of the pure synthesized diastereomers and observed that in the spectrum of the compound with the largest retention distance the C-4 proton of the lactone ring gives a signal at δ 4.39. This is the same value as found for the C-4 proton in γ-octalactone. In the spectrum of the first eluting peak the signal of this proton is shifted to higher field, δ 3.92, because of shielding by the CH_3 group, cis-positioned with respect to this proton (70). It can therefore be concluded that the first eluting peak from a Ucon column is the trans-isomer. This assignment is reverse to that of Laporte and Rambaud (71), Masuda and Nishimura (68) and Kepner et al. (69). Our results were supported by analogous observations of Paasivirta (72). The trans-isomer is present in a higher concentration than the cis-isomer.

On the basis of its retention time the third lactone identified, being β-methyl-γ-nonalactone is assumed to be the trans-isomer. An authentic pure sample was not available. It has never been reported as a constituent of alcoholic beverages.

The phenolic fraction consisted mainly of 4-ethylguaiacol. The fraction contributed to a certain value to the flavor of cognac.

The last group of miscellaneous compounds includes 44 substances. Eighteen of these possess a furan ring and are for the greater part newly found.

The structure of ethyl 2-furoate and 2-propionyl furan were confirmed by synthesis.

The compound 3-ethoxy-1-propanal was reported before as a constituent of whisky (73) and sherry (74). We also found its diethylacetal.

Addition of ethanol to β-damascenone may have resulted in the formation of 1-(2,6,6-trimethyl-1,3-cyclohexadien-1-yl)-3-ethoxy-butan-1-one. This compound has not been described before in the literature. It is present in a very low concentration. The structure was elucidated by spectroscopic analysis and confirmed by synthesis.

The most abundant representative of the 6 lactic acid esters appeared to be the 3-methylbutyl ester. Two other esters of hydroxy acids have been found. Of these ethyl 2-hydroxy-4-methylpentanoate has been described as a constituent of cognac (45), sherry (74) and of saké (75).

Ethyl 3-ethoxypropanoate, new for cognac, has been reported before as a constituent of sherry (74) and of whisky (73).

V. ACKNOWLEDGEMENT

The authors wish to thank N. van der Plasse for the interpretation of the IR spectra, L.M. van der Linde for NMR analysis and H.J. Toet for the literature search.

VI. REFERENCES

1.   Tsantalis, G., "Gas Chromatographic Investigations of the Flavor of Brandies", Thesis, University of Karlsruhe, Karlsruhe, W.Germany, 1968.

2.   Schaefer, J., and Timmer, R., J. Food Sci. 35, 10 (1970).

3. Marche, M., Faure-Goizet, A., Joseph, E., and Hélis-
    Audebert, J., Rev. Fr. Oenol. No. 57, 1 (1975) and
    Complement to No. 57, May 1976.

4. Valyuzhinich, E.N., and Popova, M.F., Biokhim. Vinodel., Sb.
    1,39 (1947).

5. Peynaud, E., and Lafon, M., Ann. Falsif. Expert. Chim. 44,
    263 (1951).

6. Gelashivili, O.S., and Murvanidze, T.G., Vinodel. Vinograd.
    SSSR 12, No. 10, 31 (1952).

7. Egorov, I.A., Tr. Kom. Anal. Khim., Akad. Nauk SSSR 6, 509
    (1955).

8. Egorov, I.A., and Borisova, N.B., Biokhim. Vinodel., Sb. 5,
    27 (1957).

9. Lichev, V.I., and Panaiotov, I.M., Vinodel. Vinograd. SSSR
    18, No. 4, 10 (1958).

10. Lichev, V.I., and Panaiotov, I.M., Bulg. Akad. Nauk. Izv.
    Khim. Inst. 6, 167 (1958).

11. Fouassin, A., Rev. Ferment. Ind. Aliment. 14, 206 (1959).

12. Gogichaishvili, E.A., Vopr. Biokhim. Vinodel., Sb. 1961,
    210.

13. Baraud, J., Bull. Soc. Chim. Fr. p 1874 (1961).

14. Ronkainen, P. Salo, T., and Suomalainen, H., Z. Lebensm.
    Unters. Forsch. 117, 281 (1962).

15. Bober, A., and Haddaway, L.W., J. Gas Chromatogr. 1, No. 12,
    8, (1963).

16. Baraud, J., Qual. Plant. Mater. Vegetab., 11, 207 (1964).

17. Otsuka, K., Imai, S., and Morinaga, K., Agric. Biol. Chem.
    29, 27 (1965).

18. Ronkainen, P., and Suomalainen, H. Suom. Kemistil. B 39,
    No. 12, 280 (1966).

19. Drawert, F., Heimann, W., and Tsantalis, G., Z. Anal. Chem.
    228, 170 (1967).

20. Deluzarche, A., Maillard, A., Maire, J-C., Sommer, J-M., and
    Wagner, M., Ann. Falsif. Expert. Chim. 60, 173 (1967).

21. Nilov, V.I., and Vysotskaya, L.E., <u>Vinodel. Vinograd. SSSR</u>
    28, No. 2, 4 (1968).

22. Nykaenen, L., Puputti, E., and Suomalainen, H., <u>J. Food Sci.</u>
    33, 88 (1968).

23. Reinhard, C., <u>Dtsch. Lebensm. Rundsch.</u> 65, 223 (1969).

24. Vostrikova, E.I., and Yatsyna, A.N., <u>Vop. Ekon. Vinodel.</u>
    <u>Vinograd. Automat. Mekh. Proizvod. Protsess.</u> No. 2, 87
    (1970).

25. Mamakova, Z.A., Lipis, B.V., and Maltabar, V.M., <u>Tr. Mold.</u>
    <u>Nauchno-Issled. Inst. Pishch. Promsti.</u> 9, 93 (1970).

26. Bricout, J., <u>Ann. Technol. Agric.</u> 19, 197 (1970).

27. Rothe, M., and Woelm, G. <u>Ernaerungsforschung</u> 15, 309 (1970).

28. Pietsch, H.P., and Kasprick, D., <u>Ernaerungsforschung</u> 15, 319
    (1970).

29. Miskov, O., and Bourzeit, M., Int. Symp. Chromatogr.
    Electrophor. Lect. Papers, 6 th, 1970, 488, Ann Arbor Sci.
    Publ. Inc., Ann Arbor, Mich.

30. Belchior, A.P. da C., and Garcia, A.S.C., <u>Vinea Vino Portug.</u>
    <u>Docum.</u>, Series II: Enologia 6, No. 2 (1971).

31. Askew, B., and Lisle, D.B., <u>J. Sci. Food Agric.</u> 22, 102
    (1971).

32. Maltabar, V.M., Frolova, Z.N., and Mamakova, Z.A., <u>Sadovod.</u>
    <u>Vinograd. Vinodel. Mold.</u> 26, No. 3, 28 (1971).

33. Dobos, A., Orszagova, M., and Marcina, J., <u>Kvasny Prum.</u> 17,
    No. 3, 60 (1971).

34. Petrosyan, T.L., and Djanpoladyan, L.M., <u>Vinodel. Vinograd.</u>
    <u>SSSR</u> 31, No. 8, 16 (1971).

35. Reinhard, C., <u>Dtsch. Lebensm. Rundsch.</u> 67, 349 (1971).

36. Cordonnier, R., <u>Bull. Off. Int. Vin</u> 44, 1128 (1971).

37. Guymon, J.F., and Crowell, E.A., <u>Am. J. Enol. Vitic.</u> 23, 114
    (1972).

38. Nacheva, T.A., Salnikova, G.M., Knyazeva, A.A., and Yashin,
    Y.I., <u>Vinodel. Vinograd. SSSR</u> No. 6, 25 (1972).

39. Sisakayan, N.M., Egorov, I.A., and Rodopulo, A.K., in
     "Biokhim. Osn. Konyachnogo Proizvod". ("Biochemical
     Principles of Cognac Production", I.A. Egorov, Ed.), p 7,
     Moscow, 1972.

40. Skyrikhin, I.M., and Efinov, B.N., in "Biokhim. Osn.
     Konyachnogo Proizvod.", (I.A. Egorov, Ed.), p 147, Moscow,
     1972.

41. Mndzhoyan, E.L., Rodopulo, A.K., and Bezzubov, A.A., in
     "Biokhim. Osn. Konyachnogo Proizvod.", (I.A. Egorov, Ed.),
     p 156, Moscow, 1972.

42. Rodopulo, A.K., Egorov, I.A., Bezzubov, A.A., Beridze, G.I.,
     and Kvantatiani, N.M., in "Biokhim. Osn. Konyachnogo
     Proizvod.", (I.A. Egorov, Ed.), p 169, Moscow, 1972.

43. Mndzhoyan, E.L., and Saakyan, A.S., in "Biokhim. Osn.
     Konyachnogo Proizvod.", (I.A. Egorov, Ed.), p 175, Moscow,
     1972.

44. Olschimke, D., and Junge, C., Dtsch. Lebensm. Rundsch. 69,
     115 (1973).

45. Adam, L., "Gas Chromatographic Determination of Volatile
     Constituents in Alcoholic Beverages", Thesis, Univ. Munich,
     W.Germany, 1973.

46. Khiabakhov, T., and Nechayev, L.N., Vinodel. Vinograd. SSSR,
     No. 2, 13 (1974).

47. Woidich, H., and Pfannhauser, W., Mitt. Rebe, Wein, Obstbau,
     Fruchteverwert. 24, 155 (1974).

48. Otsuka, K., Zenibayashi, Y., Itoh, M., and Totsuka, A.,
     Agric. Biol. Chem. 38, 485 (1974).

49. Lichev, V. Boidron, J.N., and Bertrand, A., Lozar. Vinar.
     23, 36 (1974).

50. Reinhard, C., Allg. Dtsch. Weinfachz. 110, 1004 (1974).

51. Postel, W., Drawert, F., and Adam, L. in "Geruch- und
     Geschmackstoffe", (F. Drawert, Ed.) p 99, Verlag Hans Carl,
     Neurnberg, W.Germany, 1975.

52. Pisarnitskii, A.F., Egorov, I.A., and Gavrilov, A.I., <u>Prikl.</u> <u>Biokhim. Mikrobiol.</u> 12, 192 (1976).

53. Kleipool, R.J.C., Tas, A.C., and van Straten, S., <u>Lebensm.</u> <u>Wiss. Technol.</u> 9, 296 (1976).

54. Dellweg, H., Miglio, G., and Niefind, H.J., <u>Brantweinwirt-</u> <u>schaft</u> 109, 445 (1969).

55. Valois, P.J. de, "Application de la Spectrometrie de Masse et de la Résonance Magnetique Nucleaire dans les Industries Alimentaires", Proc. Comm. Int. Ind. Agric. Aliment., 15 th, p 71, Bologna, 1975.

56. Schultz, T.H., Flath, R.A., and Mon, T.R., <u>J. Agric. Food</u> <u>Chem.</u> 19, 1060 (1971).

57. Szymanski, H.A., and Amabile, T. <u>J. Chromatogr. Sci.</u> 7, 575 (1969).

58. Suomalainen, H., and Nykaenen, L., <u>Process Biochem.</u> 5, No. 7, 13 (1970).

59. Williams, A.A., and Tucknott, D.G., <u>J. Sci. Food Agric.</u> 23, 1 (1972).

60. Webb, A.D., <u>Biotechnol. Bioeng.</u> 9, 305 (1969).

61. Strating, J. and Venema, A., <u>J. Inst. Brew.</u> 67, 525 (1961).

62. Schreier, P., and Drawert, F., <u>Z. Lebensm. Unters. Forsch.</u> 154, 273 (1974).

63. Kahn, J.H., Shipley, P.A., LaRoe, E.G., and Conner, H.A., <u>J. Food Sci.</u> 34, 587 (1969).

64. Kahn, J.H., <u>J. Assoc. Off. Agric. Chem.</u> 52, 1166 (1969).

65. Schreier, P., and Drawert, F., <u>Chem. Mikrobiol. Technol.</u> <u>Lebensm.</u> 3, 154 (1974).

66. Dubois, P., and Rigaud, J., <u>Ann. Technol. Agric.</u> 24, 307 (1975).

67. Liebich, H.M., Koenig, W.A., and Bayer, E., <u>J. Chromatogr.</u> <u>Sci.</u> 8, 527 (1970).

68. Masuda, M., and Nishimura, K., <u>Phytochemistry</u> 10, 1401 (1971).

69. Kepner, E.R., Webb, A.D., and Muller, C.J., Am. J. Enol. Vitic. 23, 103 (1972).

70. Jackman, L.M., and Sternhell, S., "Application of Nuclear Magnetic Resonance Spectroscopy in Organic Chemistry", Chapter 3-8, Pergamon Press, 1969.

71. Laporte, J.F., and Rambaud, R., C.R. Acad. Sc. Paris, Ser. C 262, 1095 (1966).

72. Paasivirta, J., Acta Chem. Scand. 22, 2041 (1968).

73. Kahn, J.H., LaRoe, E.G., and Conner, H.A., J. Food Sci. 33, 395 (1968).

74. Webb, A.D., Kepner, R.E., and Maggiora, L., Am. J. Enol. Vitic. 18, 190 (1967).

75. Yamanoto, A., Nippon Nogei Kagaku Kaishi 35, 616 (1961).

HEADSPACE TECHNIQUES IN MOUTH ODOR ANALYSIS

D.A.M. Mackay, M.M. Hussein
Life Savers, Inc.

Breath was analyzed for its sulfur-containing organic volatiles before and after ingestion of a number of foods, using various headspace gas chromatographic techniques and the flame photometric detector (FPD). These techniques included direct injection, head space concentration via use of short pre-columns (both porous polymer and coated support types), and also of very long open coated columns of low flow resistance. Elution of absorbed volatiles from these long columns into the analytical column was studied. Use of the standard pre-column, as an intermediate step to collect the volatiles stripped from the long pre-columns, permitted the collection of very low levels of volatiles from large volumes of unimpeded "lung breath". The standard pre-column was used to collect volatiles from the oral cavity, using 40 cc of "mouth breath".

The occurrence of methyl mercaptan and dimethyl sulfide in mouth odor was confirmed; in addition, dimethyl disulfide and dimethyl trisulfide were found in mouth breath of most individuals examined. Most intrinsic sulfur volatiles seem accounted for by saliva breakdown during sleeping ("morning mouth"). Dimethyl sulfide, however, which was found in rapidly exhaled breath, seems to have an additional, much lower concentration present in the lungs, but is not necessarily produced there.

Extrinsic sulfur volatiles were seen to be contributed to mouth breath by such foods as cabbage, sauerkraut, onions and beer. Interactions of food with saliva were observed in some instances. Breath odorization with peppermint and onion oils could be measured 45 minutes after ingestion. The natural decrease in concentration of onion oil volatiles in breath was followed for this time, and used to show the effects of various cleansing and deodorizing treatments.

INTRODUCTION AND BACKGROUND

Even the oldest civilizations have recorded efforts to mask mouth malodor using treatments such as spices, gums, berries, herbs and wine. In more recent times, the same subject has seemed to be a major concern for television if not also the public.

Interestingly, in view of the subject of this symposium, the now widely used techniques of direct headspace analysis and the use of pre-columns for analysis of larger headspace volumes were first described nearly 20 years ago in a publication on the analysis of volatiles in breath (1), some time before these techniques started to come into favor for food, flavor, and air pollution studies, although the utility and general applicability of headspace analysis to these problems had been described (2).

Part of this delay might be attributed to the domination of gas chromatography at that time by petroleum chemists who seemed to care more for precise analysis of a possibly non-representative sample than a possibly imprecise analysis of a representative sample of importance to flavor chemists. Also, about then, the argon ionization detector (AID) was replaced by the flame ionization detector (FID) with its greater linearity of range at comparable sensitivities. But lost was the flow insensitivity of the AID and its rapid re-establishment of base line, which allowed the utmost flexibility in sampling via headspace techniques. Connections to insert pre-columns could be made and broken with impunity, and their contents easily transferred if desired by adding them to the top of the analytical column. Other detectors then in use could not take that kind of abuse. For breath analysis it became clear, however, that the AID, though largely insensitive to water itself, was capable of erratic response to organics due to continuing traces of water vapor. The FID eventually became preferred because of its insensitivity to the large water content of direct breath samples, the ability to use air as a carrier gas if need be, and the wide response range which permitted analysis of traces even in swamping conditions.

The next step in breath odor analysis, as a factor of the detector employed, was the development of the sulfur-specific flame photometric detector (FPD). Earlier attempts at using sulfur-specific detectors (polarographic and coulometric) in order to relate them to organoleptic thresholds of sulfur compounds showed they have insufficient sensitivity to be generally useful for direct breath analysis, although they could be used for model systems.

It was thus not until Tonzetich (3,4) coupled the selectivity and sensitivity of the FPD to the headspace techniques described many years previously by Mackay, Lang, and Berdick (1) in their work on breath odor that the importance of nanogram quantities of sulfur compounds to the odor quality of breath was first established.

The cause and nature of non-specific oral malodor was not understood until these recent studies of Tonzetich who showed it to be due to the generation of volatile sulfur compounds in the mouth as a result of enzyme action on saliva constituents. The volatile sulfur compounds identified in malodorous breath were hydrogen sulfide, methyl mercaptan, and dimethyl sulfide. Breath malodor was attributed mainly to hydrogen sulfide and methyl mercaptan. The same three sulfur compounds were found by Tonzetich and Johnson (4) in headspace of putrefied saliva. Dimethyl disulfide, although found in the saliva headspace, was not reported in malodorous breath, however.

Earlier work (1,5) on analysis of breath by gas chromatography using argon and flame ionization detectors did not report the presence of sulfur compounds. Jansson (6) using the mass spectrometer reported hydrogen sulfide as the only odorant. He did not find the dimethyl and diethyl sulfides earlier reported (7). The objective of the studies was to correlate the patterns

of breath organics before and after oral hygiene and other breath
deodorizing treatments. The efficacy of copper chlorophyllin was
shown by measuring the reduction in headspace volatiles of onion,
and by measuring its capacity as an active ingredient against
mercaptans in onion. The method was not able to illustrate
in vivo effectiveness, however.

The newer pre-column absorbents, combined with refined collection and elution techniques now permit the organic content of
breath to be sufficently concentrated for sulfur compounds to
be measured in vivo. By concentrating the breath sample to take
advantage of the subsequent multiple enhancement of sensitivity
of the flame photometric detector (FPD) in the sulfur mode
(in which there is a square response to change in concentration),
consistent differences can be seen in the sulfur content of malodorous breaths of various individuals in their intrinsic "morning breath". The same technique permits analyzing the breath for
flavor volatiles of ingested food or beverages. Analysis for
sulfur compounds in the breath after eating onions or rinsing the
mouth with highly dilute onion oil solution (to simulate stand-
ardized ingestion of onions) also enables the effect of breath
deodorizing treatments to be measured in reducing extrinsic
mouth odor. Reduction of sulfur compounds in the intrinsic
malodorous "morning breath" after oral hygiene or eating has
been reported by Tonzetich and Ng (8).

Analysis of volatiles in breath aids in understanding any

changes that my occur in the mouth due to food components which may cause unpleasantness of the breath after ingestion. With onion and fresh cabbage, changes of this type were seen, presumably of metabolic nature.

Most work on breath odor reported to date has relied mainly on the high sensitivity of the detector permitting injection of a 10 cc breath sample directly into the gas chromatograph either with a syringe or through a sample loop (3,8,9). While direct analysis is preferred whenever possible, it suffers from the limitation on the maximum sample size (usually 10 cc) which allows detection only of constituents present at comparatively high concentrations.

Teranishi et al (10) reported on the concentration of breath and urine volatiles by collection in a 5 feet, 1/4 inch O.D. cooled stainless steel column, with the sample subsequently tranferred to the analytical column with aid of heat. Zlatkis et al (11) reported on concentration of organic volatiles in biological fluids and gases, including the breath, by collecting the sample in a porous polymer trap, followed by transfer of the sample to a cooled pre-column prior to the final transfer to the analytical column. Both methods require low temperature cooling and extra steps for sample transfer. Collection in the porous polymer trap eliminated the usual icing problem due to high moisture samples, which occurred in the former study. Neither study used sulfur specific detectors, though Zlatkis (12) has shown patterns of urinary volatile metabolites obtained by the use of FPD in conjunction with a Tenax GC pre-column, and volatile sulfur compounds from complex sources other than breath (13) using the same combination.

Conkle et al (14) recently made a very thorough study of breath from eight subjects using multistage cryogenic traps for condensing volatiles for later examination by gas chromatography and mass spectrometry. After sampling for one hour, 69 compounds were found, of which 32 also occurred in the high purity "zero" air used for the experiment. In eight subjects expired dimethyl sulfide varied from 0.54 to 53 ul per hour (0.6 to 60 ppb): only traces (0.05 to 1 ppb) of dimethyl disulfide occurred in two subjects. Dimethyl sulfide was found in 3 of 6 air cylinders at up to 18 ppb. One subject tested on three occasions showed wide variation in all volatiles: his dimethyl sulfide content varied 20-fold. The disulfide was found in traces on one occasion. No other sulfur compounds were found. Pre-columns were not used for concentration. All subjects were fasted overnight prior to testing. There was no mention of oral hygiene.

Even more recently Krotoszynski et al (15) studied breath volatiles from 28 very carefully selected subjects and found 102 organic volatiles of endogenous and exogenous origin. The six sulfur compounds (and their concentration in breath) reported were diethyl and methylpropyl sulfides (2-3 ng/l), di-(t)-butyl disulfide (1 ng/l),hexyl mercaptan (2 ng/l), thiolacetic acid (4 ng/l), ethyl 3 - mercapto-propionate (4 ng/l), and thiocyclo-

pentane (1 ng/l). The subjects were fasted overnight and allowed
to use salt water for dental hygiene the previous evening or that
morning. The technique was to use a breathing mask to fill a 20
liter Teflon bag in about 4 minutes. Subsequently the bag contents were passed through a 7 inch pre-column packed with Tenax-
GC, taking about 1 1/2 hours for the 20 liters for analysis. The
volatiles were transferred with heat to 36 inches of coiled narrow bore tubing cooled in liquid nitrogen, taking about 30 minutes. The coil was then connected to the inlet of a capillary
GLC column, heated and the volatiles transferred for analysis
by temperature programming. Only traces of 10 compounds were
found as background in dry runs of this very comprehensive system.

The present paper compares several pre-column techniques for
the collection, concentration, and subsequent analysis of breath,
using two different detectors (FID, FPD), with the emphasis on
minimum elapsed time between the start of sampling and final
analysis. Breath volatiles concentration is achieved by passing
the sample of breath either through a short pre-column (packed
with porous polymeric materials or with coated column support
materials), or through very long packed or open large-bore tubing. In neither case are the traps cooled; in fact they are
sometimes warmed to prevent breath condensation. Both short and
long pre-columns can be eluted with heat directly onto the analytical column, but the criticality of transfer from the long pre-
column is lessened if an intermediary transfer to a short one is

first made.

Use of these pre-columns for direct trapping of breath volatiles permits the worker to collect and concentrate the organic content of breath with a minimum of delay (though it may be necessary to use multiple pre-columns connected in series) and, in the case of the long "open" pre-columns, to collect a large volume of exhaled air with only slight back pressure and at short time intervals. The former factor is important if "lung" breath is to be examined; the latter if rapid sequential analysis of mouth odor is to be attempted in order to show efficacy of active agents.

The use of sampling tubes and pre-columns has been reviewed and extended by Mieure and Dietrich (16), and by Russell (17) in analysis of air and water pollutants and by many other investigators (18,19,20,21). Also, a new textbook on headspace analysis has very recently been published (22). However, a brief historical outline of the development of the pre-column technique may be useful to illustrate certain features of the present work.

The use of sample tubes for absorption of trace constituents borne in carrier gas flows has of course been long known, and was quantitatively proved at the beginning of the century for inorganic gases by the use of absorption tubes in semi-micro analysis of organic compounds by combustion trains.

Trains of organic reagents for detection of flavor volatiles are also long known, with a fairly late example being the

characterization of several types of volatile sulfur compounds
obtained by passing a carrier gas through boiling cabbage for
several days, and then through a series of various mercury salt
solutions (23). A similar technique to trap ethylene from
ripening fruit in a decomposable mercury complex has been earlier
reported (24).

Recovery of a complex mixture of materials in unchanged form
subsequent to trapping them out of a carrier gas is more recent,
though it was long attempted in many flavor studies, using the
cold finger at various temperatures, as in Haagen-Smits' 1945
work on pineapple (25).

Activated charcoal, too, has had long use in odor studies as
an efficient deodorizing system for both air and water streams.
Depending upon the type of charcoal and extent of activation,
the basic absorption phenomenon, however, is overlaid with chemi-
sorption mechanisms leading to impaired recovery of the original
mixture or creation of new chemical species. Moreover, elution
of the trapped substances requires high temperatures and is un-
certain in many cases.

The advent of gas chromatography did nothing at first to
improve or facilitate trapping or analysis of trace volatiles,
though the classic flavor study of Dimick and Corse on strawberry
flavor (26) showed the way to the employment of GLC in the analysis of minute, liquid samples obtained by conventional manipulation of flavored materials. Use of open U-traps, either cooled

to condense volatiles, or as part of a gas sampling trap to collect gas volumes up to 10 cc was also known for collection and transfer of sample.

In two engine exhaust studies (27, 28) the use of liquid oxygen-cooled liquid-coated GLC packings in the U-tube is described, but the additional use of dehydrating tubes precluded the analysis of all but hydrocarbons. In the flavor field, work by Rhoades (29) on ground coffee again described the use of a coated substrate in a liquid nitrogen-cooled U-tube to trap volatiles swept from the coffee by a helium stream. The low temperature condensation effect was sought. The substrate (Carbowax 1500) served to retain CO_2 and water while the organics were transferred with heat to another empty U-tube cooled by liquid N_2, and then swept after warming into the GLC unit for analysis.

The major advance in trapping systems for trace volatiles in headspace however, did not come until after the invention of the argon ionization detector, the first highly sensitive detector used for gas chromatography. It was now possible for the first time (1) to see that as little as 5 cc of headspace air above many food materials could be injected directly into the GLC unit to reveal the same chromatographic pattern of volatiles as shown by liquid concentrates obtained by working up possibly tons of materials. The relative insensitivity of the ionization detector to the air and moisture in headspace was a key factor in this development, as was the lack of need to replace air by helium in sample manipulation (as in cold traps) in order to prevent burn-out of the TCC detectors then in use. It then became possible to see how large a direct headspace sample could be tolerated without deterioration of the analysis. Above a certain volume, often as low as 10 cc, detection of traces by peak height was not enhanced, and became worse as larger samples were attempted. However, multiple 5 cc headspace injections into a small 2 or 3 cm long pre-column filled with the column packing known to be necessary for the analysis, but kept at a somewhat lower temperature than needed for the analysis, was shown to result in magnified peak heights of trace substances in headspace volatiles upon transfer of the pre-column, or its contents, to the analytical column. Multiple syringe injections into the capped pre-column, or gas sweeps up to a liter in volume, were able to trap trace components that were not held back in gas trains containing even liquid N_2 traps, since the vapor pressure of many organics in these traps is higher than that above their solutions in the organic substrates used to coat the solid supports (30). It was also found that efficacy of the solution traps fell off as temperature decreased, probably because of viscosity, or decreased rate of equilibrium effects.

At this point, the quality (efficiency) of the analysis is determined only by the length of the pre-column and is not in any way affected by the gas or headspace volume used for sweeping volatiles through the pre-column. However, the quantitative relationships in the mixture of volatiles suffer as soon as the breakthrough volume of the pre-column is exceeded. This may be permissible if interest is only in the minor traces that do not exceed their breakthrough volumes. Alternatively, pre-columns can be connected in series for one-by-one analysis, or a simple but essential refinement made of Nawar and Fagerson's technique (31) for collection of volatiles from foodstuffs in which a peristaltic pump cycles a small volume of headspace air back through the food being analyzed, for many subsequent passes through the trapping column. The essential difference is to replace the anhydrous K_2CO_3 drying tube they used with a pre-column containing coated column packing (at R.T. or above). The volatiles are then collected here instead of in the dry ice or liquid N_2 cooled U-tube. This cooled U-tube or cold finger can be left in the circuit but eventually will contain mainly ice. The failure of liquid N_2 traps to prevent volatile losses was noted by MacLeod and MacLeod (32) who examined the volatiles from cooked cabbage by avoiding any gas sweep at all, using only an adjacent liquid N_2 cooled trap for collection of migrating volatiles. Subsequent manipulation gave a very dilute aqueous solution which, when examined directly by FID gas chromatography, showed large amounts of dimethyl sulfide with lesser amounts of methyl mercaptan and dimethyl disulfide, a pattern of sulfur volatiles also found in the breath.

The same principle of solution trapping was extended to capillary GLC by Self et al (33) who used a few inches of coated large bore capillary tubing to trap organics from large volumes of headspace volatiles obtained from boiling potatoes and other vegetables by a gas sweep. For analysis this pre-column was simply connected to the analytical capillary column.

With the development of porous polymer packings for GLC, the pendulum seems to have swung back to pre-columns using an adsorptive type mechanism based on the capillary condensation phenomena utilized by activated charcoal, but without the chemical alterations often found with that agent. Presumably absorption due to solution phenomena still plays some part in the high separation efficiencies obtained.

In these studies, now reported for the analysis of breath odor, porous polymer and "solution" (coated column packing) traps were both utilized. The porous polymer pre-columns were more efficient, that is, did not leak as shown by a second trap in series. The second trap was a routine precaution. Coated column packings tended to lose methyl mercaptan and some dimethyl sulfide when used for trapping of sulfur compounds using the standard (40 cc) sample collected from the oral cavity.

However, the back pressure of polymer packings is too high for direct unaided breath sampling, and in this case loose or coarse column packing may be preferable in spite of the partial loss of the most highly volatile substances.

Longer pre-columns filled very loosely with column packing, or even long lengths of 1/4" open tubing with walls coated with GLC substrates, seem to be better routes for unimpeded direct sampling of large breath volumes. Otherwise, the breath must be collected in large gas syringes for later transfer to a porous polymer pre-column. However, the use of the large syringe, with its high back pressure, means that sequential analyses of breath can not be spaced closer than about 5 to 8 minutes apart. Use of 40 cc sample can permit 2 to 3 minute sequencing, but with difficulty. It was this time factor which developed the "standard" volume of breath at 40 cc maximum.

It had been hoped that the long pre-columns (or open tubes), needed for unimpeded breath samples for rapid analytical sampling without back pressure, could be eluted thermochromatographically directly onto the analytical column. Attempts at using a temperature gradient either over the whole pre-column (by spacing the heater winding so that a temperature differential was maintained as the whole column became heated), or in a moving heating section, gave elution results only marginally different from elution by passing a ring oven slowly along the pre-column without concern for a matching flow rate. In spite of the theoretical superiority of thermochromatographic elution, better results were usually obtained by stripping with the ring oven, or even easier by transfer (by heat) from the long pre-column into a standard short pre-column for analysis by the usual way.

Although it was not the intention of this work to develop a
method for measuring potency of onion and onion oil, the FPD
analysis for total sulfur in onion oil or in onion extract might
serve as a good method for this purpose. The reported methods
deal with Chemical Oxygen Demand (34), pyruvate content (35), and
FID gas chromatography (36, 37) in which some interference may
result from other non-sulfur constituents.

I.   EXPERIMENTAL

A.   Materials

1.   *Chemicals*
Dimethyl sulfide, dimethyl disulfide, methyl mercaptan, dipropyl disulfide, propyl and butyl mercaptans
and dimethyl trisulfide were obtained from commercial suppliers.

2.   *Pre-Column Packings*
. Tenax-GC (60-80 mesh) Product of Enka, N.V.,
Holland

. Coconut activated charcoal (Anasorb), 90/100 mesh,
Analabs, Inc.

. Porapak Q, 80/100 mesh, Analabs, Inc.

. 20% SE-30 on Chromosorb W(80/100 mesh), acid
washed and DMCS treated; coated in the authors'
laboratory.

3.   *Syringes*

. Gas tight 10 cc Luer Tip syringe, glass barrel,

and Teflon coated aluminum plunger with teflon tip.
Hamilton #1010.

. Gas tight 100 cc glass syringe with glass plunger
and Luer-Lok.   Becton, Dickinson & Co. #A-1601.

. Gas tight 50 cc glass syringe with Teflon coated
aluminum plunger with teflon tip. Hamilton #1050.

4. *Pre-Columns for Analysis*
. 6 Inches x 6 mm. O.D. (4 mm. I.D.) Pyrex glass tubes
are used when the auxiliary heat is external to
the injector of the chromatograph. The pre-column
fits in the auxiliary heater which is attached to
the injector with CAJON 1/4 inch fittings and
silicon rubber septum. The pre-column may be
connected directly to the injector with CAJON
fitting if another auxiliary heating source, such
as regular heating tape, is to be used.

. Glass injector insert supplied with Perkin-Elmer's
gas chromatographs (models 900 and 3920),approxi-
mately 5-1/2 inch x 3 mm. (I.D.). This type of
pre-column is used when the instrument's injection
port is the source of heat for eluting sample off
the pre-column.

B. Gas Chromatographic Conditions

a. *INSTRUMENT:*   Perkin-Elmer Model 900 with FID.

COLUMN: Dual, aluminum 8 ft. x 1/4 inch (O.D.), 0.032
inch wall thickness, packed with 10% Carbowax 20 M on

Chromosorb W 80/100 mesh (acid washed and
DMCS treated).

CARRIER GAS: Nitrogen at 50 cc/min. measured
at ambient temperature.

DETECTOR FUEL: Optimized at 18 psi H_2 and 30
psi air.

OVEN TEMPERATURE: Programmed at 6°/min. from
60 to 200°C. and held at final temperature.

INJECTOR TEMPERATURE: 250°C

MANIFOLD TEMPERATURE: 250°C

RECORDER: 5 MV at 1/2 inch per minute chart
speed.

b. *INSTRUMENT:* Perkin-Elmer Model 3920 equipped
with Perkin-Elmer flame photometric detector
(FPD) with 394 nm filter for sulfur detection.

COLUMN: Glass, 5· ft. x 1/4 inch O.D.., (4 mm.
I.D.), packed with 10% Carbowax 20 M on
Chromosorb W 80/100 mesh (acid washed and DMCS
treated.)

CARRIER GAS: Nitrogen at a flow rate of 50 cc/
min. (measured at ambient temperature). When
the sample is analyzed on a pre-column which
is heated externally and precedes the injector,
the carrier gas is split with a shut-off valve
so that 15 cc flow through the pre-column.

However, the total flow remains at 50 cc per minute.

DETECTOR FUEL: Optimized at 88 ml./min. H_2 and 104 cc/min. air.

DETECTOR MODE: Sulfur (394 nm filter)-Normal B (non-linear)

OVEN TEMPERATURE: 4 minutes at an initial temperature of 60°C. then programmed at 8°/min. to 180°C. and held at final temperature.

INTERFACE TEMPERATURE: 190°C

INJECTOR TEMPERATURE: 190°C when sample is analyzed by direct injection or on a pre-column heated externally from the injector. However, if the pre-column is the glass injector liner, it is maintained at 250°C. to elute the sample off the pre-column as rapidly as possible.

RECORDER: 1 MV at 1/2 inch per minute chart speed.

AUXILIARY PRE-COLUMN HEATING OVEN: Spex Industries' tube oven (#1022) and power supply (#1047PS), which are part of the manufacturer's headspace concentrator. The tube oven is connected directly to the chromatograph's injector. Both the insert and liner remain in the injector. A heating tape and a thermostat may be used as an auxiliary heat source for the pre-column.

PRE-COLUMN HEATING OVEN TEMPERATURE: 250°C. for 6 minutes.

c. *INSTRUMENT:* MT 220 equipped with MT flame photometric detector with 394 nm filter (for sulfur) and a 750 V. power supply.

COLUMN: Same as in (b).

CARRIER GAS: Nitrogen at 50 cc/min. measured at ambient temperature. When the sample is analyzed on a pre-column (preceding the injection port), the carrier gas is split so that 10 cc/min. flows through the pre-column. However, total flow remains at 50 cc/min.

DETECTOR FUEL: H_2 at 150 cc/min. (40 Psi), O_2 at 32 cc/min. (40 Psi), and air at 47 cc/min. (40 Psi).

OVEN TEMPERATURE: 4 minutes at an initial temperature of 60^oC, then programmed at 10°/min. to 165^oC. and held at the final temperature.

INJECTOR TEMPERATURE: 175^oC.

DETECTOR TEMPERATURE: 175^oC.

AUXILIARY PRE-COLUMN HEATING OVEN: Same as described in (b).

PRE-COLUMN TEMPERATURE: 250^oC. for 6 minutes.

RECORDER: 1 MV at a chart speed of 1/2 inch per minute.

C. Packing and Conditioning of Pre-Column

One end of the pre-column is plugged with a 1/4 inch piece of glass wool and the pre-column is packed tightly with the porous polymer material with the aid of suction and vibration. The weight of packing was determined by

weighing the pre-column before and after packing. The
amount of packing should not exceed the height of the
tube heating oven. The end of the column was plugged
with another piece of glass wool. If more than one
type of packing was desired in a pre-column, a small
piece of glass wool seperated them, and the total height
of both packings did not exceed that of the heating oven.
The pre-column was conditioned in its heating oven
(auxiliary oven or in injection port of gas chromatograph) at 250°C. for one hour with a carrier gas flow
of 50 cc/min. Conditioned pre-columns are stored in
tightly capped clean glass test tubes.

D. Cleaning of Syringes

Syringes and plungers are cleaned thoroughly by
rinsing and soaking in boiling water for 3 to 5 minutes,
and by drying with nitrogen or air flow.

E. Breath Sample Collection

1. *Direct Injection*
    A 10 cc breath sample was collected in a 10 cc
    syringe. The subject was instructed to close the
    mouth and to breath through the nose for 50 seconds
    and to stop breathing for 10 additional seconds,
    while a small eflon tube(mouth piece), which is
    connected to the Luer tip of the syringe, is
    quickly inserted in the oral cavity with the lips

tightly closed. Care was taken that the Teflon mouth piece inlet tip is not in contact with the tongue or any other parts of the mouth.

2. *Pre-Column Direct Sampling*
The desired pre-column of a particular packing was connected to a mouth piece (a short Teflon tube, 1-2 inches) containing a small wad of clean, volatile-free, glass wool. The other end of the pre-column is connected to a 50 or 100 cc syringe with a short piece of Tygon or Teflon tube. The desired volume sample is collected in 20-25 cc intervals by slow suction with the syringe while the Teflon tube mouth piece is in the oral cavity with the subject breathing through the nose, as described in the preceding section.

This is continued until the entire sample is collected. The pre-column is then capped tightly at both ends and stored in a refrigerator if it is not to be analyzed within 2 hours.

3. *Pre-Column Indirect Sampling*
The sample was collected in a syringe then transferred onto the pre-column with suction by another syringe, water aspiration or by vacuum pump at a suction rate of 60-80 cc/min. Collection of breath sample was as described in the preceding section.

4. *Pre-Column Recirculation of Sample*
    The pre-column (or pre-columns in series) was

    connected to the inlet Tygon tubing of a peristaltic

    pump. The inlet end of the pre-column and the outlet

    Tygon tubing of the pump are connected to short

    Teflon pieces which serve as mouth pieces. The

    mouth piece connected to the pre-column contains

    an extra wad of glass wool. The flow rate can be

    determined by measuring displacement volume of water

    when the outlet tube is placed in an inverted graduate

    cylinder filled with water. Both mouth pieces are

    placed in the oral cavity, one at each side of

    the mouth, with the lips tightly closed. The subject

    breathes through the nose only while timing with a

    stop watch to obtain the volume of breath circulated

    through the pre-column and the mouth.

5. *"Open Tube" Pre-Column*
    The sample was collected in 40 ft. of coiled 1/4 inch

    O.D. (3/16" I.D.) Tygon tubing, which was immersed in

    a water bath at 38°C. to minimize moisture condensation,

    by blowing directly into the tube. The volume of

    breath was measured in a large water filled graduated

    cyclinder inverted in a water tub. The sample was

    eluted from the "open tube" onto a Tenax GC pre-column

    with the aid of nitrogen at a flow rate of 40 cc/minute

    for 10 minutes while the "open tube" was immersed in a

water bath at 95°C. During collection of sample in the
"open tube", little back pressure was observed. One
liter /minute is easily collected.

F. Elution of Sample from Pre-Column for Subsequent Analysis

  The method of eluting the sample for analysis depended
on the type and geometry of the pre-column on which the
sample is trapped. If the pre-column is a glass insert
of the injector, the sample is eluted by quick insertion
of the pre-column into the injector and quick resealing,
and commencement of the analysis. The injector's
temperature is maintained at 245 to 250°C. When the
pre-column is a regular short Pyrex glass tubing, the
sample is eluted by inserting the pre-column in the
auxiliary heating oven which precedes the injector, the
carrier gas is allowed to flow through the pre-column,
and the pre-column is heated at 250°C. for 6 minutes.
Initiation of pre-column heating was done concurrently
at the start of analysis.

  When the original pre-column is open tubing, the tranfer
is made to a small standard pre-column and handled as
described in the usual manner.

  The pre-column auxiliary heating oven may be in the form
of the tube oven described in section B(b), or a heating
tape wound directly around the pre-column or around an
aluminum or stainless steel tubing, in which the pre-

column fits, and regulated by a thermostat.

The inlet side of the pre-column upon sampling is the outlet side upon elution and analysis of sample.

G. Standards and Quantitation of Sample

1. *Stock Standard*
   2.00% Dimethyl sulfide in absolute ethanol (wt./v).

   The stock standard was refrigerated when not in use.

2. *Working Standards*
   Appropriate dilutions of the stock standard were made in absolute ethanol to give a range of standards containing 1,5,10,20,50,100,200, and 400 ppm. Each 1 ppm of dimethyl sulfide is equivalent to 0.516 ppm elemental sulfur; 1 ul of 1 ppm standard solution contains 0.516 ng. sulfur. When not in use, the solutions are refrigerated. They are freshly prepared every 2 weeks.

3. *Calibration and Quantitation*
   a. *DIRECT INJECTION ANALYSIS.* 1 ul of each work-standard is analysed by direct injection. After the solvent is eluted off the analytical column, the next standard is analyzed.

   b. *PRE-COLUMN TRAPPED ANALYSIS.* To simulate, as closely as possible, the conditions of sample collections, an aliquot (1 ul) of each standard is deposited on the end of the pre-column packing (1/2 to 1 inch from packing edge) with

a 10 ul syringe, and 40 cc of air is drawn
through the pre-column by gentle suction
with a 50 or 100 cc syringe.

The area of the dimethyl sulfide peak in
each standard was measured by manual integration; (height x width at half height).
The area is plotted vs. concentration in
terms of nanogram sulfur on a log-log graph
paper. Peak areas of all sulfur compounds
in the sample are measured likewise and the
concentration of each is determined, as nanogram sulfur, from the standard calibration
log-log graph. The exact amount of a particular component can be calculated from its
sulfur content and the sulfur gravimetric
factor of the compound.

H. Determination of Breakthrough Volume or Adequate
Sample Size For Optimum Retention on Pre-Column

The desired volume of sample is trapped on 2 pre-
columns connected in series either by direct collection or by transfer from a syringe with gentle suction.
Each pre-column is analyzed; if no components are detected on the second pre-column, then the volume is
adequate for analysis on one pre-column.

An easy method with odorous samples or compounds
is to smell the effluent off the pre-column into the

suction syringe at various intervals when the sample is being deposited on the pre-column. If no odor is detected then it can be assumed that no loss occurred.

I. Mouth Odorization, Subsequent Deodorizing Treatment, and Breath Analysis

1. *Stock Onion Oil Solution*
   A 2.0% (V/V) solution of onion oil (Fritzsche-D&O , Imported, F.C.C., Extra) in absolute ethanol was prepared and stored in freezer when not in use.

2. *Diluted Onion Oil Solution*
   A 0.1% (V/V) solution was prepared by diluting 5 cc of the stock solution to 100 cc with absolute ethanol.

3. *Mouth Odorization*
   The mouth was rinsed thoroughly with 20 cc distilled water, followed by thorough rinsing for 30 seconds with 1 cc of diluted onion oil solution in 20 cc distilled water without swallowing, then followed immediately by rinsing with 20 cc distilled water for 30 seconds and expectorating the rinse. Timing with a stop watch commences immediately after the final water rinse. Breath samples at zero time, immediately after the last water rinse, or at any time interval were collected as described in section E(2); 40 cc breath samples were collected for onion breath analysis.

When the effect of a deodorizing treatment on onion breath was to be determined, the treatment was taken

at the desired time interval after the onion oil rinse.
Upon completion of the treatment or at any other desired
period following it, the breath was collected and
analyzed as in section E(2).

J. Morning and Fasting Breath, Deodorizing Treatment, and
Analysis

1. *Morning Breath*
Upon awaking and prior to oral hygiene or any oral intake, the volunteer collected the sample following the
procedure of section E(2). When 100 cc or more were
desired, the sample was collected on 2 pre-columns
connected in series. The process of breathing through
the nose was continued for 5 or 10 minutes when
collecting 100 or 200 cc. The sample was collected
in 25 cc intervals, whereby after each collection
breathing through the nose continued.

When a deodorizing treatment was to be investigated,
the breath was analyzed prior to the treatment as a
control, then the particular treatment was taken. At
conclusion of the treatment, timing was started with a
stop watch and the breath was sampled at the desired
time interval.

2. *Fasting Breath*
Fasting breath in this work is that sampled prior to
lunch which was preceded by total abstinence from
oral intake for at least 3 hours. Sampling procedure

was similar to that followed in the preceding section
for morning breath.

II. RESULTS AND DISCUSSION

Direct injection of a breath sample in gas chromatographic
analysis is ideal if one is satisfied with the compounds detectable in a 10 cc sample. Direct injection of larger volumes
is not practical due to back pressure upon injection, peak
broadening, loss of resolution in peaks of short retention
time, some loss of sample, and alteration of retention time
of early peaks. Headspace techniques of direct sample
collection on pre-columns packed with polymers, or coated
supports, or activated charcoal, offer advantages of versatil-
ity, ease, sampling of large volumes, and convenience of
sampling whereby the sample can be collected at any time
without the need for the volunteer to be in the laboratory.
The major disadvantage is that hydrogen sulfide is not
adequately retained.

Concentrating breath samples by trapping large volumes
on pre-columns packed with either Tenax GC or Porapak Q has
shown the presence of two sulfur compounds which have not
yet been reported to occur in mouth breath. Both dimethyl
disulfide and dimethyl trisulfide were noted in concentrated
'morning breath'. Identification of these compounds and
others that may be referred to in this paper is based on

retention times compared to those of pure chemicals in three different systems using polar and non-polar packings and varying
column lengths.   The presence of the two new sulfur compounds in
the breath is illustrated in Figure 1 which shows the analysis of
200 cc breath on 2 pre-columns in series.   Each pre-column con-

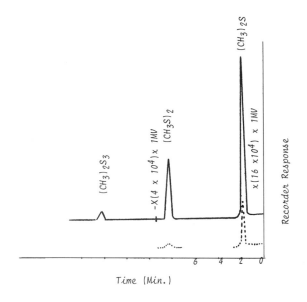

Time (Min.)

Fig. 1.   Sulfur compounds in morning breath of Subject A.
G.C. conditions c and FPD were used.

tained 200 mg Tenax-GC.   The subject showed only dimethyl sulfide,
dimethyl disulfide, and dimethyl trisulfide.   Dimethyl trisulfide
is present only in very small amount which will not be detectable
if a 10 cc breath sample is analyzed.   Methyl mercaptan is absent
but would be observable if present.

Analysis of the second pre-column (Fig. 1) shows considerable sample loss from the first pre-column, thus indicating that
a 200 cc sample is too large for this size pre-column.   The es-

cape of dimethyl sulfide, which is the most volatile component in
the sample, is more pronounced compared to the slight loss of dimethyl disulfide.

Although malodorous breath of every individual contains volatile sulfur compounds (VSC) the type and concentration of these
compounds vary among individuals. Figure 2 shows chromatograms
of 100 cc morning breath from three individuals. Each has a distinct pattern; Subject B showed methyl mercaptan in addition to
those sulfur compounds shown by Subject A plus an unknown eluting
just before dimethyl disulfide, with the same retention time as
amyl mercaptan. Subject D by contrast to A showed methyl mercaptan, but no dimethyl sulfide. Traces of dimethyl trisulfide
were shown by the three subjects. Repeats of Subject A on other
days were consistent in showing little or no mercaptan and overall reduced level of sulfur compounds compared to Subjects B and
D.

Organoleptic evaluation of morning breath of the three subjects indicated objectionability in spite of absence of methyl
mercaptan in some. This may be explained by the extremely low
odor thresholds of dimethyl trisulfide and dimethyl disulfide;
these compounds are detectable at concentrations of 0.2 and 19 ng,
respectively, per 100 cc of air. Concentrations of dimethyl disulfide (DMDS) in morning breath of the three subjects (Fig. 2)
are 12.2, 25.7, and 19.8 ng per 100 cc breath while those of dimethyl trisulfide (DMTS) are 1.4, 1.0, and 1.4 ng. All values,

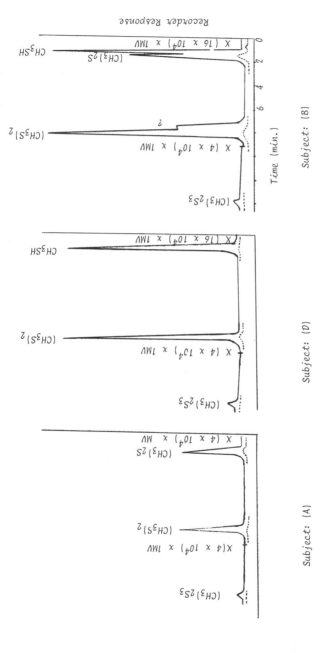

Fig. 2: – Analyses of sulfur compounds in morning breath of three different individuals (Subjects A, B, and D) – 100 cc sample from each was collected directly on 2 Tenax – GC pre-columns in series. GC conditions c and FPD were used. _____ 1st. pre-column, ...2nd pre-column.

314

except dimethyl disulfide for Subject A, are above the detectable objectionable threshold. The odor of DMTS resembles decaying cabbage.

Attention was now turned to "fasting breath" which was regularly sampled around noon time prior to lunch. "Fasting breath" is known to be malodorous, as reported by Tonzetich (8). The total concentration of VSC is much less in "fasting" than in "morning" breath. Subject B showed greatly reduced methyl mercaptan content (Fig. 3), but was consistent in showing the sulfur-containing

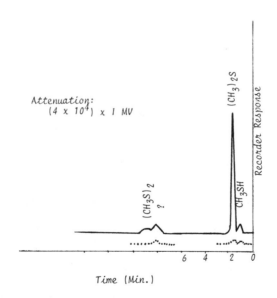

Fig. 3. Sulfur compounds in fasting (Pre-lunch) breath of
Subject B. 200 cc Sample trapped on 2 Tenax-GC pre-columns in
series. GC conditions c and FPD were used. ———— 1st. pre-
column,......2nd pre-column.

compound believed to be amyl mercaptan eluting before DMDS. Dimethyl disulfide (DMDS) is again detected as in "morning breath".

In "fasting breath" the breakthrough problem is not as serious because of lower concentrations; the second Tenax-GC pre-column after 200 cc of breath from Subject B showed only traces of the compounds found in the first pre-column

Two hundred cc of "fasting breath" from Subject A was also examined by a sharply different trapping technique (Fig. 4).

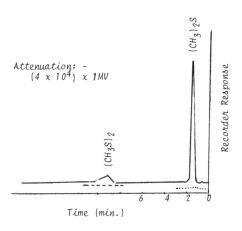

Fig. 4. Sulfur compounds in fasting (pre-lunch breath of Subject A. Sample was collected by recirculating breath via peristaltic pump for 10 minutes on 2 "Tenax-GC + activated charcoal" pre-columns in series - GC conditions c and FPD were used._____1st pre-column,.....2nd. pre-column.

The Tenax-GC was also improved upon by addition of activated charcoal to the pre-column as a layer separate from the Tenax. The Tenax layer is at the inlet side of the pre-column upon sampling, and is at the outlet upon elution of sample.

The sampling technique used was recirculation of the breath through the pre-column and back to the mouth with a peristaltic

pump at a flow rate of 20 cc/min. for 10 minutes. The equivalent of 200 cc sample was trapped on the pre-column; the procedure is outlined in Section E4. The second Tenax-charcoal
pre-column on the line showed a complete blank, thus proving no
breakthrough from the first trap. As before with this subject,
no methyl mercaptan is seen.

The use of a recirculating system strongly emphasizes
organics produced in the oral cavity and minimizes contributions
by any organics produced by the lung. An attempt was made to
compare 'lung' vs. 'mouth' breath (Fig. 5). "Fasting breath"

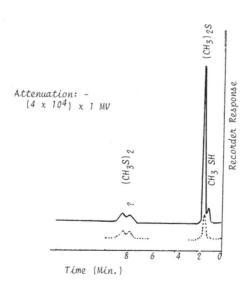

*Fig. 5. Comparison of "Mouth" vs. "lung" (exhaling) breath.
Both are fasting (pre-lunch) breath from Subject B. 100 cc
Sample was collected directly on Tenzx-GC pre-column. GC conditions c with FPD were used._____ "Mouth", and....."Lung"
breath.*

of Subject B using the two modes of breath sampling ("via mouth and breathing through nose only" compared to "strongly exhaled breath, i.e. lung breath") did not show any new components in the latter case.

The presence of sulfur compounds in exhaled breath, as shown in this particular analysis, does not necessarily suggest the lung as their origin, since they may be due to residuals in the mouth. When exhaled breath was analyzed after thorough cleansing of the mouth, teeth and tongue with a tooth brush, tri-calcium phosphate and water only a minute trace of dimethyl sulfide was now noted in both 'exhaled' and 'mouth' breath. However, use of a different sampling technique later gave evidence that dimethyl sulfide may be a constituent of "lung breath" at a far lower concentration.

Throughout this phase, the subjects were remarkably consistent in their individual patterns, although there was variation in the content of sulfur components on a day to day basis. "Morning breath" was always more odorous than "fasting breath" in all subjects and contained more sulfur compounds and always showed the dimethyl trisulfide peak. Manipulation and further concentration of samples (larger than 200 cc) will be needed to show this compound in "fasting breath".

The tentatively identified amyl mercaptan peak eluting just before dimethyl disulfide was seen only in breath of Subject B.

The pH values of saliva of the three subjects were quite

different, though fairly constant for each individual. Characteristic pH values of saliva from subjects A, B, and D were 6.4,
7.0, and 6.8 respectively. The possible significance of these
differences will be discussed later.

The presence of volatile sulfur compounds in larger amounts
in "morning breath", coupled with elimination from 'lung' and
'mouth' breath after oral hygiene clearly indicates that saliva
is the prime source of sulfur compounds in the breath, as was
previously reported by Tonzetich (3). Since methyl mercaptan
oxidizes readily to dimethyl disulfide it is not known whether
dimethyl disulfide detected in the breath is due to oxidation
of methyl mercaptan in the mouth, or due to enzymatic action on
sulfur-containing amino acids of the saliva, or to a combination
of both. This oxidation also occurs to a certain extent on the
pre-column if the sample is not analyzed immediately. The reaction of the pre-column is minimized by storing the pre-column
in a freezer or at sub-zero temperatures if it is not to be
analyzed soon after sample collection. Cold samples should be
allowed to warm up to room temperature prior to analysis.
Direct analysis of 10 cc "morning breath" indicated the presence
of the disulfide at a level comparable to dimethyl sulfide,
indicating that dimethyl disulfide does have its own prior
existence in the mouth, even though some methyl mercaptan doubt-
less can oxidize to the disulfide under the conditions of
collection and elution.

Saliva samples were collected from Subjects A and B while stimulating salivation by chewing polyvinyl acetate, a flavorless polymer. Three cc samples were incubated in 1 oz. capacity vials capped with Teflon-coated silicon rubber septa. Analyses of large headspace samples, using the same GC conditions which were used for breath analyses, show an increase of volatile sulfur compounds with time (Fig. 6). The same compounds which were seen in "morning breath" of Subject A are seen in incubated saliva headspace. After 3 hours at $37°C$, the pattern of "morning breath" and saliva headspace are almost identical. After 100 hours, the peak of dimethyl sulfide is greatly reduced but now large amounts of methyl mercaptan are seen. Some hydrogen sulfide is also noted. Although H_2S was seen as a trace in the headspace of putrefied saliva, and not seen at all in the chromatograms of mouth odor, no interpretation is possible because H_2S is poorly trapped by the pre-column, as noted by the odor of the pre-column effluent when the headspace of putrefied saliva was sampled. A new sulfur compound not detected in "fasting" or "morning" breath and eluting at about 11 minutes (the same retention time as hexyl mercaptan) is now seen for the first time in the 100 hour incubated sample. The pattern of incubated saliva headspace for Subject B is almost identical to this subject's "morning breath" including the peak believed to be amyl mercaptan. However, in saliva the usual mercaptan peak is missing, though the dimethyl sulfide is almost the same.

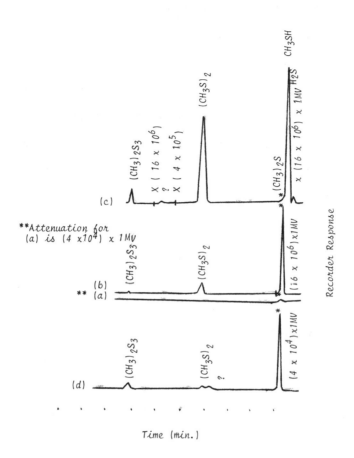

Fig. 6. - Sulfur compounds in saliva headspace. GC conditions c with FPD were used.
  a) 20 cc from fresh saliva, Subject A
  b) 40 cc after 3 hours at 37°C, Subject A
  c) 20 cc after 100 hours at RT, Subject A
  d) 80 cc after 1½ hours at 37°C, Subject B

The absence of mercaptan in this sample is probably due to the

fact that the saliva was collected soon after eating. The in-

take of food has been reported by Tonzetich (8) to reduce the number of gram negative bacteria which are responsible for generation of methyl mercaptan and H_2S in putrefied saliva.

A trace of indole was detected in the headspace of putrefied saliva (72 hours incubation at room temperature) when a 180 cc sample was collected and analyzed on a 20% SE-30 pre-column with a flame ionization detector. The indole trace was detected at a retention time of 33 minutes with GC conditions (a), which is characteristic of indole. The eluting peak had a distinct odor of indole, which was sought but not found by Larsson (6).

If the sample size is to exceed 70 cc it is necessary to use two or more standard pre-columns in series to prevent any losses of the most volatile organic compounds in the sample. Sample losses using one pre-column were shown (Fig. 1-5) with 100 and 200 cc sample sizes. The optimum sampling flow rate undoubtedly varies with the dimensions of the pre-column and the amount and type of packing. For a 6 inch x 4 mm. i.d. pre-column containing 200 mg. Tenax, the sample's organics are fully retained at up to 75 cc/min. flow. The height of 200 mg Tenax in this pre-column is 3½ inches.

Since the breath's organics can be concentrated on pre-columns it can be easily analyzed for any volatile odorants resulting from any ingested material. Because of its wide use in oral hygiene preparations, peppermint oil was chosen for analysis, and the breath was analyzed for peppermint oil components immediately after ingestion of a peppermint-flavored

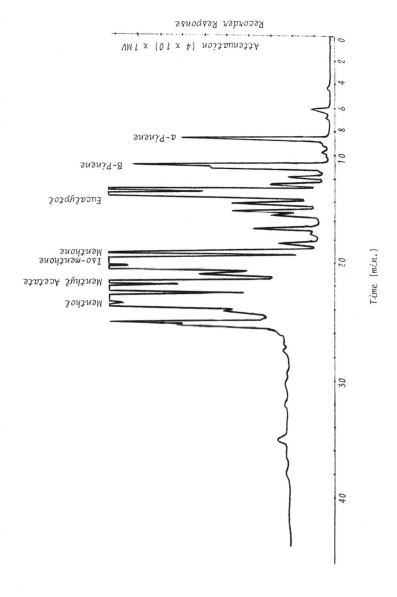

Fig. 7. Analysis of peppermint oil blend, 0.1 ul sample analyzed by direct injection. GC conditions (a) were used.

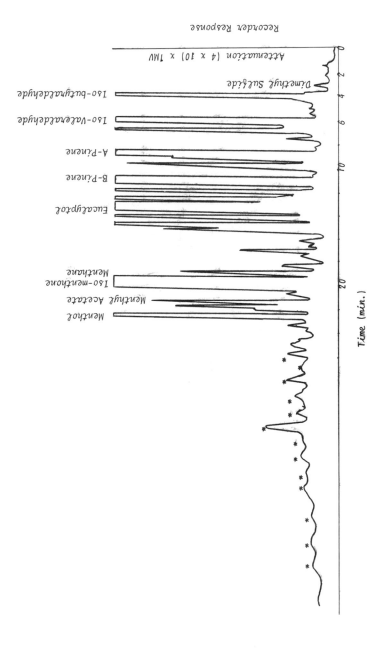

Fig. 8. Analysis of peppermint oil blend headspace (over 100 ul in 8 oz. capped bottle at RT) - 100 cc sample was analyzed as direct trap on Tenax-GC pre-column. GC conditions (a) were used.
* Artifacts probably due to thermal degradation of Tenax.

sugar fondant and at various intervals thereafter. To put the
problem into perspective Figures 7 and 8 show gas chromatographic analyses of peppermint oil (using FID) both as the oil
and as headspace collected on Tenax-GC pre-column. As expected,
the headspace analysis (Fig. 8) shows the more volatile constituents are present at a much higher proportion than in the
oil. Figure 8 shows also that the use of porous polymer pre-
column packing shows artifact peak formation due to some thermal
decomposition. These artifacts appear after the oven reaches
the final temperature and do not interfere with early eluting
components. Artifact formation is not seen using the FPD duc to
its selectivity for sulfur.

Analysis of the breath 1 minute after ingestion of 3 g
peppermint fondant (Fig. 9) gave a GC pattern qualitatively
similar to that obtained by direct analysis of the oil. The
level of peppermint in the breath 1 minute after the fondant is
high enough that direct analysis of a 10 cc sample is
sufficient and no sample concentration is necessary. The amount
of peppermint oil in this sample is about 0.3 micrograms or
0.003% of the ingested amount.

Concentration of the breath sample at 9 minutes after
taking the fondant by trapping 100 cc directly on a Tenax pre-
column (Fig. 10) gave a GC pattern qualitatively similar to
that of peppermint headspace, that is the more volatile components were proportionally higher than in the oil itself, as

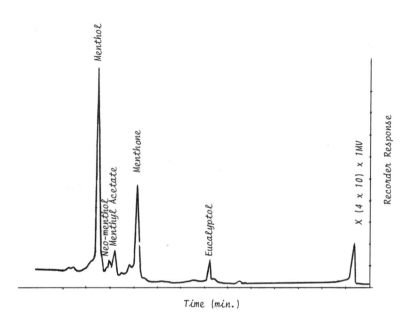

Fig. 9. Analysis of peppermint flavored breath - 10 cc sample ingected directly into chromatograph 1 minute after ingestion of 3 gm peppermint fondant. GC conditions (a) were used.

can be seen by comparing the peaks of menthone and eucalyptol to the menthol peak. Concentrating the breath greatly enhanced the peak for acetone, which has been reported many times in breath (6, 14, 15). The artifacts due to thermal decomposition of Tenax-GC are again noted.

To eliminate the artifacts due to the polymeric pre-column packing, activated charcoal was investigated. Figure 11 shows analyses of breath samples at 3, 14, and 25 minutes after eating peppermint fondant using 50 mg activated charcoal in

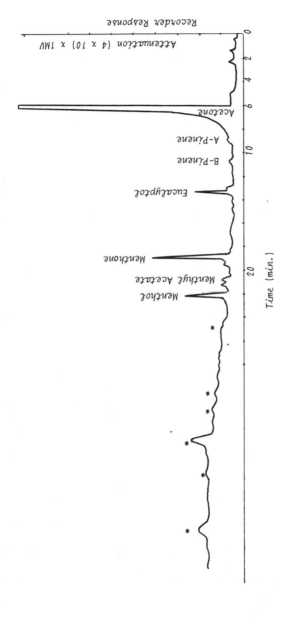

Fig. 10. Analysis of peppermint flavored breath 9 minutes after ingestion of 3 g peppermint fondant - 100 cc sample collected directly on Tenax-GC pre-column. GC conditions (a) were used.
*Artifacts which are probably due to thermal degradation of Tenax-GC.

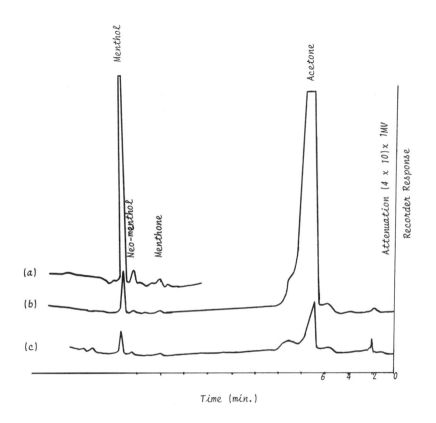

Fig. 11. Analyses of peppermint flavored breath; sampled directly on activated charcoal pre-column: (a) 3 minutes, (b) 14 minutes, (c) 25 minutes after ingestion of peppermint fondant   (a)   (b) are 100 cc samples, while (c) is re-circulated breath via peristaltic pump. GC conditions (a) were used.

the pre-column. While artifacts are not seen with charcoal,

its adverse effect on the constituents in the sample drastic-

ally negates this advantage. The only peppermint constitutents

which do not seem to be affected are menthol and neo-menthol;

the others are eliminated. The adverse effect of charcoal is

not fully understood. It may be chemical alteration or too

firm bonding or both. Smaller amounts of absorbent or higher
temperature may be indicated, but the problem of unpredictable
behaviour remains. Menthol, however was still shown to be
present in the breath 25 minutes after eating the fondant
(Figure 8 c) using this absorbent.

The use of standard coated column packings offers the
general advantages of ease of sample elution and greatly reduced
decomposition, and hence fewer interfering artifacts, whether
from the sample or pre-column packing. The disadvantage, at
least for the silicone coatings, is that they are rather less
retentive than the polymeric packings for the more volatile
organics. However, silicone coatings offer water-repellent
features which are valuable in breath analysis. Figure 12 shows
analyses of 100 cc breath 3 and 18 minutes after the peppermint
fondant using 20% SE-30 pre-columns (145 mg in injector insert).
The acetone peak, which was quite evident when either Tenax or
activated charcoal was used, was now absent, demonstrating the
likely loss of the most highly volatile constituents of this
sample. Even so the chromatogram of peppermint flavor in 100cc
of breath collected at 3 minutes shows a pattern very similar
to that of the oil's headspace, except that the peaks of
A-pinene and B-pinene are relatively low. Figure 12b shows
that other peppermint components in addition to menthol are
retained in the mouth for as long as 18 minutes after ingestion
of one candy.

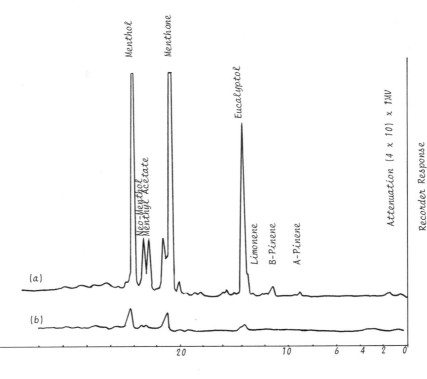

Time (min.)

Fig. 12. *Analyses of peppermint flavored breath on 20%*
SE-30 pre-column; (a) 3 minutes and (b) 18 minutes after in-
gestion of peppermint fondant. GC condition (a) were used.

Since onion is one of the most notable extrinsic mouth

odors, analysis for it in the breath offers an opportunity of

understanding its behavior in the mouth and studying the effect

of deodorizing treatments in reducing it. Rinsing the mouth

with a diluted solution of onion oil (50 ppm) and subsequent

analysis of the breath for sulfur compounds was chosen as a

model since it is more reproducible and easier than chewing

onions; any particles left in the mouth from chewing onions

present a problem. Analysis of the stock onion oil solution

(2.0%), from which the diluted rinse solution was prepared, is

shown in Fibure 13. The identifications shown for some of the

sulfur containing peaks are based on retention time comparisons

with the pure chemicals.

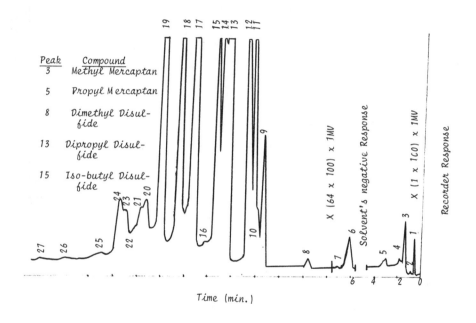

Peak	Compound
3	Methyl Mercaptan
5	Propyl Mercaptan
8	Dimethyl Disulfide
13	Dipropyl Disulfide
15	Iso-butyl Disulfide

Time (min.)

Fig. 13. Sulfur compounds in onion oil solution (2% in ethanol) - 0.1 ul sample was analyzed. GC conditions (b) and FPD were used.

Breath analyses of three different individuals after mouth

rinse with onion oil solution are shown in Figures 14, 15 and

16. The peaks are numbered to correspond to those of onion oil

analysis (Figure 13). Large differences can be seen among the

onion breaths of the three individuals, both quantitatively and in relationship of peaks to each other. The most remarkable

difference, however, is that between the chromatograms of onion

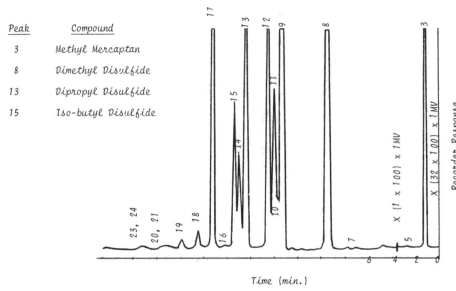

Peak	Compound
3	Methyl Mercaptan
8	Dimethyl Disulfide
13	Dipropyl Disulfide
15	Iso-butyl Disulfide

Time (min.)

Fig. 14.   Sulfur compounds in breath of Subject A immediately after rinsing mouth with 0.005% onion oil solution; 10 cc sample was analyzed by direct injection.   GC conditions (b) and FPD were used.

oil and the various breaths (Figs. 14, 15, 16) derived from it.

The large amounts of methyl and propyl mercaptans (peaks 3 and

5) are quite surprising, since both compounds are present in

onion oil only in traces. The amount of dimethyl disulfide

also increased substantially in onion breath in comparison to

the oil. The presence of volatile mercaptans, especially methyl

mercaptan, in large amounts in onion breath is undoubtedly

responsible for the unpleasantness of onion breath when com-

pared to fresh onion odor. These changes found in onion oil

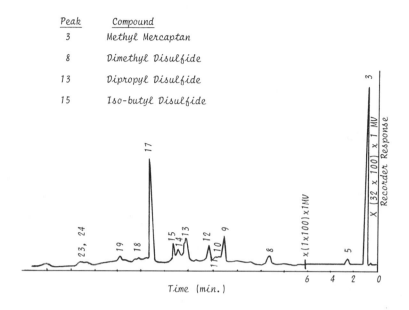

Peak	Compound
3	Methyl Mercaptan
8	Dimethyl Disulfide
13	Dipropyl Disulfide
15	Iso-butyl Disulfide

Fig. 15. Sulfur compounds in breath of Subject B immediately after rinsing mouth with 0.005% onion oil solution; 10 cc sample was analyzed by direct injection. GC conditions (b) and FPD were used.

breath were also noted in the breath after chewing fresh onions.

These thiols and probably others are presumably generated by

the action of oral enzymes on the di- and tri-sulfides in

onion oil. Action of micro-organisms to form thiols from di-

sulfides has been reported in bread cultures by Blackburn and

Challenger (38) probably via sulfide interchange reaction

mechanism.

The peaks which increased in onion oil breath, as compared

to onion oil, are 3, 5, 8, and 9, while an appreciable decrease

was shown in peaks 13 (dipropyl disulfide, the major peak of

Peak	Compound
3	Methyl Mercaptan
8	Dimethyl Disulfide
13	Dipropyl Disulfide
15	Iso-butyl Disulfide

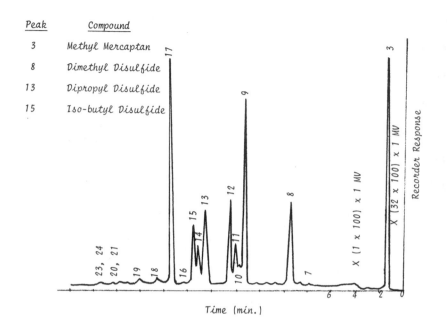

Fig. 16. Sulfur compounds in breath of Subject C immediately after rinsing mouth with 0.005% onion oil solution; 10 cc sample was analyzed by direct injection - GC conditions (b) and FPD were used.

onion oil), 16, 17, 23, and 24. Generation of methyl and propyl

mercaptans from onion and onion oil is presumably the result

of fission of di- and tri-sulfide bonds. Peak 6 shows an

appreciable but gradual increase in breath sampled 5 minutes or

more after rinsing the mouth with onion oil solution. Retention

time of this peak is identical to that of butyl mercaptan.

The volunteers, whose onion oil breath analyses are shown

(Figures 14, 15, and 16) differed in their saliva pH values

(6.4, 7.0 and 6.7 respectively for volunteers A, B. and C).

Differences in saliva pH suggest metabolic and enzymatic

differences among the individuals in their handling of onion
oil. The higher saliva pH was associated with lower concentrations of methyl and propyl mercaptans (relative to other constituents) and with lower amounts of sulfur compounds in the
breath.

The works of Boelens, et.al. (39) and Whitaker (40) provide
an excellent review of the recent work on both onion and onion
oil.

Since the concentration of volatile sulfur compounds is
high immediately after the ingestion of onion or a rinse with
onion oil solution, the breath can be analyzed easily by direct
injection of a 10 cc sample. This becomes more difficult after
a few minutes when the concentration decreases appreciably. The
comparison of breath sampled 5 minutes after a mouth rinse with
onion oil solution (Fig. 17) with breath taken immediately after
the onion oil rinse (Figs. 14, 15, 16 though the G.C. parameters
differed slightly) demonstrates the need for further concentration of sample to enhance detectability of components following
peak 5. Concentrating the breath onion volatiles by direct
trapping of larger volumes on pre-columns containing liquid
coated supports proved very satisfactory for trapping less
volatile components. An analysis of 50 cc onion oil breath
trapped on 20% SE-30 pre-column (Fig. 18) when compared with
Figure 14 shows that considerable losses occurred in the first
five peaks. Losses of peaks 9-13 were minimal and no losses

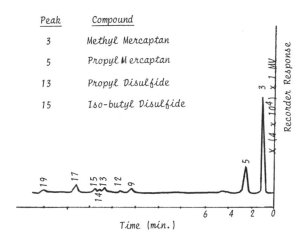

Peak	Compound
3	Methyl Mercaptan
5	Propyl Mercaptan
13	Propyl Disulfide
15	Iso-butyl Disulfide

Fig. 17. Sulfur compounds in breath of Subject B after rinsing mouth with 0.005% onion oil solution; 10 cc sample injected directly into gas chromatograph. GC conditions (C) and FPD were used.

were noted after peak 13. This was checked by subsequent

analysis of a back-up trap to the SE-30 pre-column packed with

Tenax-GC.

The porous polymers (Tenax GC and Porapak) were also found

effective for onion breath analysis. A 75 cc sample of strong

onion breath is effectively trapped with no losses of any

volatile components on 200 mg Tenax GC packed in a 6 inch x 4 mm

i. d. glass pre-column. Effective trapping is indicated by

no odor breakthrough from the trap and by analysis of a second

pre-column in series.

Suction-aided collection of a 40 cc breath sample taken

directly through a Tenax-GC pre-column and subsequent analysis

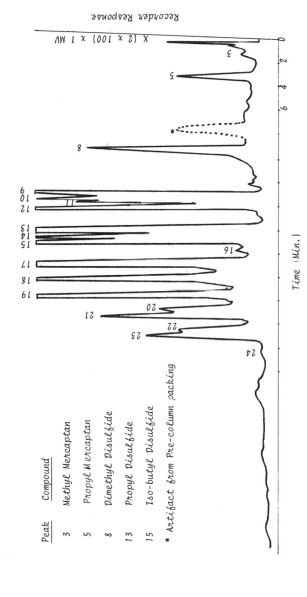

Peak	Compound
3	Methyl Mercaptan
5	Propyl Mercaptan
8	Dimethyl Disulfide
13	Propyl Disulfide
15	Iso-butyl Disulfide
*	Artifact from Pre-column packing

Fig. 18. Sulfur compounds in breath of Subject A following mouth rinse with 0.005% onion oil solution; 50 cc sample collected directly on a 20% SE-30 pre-column. GC conditions (b) and FPD were used.

for sulfur compounds by FPD was finally selected as the optimum method for determining whether breath deodorizing treatments are effective in reducing onion odor. This choice seemed the best compromise to meet different needs of rapidity, sensitivity and reproducibility of analysis. Larger volumes would obviously permit lower readings, but 40 cc is as large a breath sample as can be taken quickly and conveniently by suction with a gas syringe through the high back-pressure characteristic of that amount (and dimension) of porous polymer packing needed to give a safety factor of at least two in assurance of representative sampling. By this is meant absorption of all components characteristic of not unrealistic initial concentration of onion oil on the breath, and of the subsequent concentrations resulting either from natural decay processes or from deodorizing treatments. The initial concentration represents a strong onion odor, but is not so strong as to be a swamping condition. In any case, the comfort of panelists taking the onion oil treatment has to be taken into consideration if the panel is to have enough longevity to permit the development of instrumental correlation. Onion oil is an extremely difficult model because of its complexity of high boiling components of very low odor threshold and high persistence; but in the authors' view represents the definitive test for breath odor methodology.

The standard 40 cc was used to analyze onion breath at time zero (after the specified diluted onion oil rinses) and

at exactly 5 minutes later when a more stable value could be
obtained. Deodorization treatments, if any, were taken within
this first five minutes. This permitted evaluation of deodorizing treatments by comparison of their "5 minute values" with
each other and with that of the control. The 5 minute value is
measured as nanograms of total sulfur per 40 cc breath sample.
Typical data, shown in Table 1, are given here as percentages to
permit easier comparison of five different deodorizing treatments in one subject who showed good consistency in his 5 minute
control values (i.e. with no treatment). Each subject showed
fair to good consistency in his control values, though mean
values for each occurred within the 100 to 250 nanogram sulfur
range. Within each product class the deodorizing treatment was
made identical; but is is not intended here to go beyond the
methodological aspects since detailed results are more appropri-
ately given elsewhere.

The data already show that the deodorizing treatment, regardless of its form, reduces the concentration of onion odor
constituents in the breath. Chewing even unflavored gum base
also reduced onion odor in breath, presumably due to increased
salivation. Tonzetich (8) attributed the effectiveness of
eating in the reduction of volatile sulfur compounds in "morning
breath" to the act of chewing with subsequent enhanced salivation
removing odorant molecules from the dorsal surface of the tongue.

An example of the chromatograms upon which Table 1 is based

Table I: Typical Effect of Deodorizing Treatment on Breath Following Mouth Rinse with Diluted Onion Oil Solution; Measured as Total Amount of Sulfur in the Breath Five Minutes After Rinse with Onion Oil Solution.

Control (No deodorizing treatment after onion oil solution rinse) (ng sulfur)*	Treatment I (% of Control)	Treatment II (% of Control)	Treatment III (% of Control)	Treatment IV (% of Control)	Treatment V (% of Control)
129.3	46.5	52.0	55.5	-	-
139.4	-	-	-	47.1	51.7
138.6	26.0	-	-	-	-
113.8	-	54.8	58.2	54.2	60.9

* Expressed as ng sulfur in 40 cc breath.

Treatment I is with deodorant candy Brand A, treatment II is deodorant candy Brand B, treatment III is deodorant chewing gum Brand B, treatment IV is regular chewing gum Brand A, treatment V is teeth and tongue brushing with tooth paste.

is shown in Fig. 19 which shows analyses of onion breath 5 minutes after the onion oil rinse, with and without a breath deodorizing treatment.   Considerable reduction is effected on
every peak after the treatment, especially those of methyl and
propyl mercaptans (peaks 3, 5).   Because of the square response
of the FPD this decrease is not easily seen, though readily
shown by calculation.

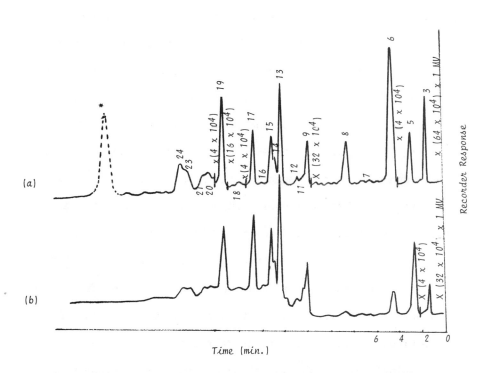

Fig. 19.   Sulfur compounds in breath of Subject B after
mouth rinse with onion oil solution followed by:(a)   no breath
deodorizing treatment (Control), (b)   one breath deodorizing
mint-treatment I.   40 cc Sample collected directly on One
Tenax-GC pre-column.   GC conditions C and PFD were used.
    *An artifact of unknown origin which occasionally appeared.

Refinements of data presentation were sought to document

the effect of deodorizing treatments over and above that due to the natural decay of onion odor in an untreated mouth. Because of person-to-person variability it is desirable to use each subject as his own control. Also, because of the lime lag between breath sampling and the completion of the chromatogram the experiment has to be "committed to" on the basis that for any one subject the zero time values for onion breath are comparable and sufficiently stable to be meaningfully analyzed.

A better understanding of the situation may be obtained by considering the results shown by rapid sequential analysis of onion breath taken at five minute intervals. In one case the natural decay of onion odor was followed and a curve obtained plotting time against nanograms sulfur. In the other, a five minute deodorizing treatment was taken immediately after time zero (the end of the onion oil rinse sequence) and nanograms sulfur again obtained at five minute intervals.

Figure 20 shows both decay curves using the same subject. The effect of treatment is shown most clearly in the first 10 minutes. Measured as a fraction of the zero time content, the 5 minute value for the treated breath is only a tenth of the original value. The untreated breath at five minutes has about a half of its original sulfur content. The effect of the one deodorizing treatment is seen to persist as a reduction in sulfur content when both measurements are followed for almost an hour, with a factor of at least two in favor of the treatment.

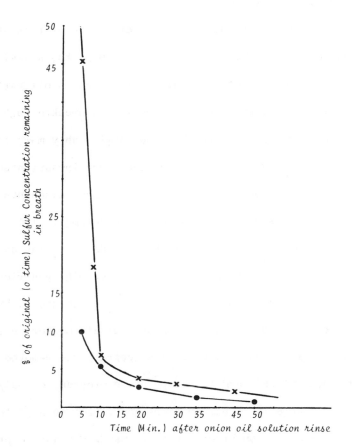

Fig. 20. *Decrease in total concentration of sulfur compounds in onion breath with time; (x) control - no breath deodorizing treatment, (o) one breath mint (treatment I) after onion oil rinse. 40 cc Samples were analyzed on Tenax-GC precolumn. GC conditions (b) and FPD were used.*

As the decay curve is followed out beyond 30 to 40 minutes, the 40 cc breath sample size is seen to become inadequate for clear representation of onion oil on the breath. In addition, the background of natural sulfur compounds in breath becomes visible as sulfur compounds not characteristic of onion oil.

At least one compound from onion oil appears to increase with time, however.

Taking larger breath samples of 250 or 500 cc at this stage permits large enhancement of the chromatogram peaks, allowing definite identification of the characteristic onion oil pattern. Two traps (in series) are needed to handle the breakthrough, necessitating two separate analyses and considerably more time.

A single 18" long, pre-column was therefore investigated for collection of large breath volumes for trace components, using 600 mg of Tenax-GC (12" x 4 mm in the column). This was stripped onto the analytical column using a movable ring oven at $250°C$, moving at $\frac{1}{2}$" per minute with a 15 cc/min. gas flow. The first few inches of the analytical column were cooled by wrapping with a plastic tube containing ice/salt mixture until the transfer was judged complete. The ice/salt was removed, the column oven closed, and the temperature programmed analysis begun. Some change in retention times and slight loss of the initial volatiles was observed. Results using a standard pre-column insert for receipt of the stripped volatiles from the long pre-column were as good, and more conveniently obtained.

For proof of efficacy of deodorizing treatment up to 25 minutes or so, the 40 cc sample will probably suffice, and has practical advantages over the long pre-column method.

Attention was now turned to other breath odorants, such as sulfur-rich foods like cabbage, where enhanced enzymatic action

in saliva could be expected. Chopped cabbage by itself under-
goes well known enzymatic changes to isothiocyanates and related
intermediates such as nitri es.

Figure 21 shows changes in sulfur compounds which occur in
headspace of chopped cabbage at room temperature.

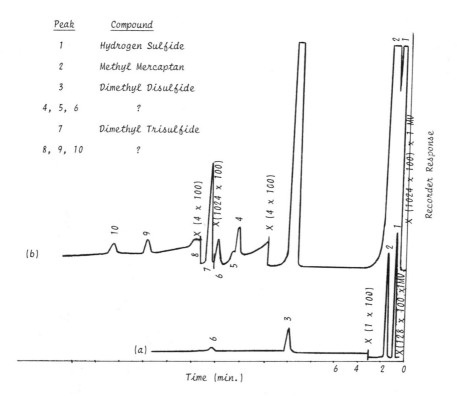

Peak	Compound
1	Hydrogen Sulfide
2	Methyl Mercaptan
3	Dimethyl Disulfide
4, 5, 6	?
7	Dimethyl Trisulfide
8, 9, 10	?

Fig. 21. Sulfur compounds in chopped cabbage headspace
(50 g in 8 oz. capped bottle) - 10 cc direct injection into
chromatograph; (a) freshly chopped cabbage, (b) 71 hours at
room temperature, GC conditions (b) and FPD were used.

The only compounds noted in headspace of freshly chopped

cabbage (Fig. 21a) are hydrogen sulfide, methyl mercaptan, a

very small amount of dimethyl disulfide, and an unknown

(peak 6). After aging for 71 hours, a large increase is noted
in peaks 1, 2 and 3, and dimethyl trisulfide (peak 7) is generated in large amounts. The unknown (peak 6) is increased
slightly, while other unknowns are also generated (peaks 4, 5,
8, 9, 10). The strongly objectionable odor of rotting cabbage
seems due to compounds of peaks 1, 2, 3 and 7 with peak 7 (dimethyl trisulfide) providing the most distinct rotten cabbage
odor. This compound was reported by Maruyama (41) to be the
main cause of stale cooked cabbage odor.

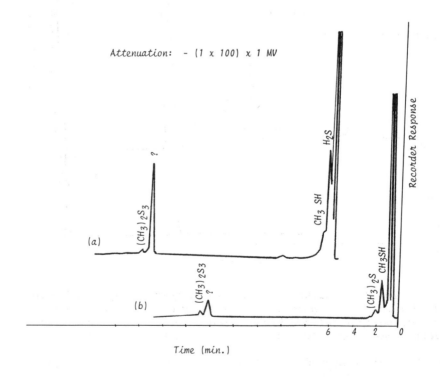

Fig. 22. Sulfur compounds in breath after ingestion of
cabbage (50 gm) - 10 cc Sample injected directly into chromatograph; (a) breath of Subject A, (b) breath of Subject (B) -
GC conditions (b) and FPD were used.

Analysis of the breaths of subjects after eating 50 g fresh cabbage (Fig. 22) showed that dimethyl trisulfide (peak 7) is generated in the breath and the unknown (peak 6) is enhanced, although in different proportions. The appearance of dimethyl trisulfide in cabbage breath, while not noted in fresh cabbage headspace was interesting. While the breath of Subject B additionally contained methyl mercaptan and dimethyl sulfide, the breath of Subject A contained hydrogen sulfide and methyl mercaptan, suggesting oral enzymatic differences.

Eating sauerkraut, which is no longer affected by enzymes, did not cause any new sulfur compounds on the breath. Figure 23 shows analyses of sauerkraut headspace and of breath after ingestion of 50 g sauerkraut. Only methyl mercaptan and di-methyl sulfide, which are the major sulfur compounds in sauer-kraut headspace, were detected in the breath.

In the examples quoted quantitation of sulfur compounds in the breath was accomplished by manual integration of peak areas by the "height x width at half height" method, and determining the amount of elemental sulfur in the sample from a log-log calibration of standards ranging in concentration from 0.5 to 300 ng sulfur. The standards were solutions of dimethyl sulfide in absolute ethanol. To minimize errors due to differ-ence in matrix, the standard was analyzed in the same manner as the sample by depositing 1 ul of standard at the end of the pre-column packing and passing a volume of air equal to the sample

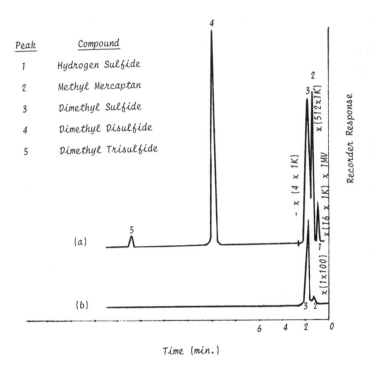

Peak	Compound
1	Hydrogen Sulfide
2	Methyl Mercaptan
3	Dimethyl Sulfide
4	Dimethyl Disulfide
5	Dimethyl Trisulfide

Fig. 23. Sulfur compounds in sauerkraut headspace and "sauerkraut breath" - (a) sauerkraut headspace (over 15 g in 30 cc vial). (b) breath after 40 g sauerkraut. 10 cc Samples were analyzed by direct injection. GC conditions (b) and FPD were used.

volume through the pre-column at the flow rate used in sample collection.

The choice of dimethyl sulfide as the standard is for speed of analysis, due to its short retention time allowing frequent calibration, and to the fact that the bulk of concentration of sulfur compounds in the breath is composed of volatiles of relatively short retention times. In spite of the differences in retention times between the standard and slower eluting compounds such as dimethyl disulfide and dipropyl disulfide, good recoveries were obtained for the latter two components, ranging from 85 to 96%.

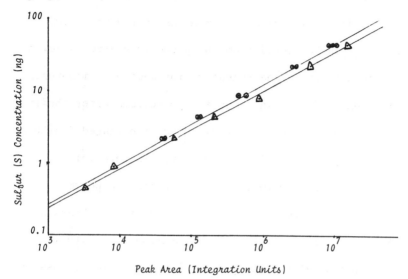

Fig. 24. *Calibration of dimethyl sulfide standards with direct injection and by analysis on pre-column; (a) pre-column analysis, (b) direct injection of the equal amount.*

Analysis via pre-column does result in loss of sample. Comparison of log-log calibrations (Fig. 24) of identical sets of standards analyzed by direct injection of 1 ul and by trapping of the same amount of Tenax - GC pre-column by simulated breath sampling shows that direct analysis consistently gives a higher response than does pre-column trapping and analysis.

Very low boiling components such as dimethyl sulfide are effectively eluted from the pre-column after 1 minute at 250°C, while high boiling components are effectively eluted after 4 minutes. Heating the pre-column for 6 minutes was adopted for this work. High boil-

ing components (of retention times longer than dimethyl disulfide), especially when present at high concentrations, are not
completely eluted off the pre-column even after a prolonged
heating period; a residual amount remains on the pre-column.
This residual can be eluted from the pre-column after allowing
the pre-column to cool, and reheating for another 6 minutes.
The sulfur compounds remaining on the pre-column after the intended elution of 200 ng of dipropyl disulfide ranged from 6 to
12 ng i.e. 3 to 6% of the initial amount. The problem of
trapped residuals on pre-columns is not unique to polymer
packings, but was noted also with support-coated packings such
as 20% SE-30. Prolonging the initial heating period to 18
minutes did not eliminate the problem and the residual loss remained in the 3 to 6% range. To compensate for errors due to
residual entrapment, the pre-column can be stripped again after
cooling, but usally it is enough, if an "echo" of the first
analysis is obtained, to gain an indication of the pre-column
behavior and to prepare the pre-column for the next analysis.

No loss of sample volatiles was noted up to 3 hours after
the collection of the sample on the pre-column when both ends
were capped tightly while the pre-column was stored at room
temperature. Storage of the tightly capped pre-column in a
refrigerator for 24 hours resulted in no loss in sample volatiles.

The use of open tubes as "collection" pre-columns for very

large breath volumes offers at least theoretical advantages over large packed pre-columns in sample handling, and perhaps for avoiding residual entrapment characteristic of highly absorptive substances by using a larger amount of a weak absorbent in a favorable physical configuration. Illustrative of their use was an experiment using nearly 40 feet of 3/16 inch i.d. Tygon tubing, coiled and immersed in a warm water bath (38°C). Prior to use, the tubing is conditioned by a gas sweep at 100°C to obtain a zero blank with the FPD, though not with the FID. The Tygon is so well plasticized that the tubing wall is effectively "coated". The volume of such a "collecting pre-column" was 217 cc; the back pressure was slight. One exhalation of about 1 liter can be achieved through the column with comfort in 1 minute. At the temperature of the bath it is clear that breath condensation inside the Tygon is minimal. Onion breath is not detected (by odor) at the column exit even after several breaths, indicating it is functioning as a collection device in spite of its poor efficiency as a chromatographic device.

Four long exhalations (4 liters) of onion breath were passed through this Tygon "pre-column" in about 4 minutes. The Tygon coil was then transferred to a 95°C water bath and back-flushed for 10 minutes with nitrogen at 40 cc/minute. The desorbed volatiles were passed through a standard Tenax pre-column at room temperature, and the pre-column was then analyzed in the normal manner (Fig. 25). The pattern of sulfur volatiles

was almost identical to that of 200 cc onion breath collected

by blowing directly on the small pre-column; the principal

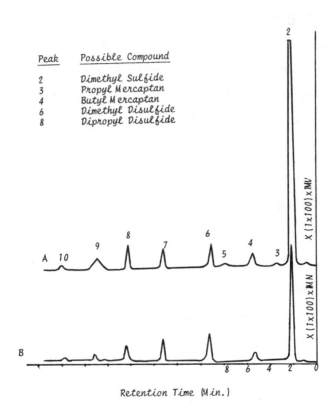

*Fig. 25. Sulfur compounds in "onion breath" 5 minutes
after mouth rinse with onion oil solution; (A) 4 liters
collected by blowing in 40 ft., ¼" O.D. Tygon tubing, (B)
200 cc collected by blowing directly on Tenax-GC pre-column.
GC conditions (b) and FPD were used.*

difference was large increase in the dimethyl sulfide peak ob-

tained from the Tygon "pre-column" suggesting the possibility

of an additional source of this compound. The dimethy sulfide

has apparently come from the lungs but was not necessarily

produced there.

Traces of dimethyl sulfide were always found in breath, how-ever, no matter how thorough the prior oral hygiene. The 20-fold increase in sample volume did little to increase the other onion volatiles, suggesting a similar degree of dilution for them as the mouth odor was mixed with the rapidly exhaled lung breath. Incomplete elution from the "collection" pre-column may also be a factor, though easy elution from a weak absorbent would be ex-pected to avoid this possibility.

Good prospects for breath analysis might be found to lie in long open pre-columns of this type, particularly if interest de-velops in the trace volatiles in lung breath, requiring larger sampling methodologies. This is not to say that the direct sampling and packed pre-column techniques described here are not capable of future development, but suggests long collection columns of weak absorption power may have a place besides the standard ones if easy desorption can be a useful factor.

As referred to earlier, a large sample of onion breath was directly examined with some difficulty with syringe-aided suc-tion through a Tenax-GC pre-column at "time zero plus 30 minutes" when the standard 40 cc volume of mouth breath was giving only a marginal response for sulfur compounds (Fig. 26). The pre-column enriched with volatiles from the 500 cc sample gave very clear evidence of sulfur compounds from onion oil. However, it also showed a large background of intrinsic sulfur volatiles

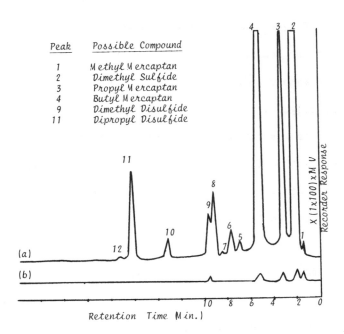

Peak	Possible Compound
1	Methyl Mercaptan
2	Dimethyl Sulfide
3	Propyl Mercaptan
4	Butyl Mercaptan
9	Dimethyl Disulfide
11	Dipropyl Disulfide

Fig. 26. Sulfur compounds in "onion breath" 30 minutes after mouth rinse with onion oil solution; (a) 500 cc, (b) 40 cc. Samples were collected and analyzed on Tenax-GC precolumn.GC conditions (b) and FPD were used.

(DMS and DMDS) seen earlier in "morning" and "fasting" breath, resulting in some confusion as to the source of some substances.

Techniques which help distinguish lung breath from mouth breath, such as open "collection" pre-columns will be needed especially to meet the short time requirements of sequential analysis. Techniques like the cyclic enrichment system, which maximize the effects of events in the oral cavity, should also prove useful in separating intrinsic from extrinsic factors.

ACKNOWLEDGEMENT

. The authors acknowledge the invaluable assistance of A. R. Pidel in the performance of the analyses and greatly appreciate his and other coworkers' efforts in participating in some of the experiments.

REFERENCES:

1. Mackay, D.A.M., Lang, D.A., Berdick, M., The Toilets Goods Association 32, 45 (1959).

2. Mackay, D.A.M., "Gas Chromatography 1960", (R.P.W. Scott, Ed.), p. 357.William Clowes and Sons Ltd., London, 1960.

3. Tonzetich, J., Arch. Oral Biol. 16,587 (1971).

4. Tonzetich, J., Johnson, P.W. Arch Oral Biol. 22,125 (1977).

5. Mackay, D.A.M., Lang, D.A., Berdick, M., Anal. Chem. 33, 1369 (1961).

6. Jansson, B.O., Larsson, B.T., J. Lab. & Clin. Med. 74., 961 (1969)

7. Anonymous, Chem. Eng. News. March 14, 36 (1960).

8. Tonzetich, J., Ng, S.K., Oral Surg. 42,172 (1976).

9. Larsson, B.T. Acta Chemica Scandinavica 19,159 (1965).

10. Teranishi, R., Mon, T.R., Robinson, A.B., Cary, P., Pauling, L., Anal. Chem. 44.18 (1972)

11. Zlatkis, A., Lichtenstein, H. A., Tishbee, A., Chromatographia 6, 67 (1973).

12. Zlatkis, A., Lichtenstein, H. A., Tishbee, A., Bertsch, W., Shunbo, F., Liebich, H.M., J. Chrom. Sci. 11, 299 (1973)

13. Fletcher, J. C., U. S. Patent 4003257, Jan. 18, 1977

14. Conkle, J. P., Camp, B. J., Welch, B. E., Arch. Env.Health 30, 290 (1975).

15. Krotoszynski,B., Gabriel, G., O'Neill, H., Claudio, M.P.A. J. Chrom. Sci. 15, 239 (1977)

16. Mieure, J. P., Dietrich, M.W., J. Chrom Sci. 11,559 (1973).

17. Russell, J.W., Environmental Sci & Tech. 9, 1175 (1975)

18. Novotny, N., Lee, M.L., Bartle, K.D., Chromatographia 7, 333 (1974).

19. Darbre, A., Islam, A., J. Chromatog. 49, 293 (1970)

20. Cramers, C.,A., Van Kessel, M.M., J. Chromatog. 6, 577 (1968)

21. Brown, D.F., Dollear, F.D., Dupuy, H.P., J. Am. Oil Chem.Soc. 49, 81 (1972)

22. Hachenberg, H., Schmidt, A.P., "Gas Chromatographic Head-space Analysis", Heyden & Sons Ltd, London, 1977.

23. Dateo, G.P., Clapp, R.C., Mackay, D.A.M., Hewitt, E.J., Hasselstrom, T., Food Res. 22,440 (1957)

24. Young, R.E., Pratt, H. K., Baiale, J.B., Anal. Chem., 24, 551 (1952).

25. Haagen-Smit, A.J., Kirchner, J.G., Prater, A.N., Deasy, C.L., JACS. 67. 1646 (1945)

26. Dimick, K.P., Corse, J., Food Tech. 10,360 (1956)

27. Eggertsen, F.T., Nelsen, F.M., Anal. Chem. 30, 1040 (1958)

28. Farrington, P.S., Pecsok, R.L., Meeker, R.L., Olson, T.J., Anal. Chem. 31, 1512 (1959)

29. Rhoades, J.W., J. Agr. Food Chem. 8, 136 (1958)

30. Birchfield, H.P., Storrs, E.E., "Biochemical Applications of Gas Chromatography", Pages 208, 212, Academic Press, New York, 1962.

31. Nawar, W.W., Fagerson, I.S., Anal. Chem. 32, 1534 (1960)

32. MacLeod A.L., MacLeod, G., J. Sc. Fd. Agr. 19, 273 (1968).

33. Self, R., Casey, J.C., Swain, T., Chem. & Ind., p. 863 (1963)

34. Saguy, M., Mannheim, C.H., Peleg, J. Food Tech. 24, 165 (1970)

35. Schwimmer, S., Guadagni, D.G., J. Food Sci.33, 193 (1968)

36. Bernhard, R.A., J. Food Sci. 33, 298 (1968)

37. Brodnitz, M.H., Pollock, C.L., Food Tech. 24, 78 (1970).

38. Blackburn, S., Challenger, F., J. Chem. Soc. 1872 (1938)

39. Boelens, M., de Valois, P.J., Wobben, H.J., Van der Gen, A. J. Agr. Food Chem. 19, 984 (1971).

40. Whitaker, J.R., "Development of Flavor, Odor, and Pungency of Onion and Garlic", Advances in Food Research, Vol. 22 p. 73, Academic Press, New York, 1976.

41. Maruyama, F.T., J. Food Sci. 35,540 (1970)

HEADSPACE TECHNIQUES USED IN THE ANALYSIS OF
VOLATILE COMPONENTS FROM LIPOXYGENASE CATALYZED REACTIONS

J. A. SINGLETON AND H. E. PATTEE

USDA, Mid-Atlantic Area, SR, ARS, North Carolina State University

Many volatile compounds that contribute to the flavor of
fruits and vegetables are formed by enzymatic action during
maceration of the tissue. In peanuts, soybeans, tomatoes,
potatoes, and cucumbers the major volatiles in the flavor
profiles arise via the breakdown of hydroperoxides produced by
lipoxygenase from polyunsaturated acids containing a 1,4
cis,cis pentadiene system in the presence of molecular oxygen.
Various isolation techniques and subsequent sampling methods for
gas-liquid chromatography and mass spectrometry have been
employed to study the biochemistry of enzymatic flavor production
and mechanisms involved. Headspace preconcentration methods and
sampling techniques offer some unique advantages in this area.
Volatiles can be preconcentrated and analyzed using a minimum of
time under mild conditions which decreases the risk of possible
artifact formation. The method of choice for preconcentration
of headspace vapors depends on sample size, vapor pressure,
concentration, boiling point range of volatiles to be studied,
and information desired. Preconcentration methods, sampling
techniques, interpretation of volatile profiles, and problems
encountered in vapor phase analysis will be discussed. Data
presented represents an application of headspace techniques to

the study of biochemical production of volatile components from
lipoxygenase catalyzed reactions.

I.   CHARACTERISTICS AND APPLICATIONS OF HEADSPACE TECHNIQUES

The composition of vapors above foodstuffs and beverages
depends to a great extent on the vapor pressure of the components
present and the nature of the substrate matrix. For example, if
two systems are chemically similar in total volatile analysis yet
vary in their lipid content, headspace analysis would result in
different volatile profiles, and the odor perceived would be
quite different. Since threshold levels and concentration of
the components present in the vapors above food products actually
determines the odor sensation perceived by our olfactory system,
headspace analysis can be used effectively to show the relative
importance of a specific component to overall odor perception.
The term "volatile", as used in a composition analysis, is a
functional term and includes compounds possessing a wide range of
boiling points. The compounds may be non-condensable gases to
compounds that require high vacuum degassing and molecular
distillation for removal. One of the major difficulties in
volatile analysis is the separation of water which is generally
the major volatile present in aqueous systems from the trace
constituents of interest. Therefore, the criteria used to select
a volatile analysis method or combinations of techniques should
be based on the volatility of the constituents, their relative
concentrations, lability, polarity, and the nature of the
substrate matrix. Techniques such as direct vapor analysis,
various preconcentration methods, and combinations of high
vacuum degassing and vapor sampling have been used in volatile
analysis since the advent of gas-liquid chromatography. All of
these techniques have advantages or special applications,
depending on the system being analyzed.

Direct vapor sampling has been used frequently for the analysis of volatiles over a wide variety of products. Approximately 5-10cc of headspace vapor over a product is sampled by syringe and injected directly into a gas-liquid chromatograph. This technique has proved useful in numerous applications: monitoring rancidity development in potato granules during storage, showing the qualitative and quantitative changes in volatiles that occur in ripening bananas, analyzing the flavor components of vinegar and off-flavor development in peanuts, determining the flame response ionization response to various carrier gases, and facilitating study of the enzymatic production of volatiles in tomato and peanut homogenates (1,2,3,4,5,6,7). These applications illustrate the usefulness of direct sampling to obtain different types of information.

Although the direct headspace sampling technique offers some unique advantages, the concentrations of vapor components can sometimes be limiting; therefore preconcentration of headspace vapor is often necessary. Recycling of vapors, N_2 gas sweeping, and high vacuum degassing are preconcentration techniques that have been used in the study of headspace volatiles (8-11). More recently, porous polymers have been used to preconcentrate headspace vapors (12-16). These polymers have relatively high absorptive characteristics for most organic compounds but very little affinity for water vapor. Polymers have been used to concentrate volatiles in the headspace over alcoholic beverages, and food products, as well as volatiles produced enzymatically.

Lipoxygenase catalyzes the oxidation of polyunsaturated acids in the presence of molecular oxygen and the isomeric hydroperoxides produced decompose into volatile aldehydes having characteristic odor and flavor properties. Even though the exact physiological role of lipoxygenase remains enigmatical, there has been renewed interest in its effect on lipid peroxidation. Headspace analysis techniques have proven useful to

analyze the volatile end products. Various techniques used to
analyze the vapors from different lipoxygenase systems will be
emphasized in the following sections (6,7,8,17,18).

II.   VAPOR ANALYSES USING DIFFERENTIAL CRYOGENIC TRAPPING AND
SYRINGE TECHNIQUES

A.   Volatile Fraction Isolation

1.   *Equipment Design Description*
     Fractionation and isolation of volatile constituents from
food products is probably the least glamorous and most tedious
aspect of volatile analysis. However, vacuum distillation
equipment design and control of operating parameters are of
prime importance to ensure a volatile fraction free of artifacts
and reminiscent of the starting material. Consideration must
also be given to the amount of starting material available and
the boiling point range of the components of interest.

     A vacuum system has been designed to incorporate differential
cryogenic trapping and a liquid-N_2 isolate trap adapted specifically for vapor analysis using a syringe sampling technique.
Fig. 1 shows the design of the isolate trap removed from the
cryogenic entrainment system.

     Vacuum stopcocks are placed on both arms of the trap
allowing complete isolation of trapped volatiles prior to
removal from the vacuum system. The volatiles can then be
sampled by syringe via the rubber septum at the top and analyzed
directly by gas-liquid chromatography. The rest of the system
preceding the trap consists of cryogenic traps and an allihn
condenser attached to the distillation flask. This type of
condenser has sufficient bore size to allow water reflux.
Ethylene glycol (-20 C) is used as the coolant. Reflux action
in the condenser prevents water from blocking the other cryogenic
traps and provides a stripping action as vapors move upward

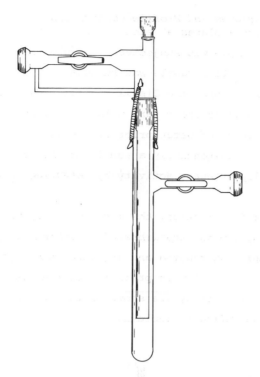

Fig. 1. Liquid-N$_2$ trap for isolation of volatiles.
through the column. This reflux process increases the efficiency
of volatile extraction from the sample. Other in-line traps
consist of wet ice and dry ice-acetone traps, which provide a
cryogenic temperature differential. This particular system has
been used to isolate volatiles produced from peanuts produced at
various stages of maturation and to demonstrate a relationship
between the lipoxygenase activity and certain volatile constituents (19).

2. *Plant Material and Sample Preparation*
    Peanuts were harvested weekly beginning 6 weeks from the
initial pegging and thereafter every week through the fifteenth
week. Samples were selected for uniformity of size according to
physiological maturity (20). The average length of time from
harvest to vacuum distillation was 3 hours.

3. *Analyses Techniques and Profile Comparisons*
Volatiles were isolated at each stage of maturity. A
200-gram aqueous sample was subjected to vacuum distillation and
cryogenic trapping. Each sample was subjected to a vacuum at
5×10^{-3} torr for 3 hours; the distilling flask was held at 25 C.
Volatiles were distilled under very mild conditions using this
system and the removal of water prior to the isolate traps was
very effective. Correspondingly a sample of the same maturity
was assayed for lipoxygenase activity by measuring O_2 uptake
(19).

After vacuum distillation, the liquid-N_2 trap was removed
from the vacuum system and equilibrated to ambient temperature.
A 5-ml vapor sample was removed and injected into a gas chroma-
graph. Representative volatile profiles for peanuts at
different stages of maturity are shown in Fig. 2, and the
components are identified in Table 1.

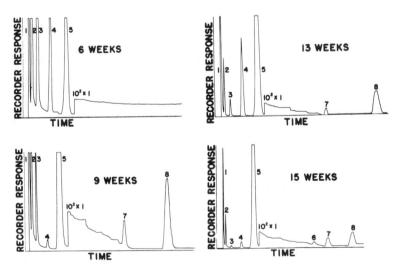

*Fig. 2. Influence of maturation on the volatile profile of
peanuts. (Reproduced with permission of Journal of Agricultural
and Food Chemistry.)*

TABLE 1

Identification of Volatile Components Isolated from Peanuts During Maturation.

==

Peak No.	Compound
1	Methanol
2	Acetaldehyde
3	Ethanol
4	Acetone
5	Pentane
6	Unknown
7	Pentanal
8	Hexanal

Reproduced with permission of Journal of Agricultural and Food Chemistry.

These chromatograms show that both qualitative and quantitative changes in volatile content occur throughout the maturation of peanuts and that vapor analysis can be used to monitor these changes.

Hexanal has been used as a indicator of rancidity in breakfast cereals, dehydrated potatoes, and breading mixes; but hexanal is also an important flavor contributor in tomatoes and peanuts (6,20,21).

Fig. 3 shows the relationship of changes in pentane and hexanal contents to lipoxygenase activity during the maturation of peanuts, and the effectiveness of using headspace techniques to relate volatile production with enzymatic reactions occurring in plant material. A cryogenic vacuum entrapment system in combination with headspace analysis enables the researcher to concentrate volatiles of diverse polarity under very mild conditions.

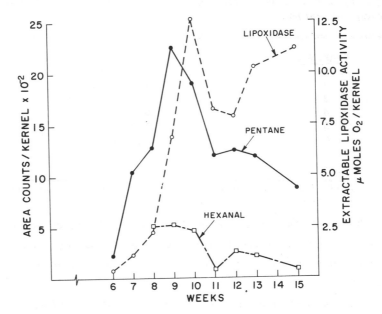

Fig. 3. Relationship of lipoxidase activity to the production of pentane and hexanal in peanut kernels during maturation. (Reproduced with the permission of Journal of Agricultural and Food Chemistry.)

III.   SIMULTANEOUS MEASUREMENT OF PRIMARY AND SECONDARY REACTION PRODUCTS

A.   Analysis and Technique Description

Lipoxygenase catalyzes the oxidation of linoleic acid and other polyunsaturated acids having a methylene-interrupted system with a *cis,cis* configuration producing hydroperoxide isomers as the primary reaction products. Simultaneously, secondary volatile products are produced during the reaction. Some plant sources have lipoxygenase systems that produce a predominance of the 13-hydroperoxide isomer from which pentane

is derived. Since O_2 uptake in lipoxygenase reactions is related
to primary product formation, a method was developed to measure
pentane, a secondary reaction product, concomitantly with lipoxygenase activity in a small reaction mixture.

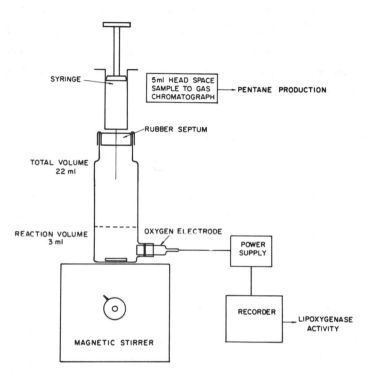

*Fig. 4. Apparatus for the measurement of lipoxygenase
activity and pentane production. (Reproduced with permission of
the Journal of The American Oil Chemists Society.)*

Fig. 4 shows the apparatus used for the measurement of
reaction products. A 22-ml volume vial was fitted with a Clark
oxygen electrode to measure lipoxgyenase activity by oxygen
consumption. A total volume of 3 ml was used for the lipoxy-
genase-substract mixture. After addition of the enzyme, the
reaction vessel was sealed with a rubber septum for headspace
analysis of pentane. The vapor (5 ml) above the reaction
mixture was sampled after a predetermined time and injected into
a gas-liquid chromatograph by the direct syringe injection

technique. This is an excellent technique for this particular
application since pentane production relates to primary product
specificity of soybeans lipoxygenase (pH 9) and peanut
lipoxygenase (22,23). A simple chromatogram was obtained
showing pentane as the major component. This was a definite
advantage since pentane was the only component of major interest
for this particular assay. However, the gas liquid chromatograph
must operate near its theoretical detection limits with this type
of system analysis.

B. Characterization of System

Lipoxygenase, fatty acid substrates, and molecular O_2 are required for the production of hydroperoxides and subsequent formation of volatile hydrocarbons and carbonyls. Fig. 5 shows the
relationships of O_2 consumption and pentane production with time.

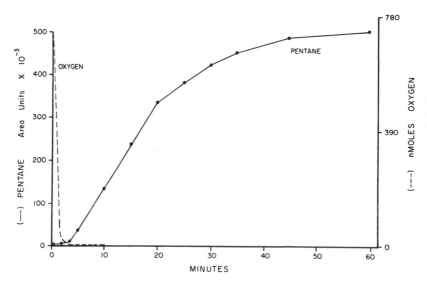

*Fig. 5. Pentane production and oxygen consumption as a
function of time. (Reproduced with permission of the American
Oil Chemists Society.)*

For this particular reaction, the soybean pH 9 isozyme was used. This isozyme produces a predominance of the 13-hydroperoxide as the primary product; and therefore, pentane is produced as one of the principal secondary reaction products. As molecular O_2 was depleted, pentane production became measurable. This reaction represents the anaerobic production of primary and secondary products; however, lipoxygenases will produce pentane under aerobic conditions (24). Pentane production increased for sixty minutes but was linear for approximately the first 15 minutes.

Enzyme concentration, amount of available substrate, pH, molecular O_2, and other environmental factors can affect primary product specificity and subsequent volatile production. The effect of enzyme concentration on pentane production is shown in Fig. 6.

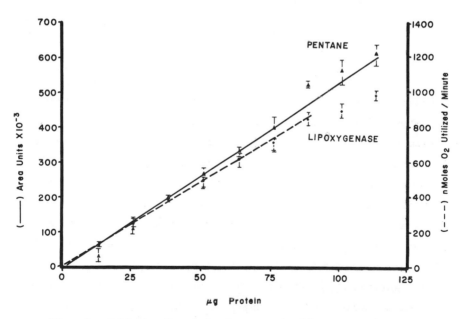

Fig. 6. Effect of catalyst concentration on pentane production and lipoxygenase activity. (Reproduced with permission of the Journal of Agricultural and Food Chemists.)

The rate of O_2 consumption was linear between 12 and 87 μg of protein, and pentane production was linear from 35 to 75 μg of protein. Approximately 1.5 to 2 minutes were required for the system to reach anaerobosis. Systems with lower protein concentrations required 5 to 11 minutes to reach anaerobic conditions; consequently, pentane values were lower. Figs. 5 and 6 show the effectiveness of measuring O_2 consumption by lipoxygenase concomitantly with volatile secondary product formation by headspace analysis. This technique could be used in any reaction which requires O_2 uptake and produces volatile products.

IV. DIRECT HEADSPACE ANALYSIS OF FLAVOR VOLATILES FROM A LIPOXYGENASE MEDIATED REACTION

A. Biochemical Aspects of Volatile Production

Many of the aroma producing compounds detected in raw and processed foods can be traced to the lipid fraction. Oilseeds, beans, potatoes, corn, tomatoes, eggplant and other fruit and vegetables vary in their lipid content; but all possess the very potent catalytic lipid peroxidizing enzyme lipoxygenase. This enzyme has an activation energy of 12-20 kg mol^{-1} and a high specificity for linoleic and linolenic acids producing hydroperoxides as primary reaction products and an array of volatile aldehydes, saturated and unsaturated, with characteristic odor and flavor properties. Even though odor and flavor are very complex entities involving synergistic effects of many components, media, and environmental parameters, some volatile components impart characteristic flavor notes to certain foods. For example, the characteristic taste and aroma of the cucumber has been attributed to hexanal, *trans* 2-nonenal, and *trans* 2, *cis* 6-nonadienal and in unprocessed peanuts and tomatoes, hexanal and hexenals impart characteristic flavor notes

respectively (25-28,21,6). All of these components are derived
from the lipid fraction and are produced upon disruption of the
tissue by the oxidizing action of lipoxygenase on polyunsaturated
fatty acids containing a *cis,cis*, 1,4 pentadiene system.

Most of the research relating lipoxygenase-produced aroma
compounds to odor and flavor has been made with model systems
that include the enzyme and linoleic acid. However, a limited
amount of work has been done relating lipoxygenase to volatile
production in food homogenates (6-8). In order to elucidate
some of the biochemical and analytical aspects of enzymatic
production to volatile components in unprocessed peanuts,
different parameters were applied to macerated tissue and the
volatiles analyzed by headspace analysis. The apparatus used
for headspace sampling is shown in Fig. 7. It consisted simply
of a 500 ml Erylenmeyer flask fitted with a rubber stopper with a
sampling septum inserted for needle insertion. The seeds were
macerated by blending with water and placed in the reaction flask
for headspace sampling using the direct syringe injection
technique.

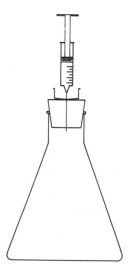

Fig. 7. Headspace sampling flask.

B. Enzymatic Reactions in Homogenates and Profile Comparisons

1. *Homogenate Reactions*

The enzymatic mediated affect of volatile production in peanut homogenates was shown by a series of experiments using acetone powders, water extracts of acetone powders, exogenous linoleic acid, and known lipoxygenase inhibitors in peanut homogenates. Volatiles were analyzed by sampling the headspace above the homogenates using the direct syringe injection technique. Headspace analysis of the homogenates showed (Table 2) that volatiles were produced from the available endogenous substrate and that the production required enzyme-mediation.

TABLE 2

Effects of Acetone Powder, Aqueous Acetone Powder Extracts and Linoleic Acid on Volatile Production in Peanut Homogenates[a]

	Acetal-dehyde	Pen-tane	Penta-nal	Hexa-nal
	Peak areas in integrator units X 10^{-3}			
Raw	13	168	16	115
Control	1	2	7	22
Control + 5 g of acetone powder	23	131	12	35
Control + water extract from 5 g acetone powder	15	306	7	65
Control + heat inactivated water extract from 5 g acetone powder	9	15	4	24
Raw + 0.1 ml of linoleic acid	14	192	15	212

[a] Each value is the mean of three replications. (Reproduced with permission of the Institute of Food Technologists.)

The water extract was more effective than the acetone powder treatments in inducing volatile production especially pentane. The addition of exogenous substrate (linoleic acid) to the non-deactivated homogenate caused an increase in the production of pentane and hexanal, but not to the extent expected. This phenomenon may have been due to incomplete solubility of the exogenous substrate and its failure to form a homogenous mixture with the endogenous substrate. To demonstrate further the enzymatic production of volatile components, known

lipoxygenase inhibitors and chelating compounds were added to
the homogenates prior to the maceration of the seeds.   Table 3
shows that propyl gallate and hydroquinone effectively inhibited
pentane production in peanut homogenates.

TABLE 3

*Effects of Antioxidants and Chelates on Production of Volatiles
by Peanut Homogenates*[a]

Antioxidant chelate	Conc (mM)	Acetal- dehyde	Penta- nal	Hexa- nal	Pen- tane	Pentane Produc- tion
		Peak areas in integrator units X 10^{-3}				(% of Control)
None		40	23	258	210	100
Hydroquinone	1.5	17	20	274	153	73
Propyl gallate	1.5	34	16	273	88	42
NDGA	0.1	-	-	294	241	115
EDTA	1.5	64	31	391	227	108
Ascorbic acid	2.4	68	20	340	237	113
	18.9	32	36	367	229	109
	56.8	21	57	405	38	18
	94.7	3	28	256	5	2

[a]Each value is the mean of three replications.   (Reproduced with
permission of the Institute of Food Technologists.)

However, inhibitors were more effective in the model systems
than in homogenates, possibly because of a protective effect of
protein in food homogenates.   Chelates had no effect, and
ascorbic acid was an effective inhibitor of pentane production
only at relative high concentrations.   Numerous samples were
required to yield the gas-liquid chromatography data; therefore,
headspace sampling and the direct syringe injection technique
were the methods of choice to analyze rapidly the large number
of samples.

2.   *Parameters of Gas-Liquid Chromatography for Headspace
Analysis and Profile Comparisons*
        Since pentane is one of the major secondary reaction
products of lipoxygenase-mediated reactions, a column was sought
that would give a reasonable retention time for pentane as well

as separate other components of interest. Also, when a large number of analyses are to be made, the column selected must maintain both its capability to make the separations and its physical characteristics over an extended period.

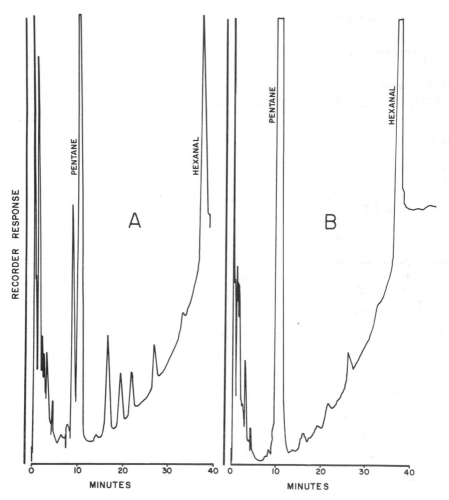

Fig. 8. Typical chromatograms of volatiles from a peanut lipoxygenase-linoleic acid model system (A) and a peanut homogenate (B). (Reproduced with permission of the Institute of Food Technologists.)

Chromosorb 102, a styrene divinyl benzene polymer, was selected because of its inert properties, stability over extended periods of use, retainability of pentane, and resolution of the components of interest. Chromatograms of enzymatically produced volatiles that were separated on a Chromosorb 102 column are shown in Fig. 8. Temperature programming was used in the analysis to reduce elution time and to enhance resolution. However, it caused some unavoidable column bleed. This was made evident by signal amplification (4 x 10^{-12} afs), which was necessary for detection. Column bleed is one of the major disadvantages of the direct syringe injection method because often, the concentrations of volatiles are near the theoretical detection limits.

Fig. 8A is a chromatogram of volatiles in the headspace of a reaction between a purified lipoxygenase preparation and linoleic acid; and Fig. 8B is a profile of enzymatically produced volatiles from a peanut homogenate. Both chromatograms contain the major lipoxygenase-mediated secondary reaction products pentane and hexanal. Since hexanal imparts a distinctive flavor note to peanuts and other food products, the oxidizing action of lipoxygenase on the lipid fraction is a factor to be considered during food processing and new-product development.

V.   PRECONCENTRATION OF HEADSPACE VAPORS FROM LIPOXYGENASE MEDIATED REACTIONS BY POLYMER TRAPPING.

A.   Equipment
1.   *Polymer Column Design and Operation*
     Preconcentration of volatiles by polymer trapping prior to gas-liquid chromatography is gaining widespread interest. Unique absorption and desorption characteristics and other physical properties of polymers make this technique desirable for pre-concentration of volatiles. Fig. 9 shows a preconcentration polymer trap made with a glass insert which normally serves as a

liner in the injection port of a gas liquid chromatograph.

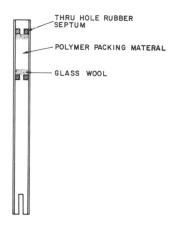

SECTION THROUGH SAMPLING TUBE

Fig. 9.   Injector-insert polymer trap.

The glass column was approximately 83 mm long and had a 4-mm
inside diameter; and was packed with Poropak Q, 80-100 mesh
(Waters Associates). The polymer packing material, ca 13 mm
deep, was sandwiched between two silinized glass wool plugs and
two septum injector washers. Retainer washers were necessary to
hold the packing material in place during volatile collection.

Injector polymer traps of the design shown in Fig. 9 are
conditioned by placing the trap in the injector port of the gas-
liquid chromatograph for at least an hour, or longer if time
permits, at 200 C with carrier gas flowing through the column at
25 ml/min. Insertion of the trap into the injector port is
simplified by drilling out the injector port which allows passage
of the column into the injector system simply by removing the
septum retainer nut. This modification of the gas-liquid
chromatograph eliminates the need for external heaters and
carrier gas connections for polymer trap conditioning. Also with

a dual column instrument, a conditioned injector column can be available without interruption or delay of any analytical analysis.

2. *Reaction Apparatus and Entrainment System*
When plant tissues containing lipoxygenase are macerated with water, primary and secondary reaction products are formed from the available endogenous substrate very quickly. The reaction apparatus and entrainment system that incorporates the polymer trap are shown in Fig. 10.

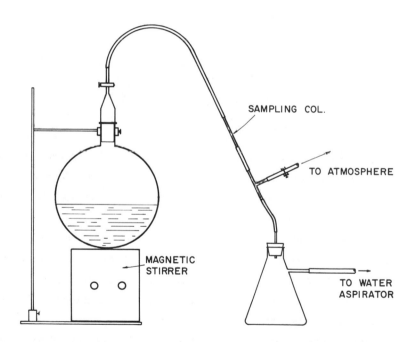

Fig. 10. Apparatus for polymer trapping of headspace volatiles.

A 1-liter round-bottom flask with a 24/40 ground-glass joint fitted with a vacuum stopcock was used as the reaction flask. The stopcock allowed the reaction system to be isolated from the entrainment section.

The entrainment system consist of a injector insert polymer
trap, glass tee with screw clamp, suction flask used as a water
trap, and connecting tubing. This entire system was attached to
a water aspirator operating at approximately 30 psi. In a
previous study N_2 was used to purge the volatiles from reaction
systems (13); however, more water is forced through the polymer
trap by this method than by the water aspirator method.

B.   Characterization of the System

1.   *Polymer Trapping of Lipoxygenase-Produced Volatiles*
     Lipoxygenase-mediated production of volatiles from peanut
and soybean homogenates was used for the evaluation of the
polymer trapping system. A 100-g sample of material was blended
with water forming an aqueous slurry. The slurry was placed in
the reaction flask and stirred with the stopcock closed. After
20 minutes of enzymatic reaction the vacuum stopcock was opened
and the volatiles were collected by water aspiration. The
polymer column was then removed and inserted into the injector
port for gas-liquid chromatography analysis. This method does
not require any development of the polymer column by carrier gas
purging or backflushing into cold traps prior to gas chromatography.

Chromatograms of lipoxygenase produced volatiles from
peanuts and soybeans are shown in Fig. 11 A and B respectively.
In both chromatograms, the major lipoxygenase-produced volatiles
are pentane, pentanal, and hexanal. The chromatographic
evidence indicating the presence of several minor volatiles in
the soybean homogenates attests to the trapping efficiency of the
polymer method. Differences between the two homogenates in the
amounts of the major products produced were also detectable;
peanut homogenates produced more pentane and less pentanal than
soybean homogenates. These profiles show that the injector insert
polymer trapping method is apparently sensitive enough to
differentiate samples.

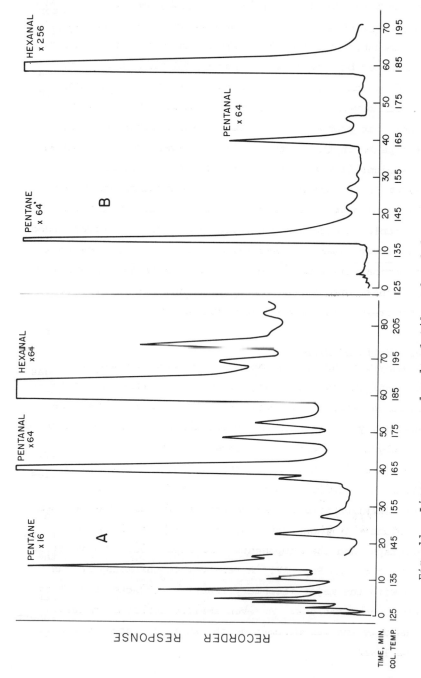

Fig. 11. Lipoxygenase-produced volatiles eluted from polymer traps. (A) Soybean homogenate (B) Peanut homogenate.

2. *Considerations of Collection Parameters*

In the development of a polymer trapping method, consideration must be given to the volatility, polarity, and concentration of the components of interest. Column dimensions and collection parameters must be optimized so that useful information would be obtained from the analysis of headspace vapors. For example, in alcoholic beverages, the concentration of ethanol can be a chromatographic problem. The ethanol peak obliterates other component peaks in the profile (13). However, usable profiles can be obtained if the development time of the column is increased. In the preconcentration of lipoxygenase-produced volatiles from peanut homogenates, pentane became a chromatographic problem due to its concentration. This is circumvented in the injector insert polymer trapping method by increasing the collection time which allows some of the pentane to pass through. Therefore, a usable and representative profile of volatiles present in the headspace can be obtained.

3. *Sensitivity of Method*

In many instances, the amount of material available for volatile analysis is a limiting factor. Therefore, the preconcentration method used should be as sensitive as possible. The sensitivity of the polymer entrapment method was demonstrated by the analysis of volatiles produced by 1 g of material (one peanut) macerated with 10 ml of water. The reaction mixture was held in the closed system for 20 minutes as described and then the volatiles were collected for 10 minutes. The polymer insert column was placed into the injector port of the gas chromatograph, and the components were separated. The volatile profile is shown in Fig. 12. A very usable chromatogram was obtained with the major secondary reaction products present in excellent concentrations. An even smaller amount of material can be used if the gas chromatograph can be operated at a more sensitive level.

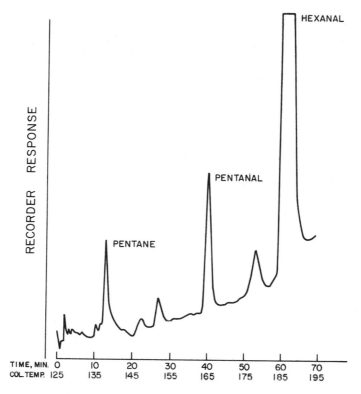

Fig. 12. Polymer trapping of headspace volatiles from one gram of peanuts.

4. *Storage of Polymer-Trapped Volatiles*
    It is often desirable and sometimes necessary to store trapped volatiles for later analysis by gas chromatography. They are then usually backflushed from the polymer trap into glass traps held at very low temperatures. The injector-insert polymer trap, however, can simply be stored at room temperature for extended periods until analyzed. Fig. 13A is a chromatogram of a sample analyzed immediately after collection of volatiles on a polymer trap; and Fig. 13B, a chromatogram of volatiles eluted from a polymer trap stored for 70 hours at ambient temperature in a small brown glass bottle. These profiles show that volatile components can be collected on polymer traps, stored at room temperature, and chromatographed later without any apparent component interaction or significant loss of volatile material.

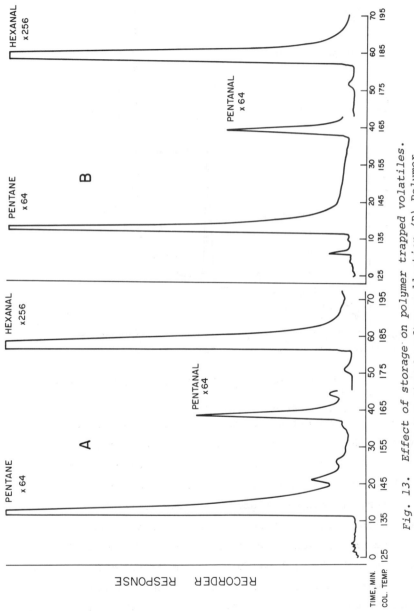

Fig. 13. Effect of storage on polymer trapped volatiles.
(A) Chromatographed immediately after collection (B) Polymer
trap stored for 70 hours at ambient temperature prior to
GLC analysis.

This technique would simplify the storage and manipulation of headspace vapors with preconcentrated polymer traps.

5. *Multiple Polymer Trapping*
    In some systems, a particular component may be present in relative high concentrations as compared to other components in the system. When this situation arises, usually a chromato-graphic problem will exist in polymer trapping methods. For example, in the preconcentration of headspace vapors of alcoholic beverages by polymer trapping, ethanol becomes a major chroma-tographic problem because of the concentration levels (13). Therefore, the amount must be reduced in the development phase of the column otherwise many other components of interest will not be seen. In the analysis of lipoxygenase produced volatiles pentane concentration creates a similar problem. However using the injector insert polymer trapping method, the amount of pentane produced in any particular system can be concentrated by the use of more than one trap without creating any chroma-tographic problem. Both polymer traps can be analyzed resulting in usable simplified chromatograms. The chromatograms shown in Fig. 14 A and B are the result of using two polymer insert traps in tandem isolating the volatiles from the same reaction mixture. Pentane was collected in both traps due to its concentration and volatility. If only one trap had been used to collect all the pentane and other volatiles, the chromatographic analysis would have been more difficult. Therefore in this particular case, chromatographic problems were avoided by the use of two traps. Also advantageous would be the use of traps with different polymer material so that each would absorb different components. Such a system of traps could greatly simplify certain chromatographic analyses.

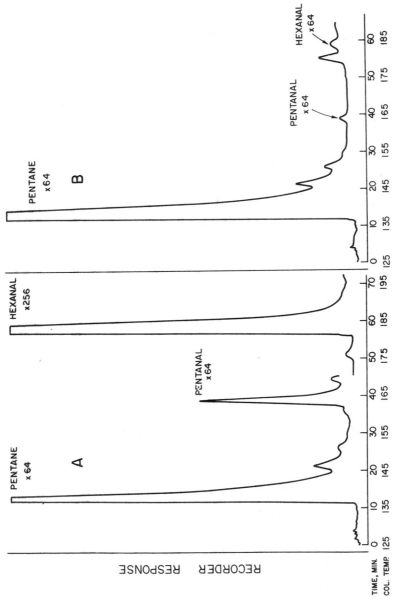

RECORDER   RESPONSE

TIME, MIN.
COL. TEMP.

Fig. 14. Example of multiple polymer trapping of headspace volatiles (A) First polymer column (B) Second polymer column in the entrapment system.

VI. HEADSPACE VAPORS AND THEIR RELATIONSHIP TO PRECURSOR
FORMATION IN A LIPOXYGENASE MEDIATED REACTION

A. Headspace Analysis of Volatiles From a Lipoxygenase-Linoleic
Acid System

Product formation by the degradation of lipid material by
enzymes can be generally classified as isomerization reactions,
vinyl ether production, epoxidation, and volatile aldehyde
production. In a peanut lipoxygenase-linoleic acid system the
major secondary products produced are volatile aldehydes.
Fig. 15 is a chromatogram of volatiles isolated from a peanut
lipoxygenase-linoleic acid reaction mixture.

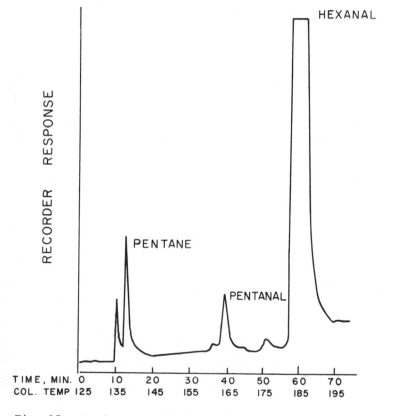

*Fig. 15. Headspace volatiles from a peanut lipoxygenase-
linoleic acid reaction mixture (polymer trapping method).*

The reaction mixture consisted of a water extract of 10 g of acetone powder with lipoxygenase activity of 4615 units/ml and an aqueous solution of linoleic acid (270 mg.). Reaction time was 20 minutes at pH 6.7. Headspace volatiles were preconcentrated on an injector polymer trap.

The same major secondary lipoxygenase reaction products were produced in the model system and in the homogenates. However with acetone powder extracts, it appears that less pentane is produced relative to hexanal than in the homogenate systems. Possibly, the enzyme is slightly altered during the extraction of acetone powder.

B.   Precursors and Volatile Production

Primary reaction products of lipid degradation by lipoxygenase are isomeric hydroperoxides. Product specificity varies with the plant source used, but the hydroperoxides produced from linoleic acid are the two positional isomers 13-hydroperoxy-cis-9, trans-11-octadecadienoic acid (13-LOOH) and 9-hydroperoxy trans-10, cis-12-octadecadienoic (9-LOOH). Geometrical isomers are also present resulting from isomerization reaction of the cis, trans isomers to the more stable trans,trans configuration. Fig. 16 shows the separation by high performance liquid chromatography (HPLC) of the hydroxydiene analogues of the hydroperoxides isolated from a peanut lipoxygenase-linoleic acid reaction mixture. Positional and geometrical isomers were isolated and separated, and 13-LOOH was the major hydroperoxide produced. Ratios of the isomeric hydroperoxides produced can vary, depending upon conditions of the reaction (28). Also, the ratio of carbonyl fragments isolated to the amounts of hydroperoxides produced varies with incubation parameters (29).

The volatiles identified in Fig. 15 are apparently derived from the 13-LOOH, since approximately 80% of the total hydroperoxides produced in the peanuts is 13 cis,trans isomer. A schematic diagram showing the product specificity of peanut

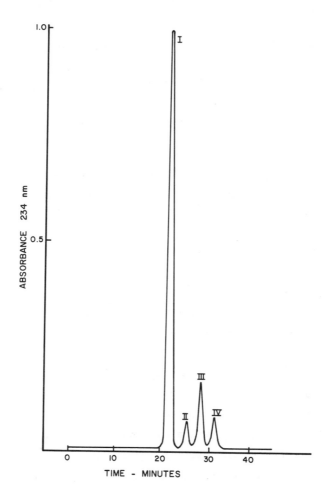

*Fig. 16. HPLC of the hydroxydiene analogues of positional
and geometric hydroperoxide isomers from a peanut lipoxygenase-
linoleic acid reaction. (I) Methyl 13-hydroxy-cis-9, trans-11
octadecadienoate. (II) Methyl 13-hydroxy-trans-9, trans-11-
octadecadienoate. (III) Methyl 9-hydroxy-trans-10, cis-12-
octadecadienoate. (IV) Methyl 9-hydryoxy-trans-10, trans-12-
octadecadienoate.*

lipoxygenase, and the subsequent production of volatiles from

that product is presented in Fig. 17. Cleavage of the C-C bond

to the left of the hydroperoxy group would yield an alkyl radical

$[CH_3(CH_2)_4]$ and a vinyl aldehyde. If the C-C bond is disrupted

to the right of the hydroperoxy group, hexanal and a vinyl

radical would be formed.

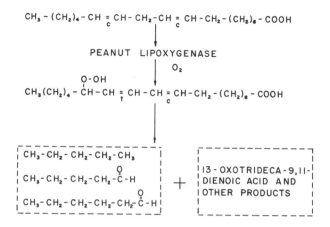

Fig. 17. Primary and secondary reaction products of a peanut lipoxygenase-linoleic acid reaction.

The cleaved alkyl radical $[CH_3(CH_2)_4]$ can abstract a hydrogen forming pentane (derived from 13-LOOH isomer). Hexanal would be formed by cleavage of the 13-LOOH at the C-C bond to the right of hydroperoxy group via the enolic mechanism for the formation of aldehydes. Pentanal, the other major secondary aldehyde reaction product, would likely be formed in two steps: reaction of the 5-C alkyl radical with a hydroxyl radical and then conversion of the product via the enolic form to the aldehyde. Since pentane production is linear with time, the volatiles from the peanut lipoxygenase system might be produced via an enzyme controlled free radical mechanism. There is spectrometric evidence for the production of oxo-compounds in peanut lipoxygenase systems which would account for the 13-oxo compound shown in the operational schematic (8).

VII.   GENERAL CONCLUSIONS

The use of headspace analysis for determining the chemical composition of vapors above beverages and edible products affords analytical and flavor chemists with a technique which allows the detection of many volatile components without extensive sample preparation or distillation equipment. Usually only small amounts of material are required to produce enough volatiles for chromatographic analysis. Headspace analysis is also an excellent technique to determine the relative importance of a particular compound to the overall odor perceived from the food product. Although there are certain advantages to vapor analysis, this technique can confront the analyst with a multifaceted problem. Vapor pressure, polarity, concentration, boiling point range of components of interest, and sensitivity of instrumentation must be considered carefully in developing methodology. In many cases, a relatively high concentration of a particular component in headspace analysis presents a chromatographic problem by completely masking other components of interest, i.e. ethanol in alcoholic beverages. Therefore the selection of a vapor analysis technique or combination of techniques should be based on the material being analyzed and the desired information to produce a useful chromatogram which is representative of the headspace composition.

REFERENCES

1. Buttery, R. G. and Teranishi, R. (1963). J. Agr. Food Chem. 11, 504.
2. McCarthy, A. I., Palmer, J. R., Shaw, C. P. and Anderson, E. E. (1963). J. Food Sci. 28,379.
3. Aurand, L. W., Singleton, J. A., Bell, T. A. and Etchells, J. L. (1965). J. Food Sci. 30,288.
4. Pattee, H. E., Beasley, E. O. and Singleton, J. A. (1965). J. Food Sci. 38,388.
5. Singleton, J. A., Aurand, L. W. and Bell, T. A. (1965). J. Gas Chrom. 3,357.
6. Kazeniac, S. J. and Hall, R. M. (1970). J. Food Sci. 35,519.
7. Singleton, J. A., Pattee, H. E. and Sanders, T. H. (1975). J. Food Sci. 40,386.
8. Singleton, J. A., Pattee, H. E. and Sanders, T. H. (1976). J. Food Sci. 41,148.
9. Hornstein, I. and Crowe, P. F. (1962). Anal. Chem 34,1354.

10. Morgan, M. E. and Day, E. A. (1965). J. Dairy Sci. 48,1382.
11. Flath, R. A., Forrey, R. R. and Teranishi, R. (1969). J. Food Sci. 34,382.
12. Singleton, J. A., Pattee, H. E. and Johns, E. B. (1971). J. Agr. Food Chem. 19,130.
13. Jennings, W. G., Wohleb, R. and Lewis, M. J. (1972). J Food Sci. 37,69.
14. Lindsay, R. C., Withycombe, D. A. and Micketts, R. J. (1972). Proc. of the Ann. Meeting of the Amer. Soc. of Brewing Chemist, Inc.
15. Withycombe, D. A. and Lindsay, R. C. (1973). Tech. Quarterly 9,XXVII.
16. Jennings, W. G. and Filsoof, M. J. (1977). J. Agr. Food Chem. 25,400.
17. Leu, K. (1974). Lebensm-wiss. U Technol 7,98.
18. Johns, E. B., Singleton, J. A. and Pattee, H. E. (1974). J. Amer. Oil Chem. Soc. 51,32.
19. Pattee, H. E., Singleton, J. A., Johns, E. B. and Mullins, B. C. (1970). J. Agr. Food Chem. 18,353.
20. Fritsch, C. W. and Gale, J. A. (1977). J. Amer. Oil Chem. Soc. 54,225.
21. Pattee, H. E., Singleton, J. A. and Cobb, W. Y. (1969). J. Food Sci. 34,625.
22. Garssen, G. J., Vliegenthart, J.F.G. and Boldingh, J. (1971). Biochem. J. 122,327.
23. Johns, E. B., Pattee, H. E. and Singleton, J. A. (1973). J. Agr. Food Chem. 21,570.
24. Pattee, H. E., Singleton, J. A. and Johns, E. B. (1974). Lipids 9,302.
25. Forss, D. A., Dunstone, E. A., Ramshaw, E. H. and Stark, W. (1962).
26. Fleming, H. P., Cobb, W. Y., Etchells, J. L. and Bell, T. A. (1968). J. Food Sci. 33,572.
27. Kemp, T. R., Knavel, D. E. and Staltz, L. P. (1974). J. Agr. Food Chem. 22,717.
28. Singleton, J. A., Pattee, H. E. and Nelson, M. S. In press. 1977.
29. Galliard, T. and Phillips, D. R. (1976). Biochem. et Biophys. Acta 431,278.

INDEX

A

B

C